The Origins of the First World War

Controversies and Consensus

The Origins of the First World War

Controversies and consensus

Annika Mombauer

Longman

An imprint of Pearson Education

London • New York • Toronto • Sydney • Tokyo • Singapore • Hong Kong • Cape Town
New Delhi • Madrid • Paris • Amsterdam • Munich • Milan • Stockholm

PEARSON EDUCATION LIMITED

Head Office:
Edinburgh Gate
Harlow CM20 2JE
Tel: +44(0)1279 623623
Fax: +44(0)1279 431059

London Office:
128 Long Acre
London WC2E 9AN
Tel: +44(0)20 7447 2000
Tel: +44(0)20 7240 5771
Website: www.history-minds.com

First published in Great Britain in 2002

ISBN 0 582 41872 0

British Library Cataloguing in Publication Data
A CIP catalogue record for this book can be obtained from the British Library

Library of Congress Cataloging in Publication Data
A CIP catalog record for this book can be obtained from the Library of Congress

10 9 8 7 6 5 4 3 2
06 05 04 03

Typeset by Fakenham Photosetting Limited, Fakenham, Norfolk
Printed in Malaysia, PJB

The Publishers' policy is to use paper manufactured from sustainable forests.

Contents

Acknowledgements

In preparing this book, I benefited greatly from the advice and expertise of colleagues and friends who read parts, or even all, of the manuscript, suggested many improvements, and spared me some of the worst omissions. I am grateful to Paul Lawrence, Matthew Stibbe, Holger Afflerbach, Robert Foley, Clive Emsley and Antony Lentin for their help, and for making this a better book than it would otherwise have been.

My particular thanks are due to a great scholar and inspiring teacher, John Röhl, whose work has contributed so significantly to the controversy which is analysed in this book. He introduced me to the debate on the origins of the First World War some ten years ago, and his help and continued friendship over the years have been invaluable. This book is dedicated to him with thanks.

The publishers are grateful to the following for permission to reproduce copyright material:

Maps redrawn from *First World War Atlas*, published and reprinted by permission of Routledge (Gilbert, M. 1970).

In some instances we have been unable to trace the owners of copyright material, and we would appreciate any information that would enable us to do so.

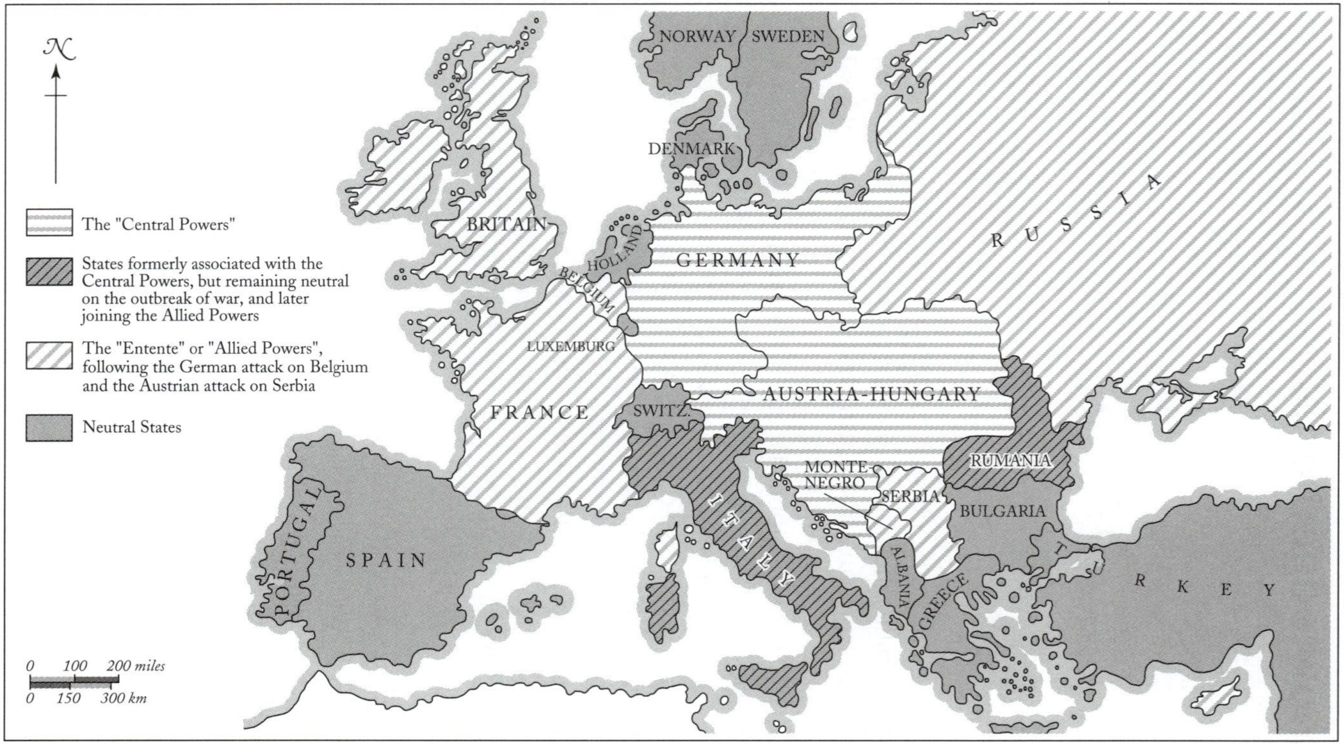

Map 1 European alliances before the First World War
Source: Redrawn from Gilbert, M. (1970) *First World War Atlas*.

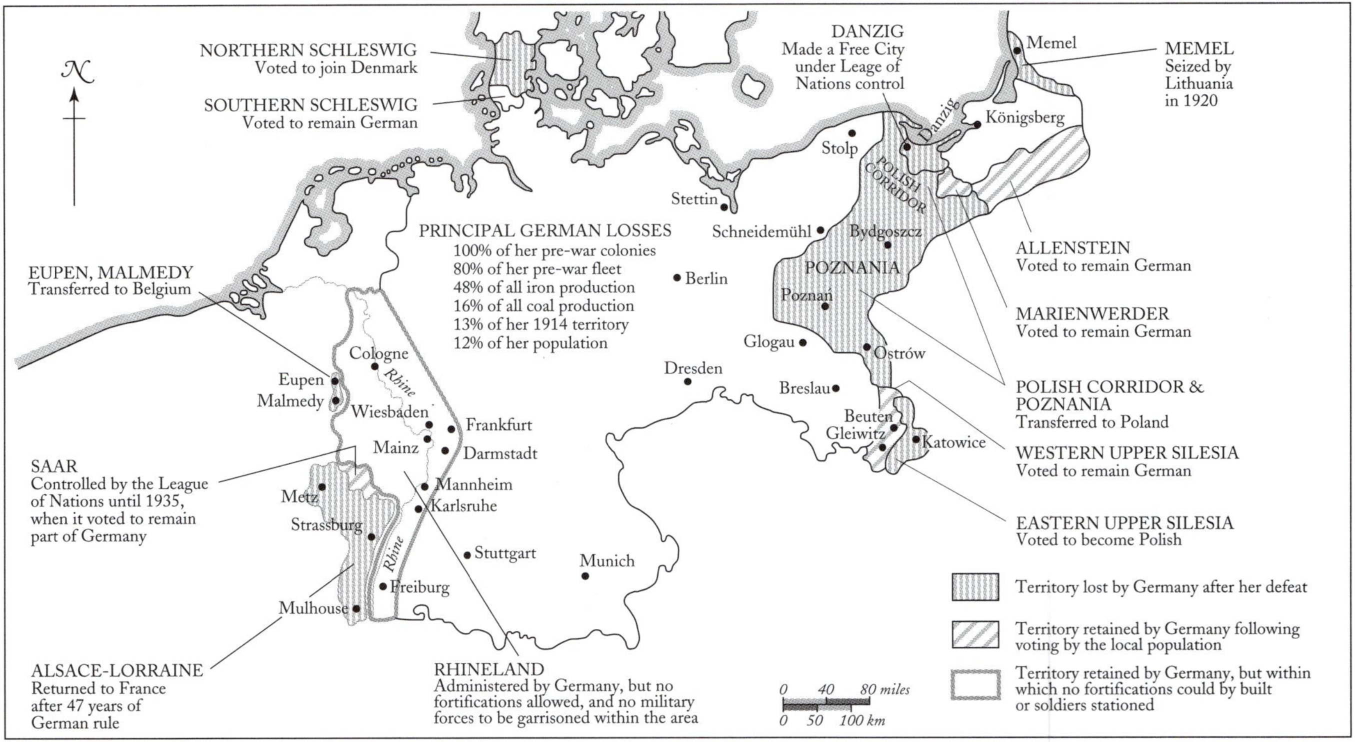

Map 2 German territorial losses following the Treaty of Versailles
Source: Redrawn from Gilbert, M. (1970) *First World War Atlas*.

Introduction

It is part of the tragedy of the world war that every belligerent can make out a case entirely convincing for itself. George P. Gooch[1]

The origins of the First World War have occupied and intrigued historians for decades and, nearly ninety years after its outbreak, continue to pose challenging questions. The following account attempts to explain why the search for an explanation of the outbreak of the war has been 'almost obsessive'.[2] As well as providing a guide through the maze of interpretations on the origins of the war, its aim is to analyse why such an abundance of studies have been published since the 1920s, and why it has continued to be difficult to establish the precise reason for war breaking out in 1914.

It will be suggested that there are several underlying reasons behind this ongoing quest to apportion responsibility. In part, emotional reactions to the horror of the war led to an understandable desire on the part of the victorious Allies to find someone to blame. They blamed the Central Powers, and Germany in particular. At the same time, national pride led to a strident denial of this alleged responsibility within Germany. A further motive for investigating the origins of the war was the desire to establish how to avoid another escalation of a conflict into full-scale war in the future. The international crises which followed both world wars led to a quest to find a universal answer to the problem of wars, and in studying the origins of the First World War, historians have attempted to solve the mystery of why international crises, at times, escalate into armed conflict.

After the Second World War, the renewed interest in the origins of the war of 1914 can partly also be explained by the perception that the First World War had been in many ways '*the* great seminal catastrophe' of the twentieth century.[3] Understanding the history of that century necessitated an awareness of the war that had defined it and had determined its course. A perception that there were direct links leading from the First to the Second World War (and that both wars might even be regarded as a thirty-years war) prompted renewed interest in its causes – particularly, of course, in Germany, where questions of continuity from the First to the Second World War had to be addressed.

Germany occupies a central part in this account of the debate on the origins of the war, for a number of reasons. Because Germany was blamed for the outbreak of the war by the Allies at the Versailles Peace Conference, it was in that country that most effort was expended to prove them wrong, although by no means all of those seeking to exonerate Germany were, or are, German. Secondly, given that Germany was initially considered responsible for the outbreak of the war by her enemies, much subsequent research has taken this position as a starting point and has primarily argued either for or against German culpability. Only relatively recently have the actions of other belligerents been studied to a similar degree. Moreover, the current consensus among most historians attributes the largest share of responsibility to the decisions made by German leaders in 1914. It is thus only right that Germany's prewar policies should be central to an investigation of the origins of the First World War, and that the debate as it developed among German historians should be a focal point of this investigation.

This book will also consider why, at certain times, a particular view of the origins of the First World War was advocated in a particular country. It will become apparent that these widely differing interpretations often had much to do with contemporary political and ideological concerns than necessarily just with the conviction that a particular interpretation of events was the right one. The focus here is thus less on an investigation of the events that led to war (although these will be analysed briefly in the Introduction), but more on the circumstances that fuelled this 'long debate'[4] and continue to do so. As we will see, the debate on the origins of the war has been complicated by falsifications and censorship, and by a confusing array of interpretations. Often, the arguments between one school of thought and another hinge on the analysis of minute details. Often, too, it is difficult to understand the hostility of the reactions of opponents in the debate. Hundreds of books and articles have been published on the subject over the decades, thousands of documents have been unearthed in archives and made available to historians – but nonetheless key issues are still far from resolved, and publications on the First World War and its origins continue in abundance.

The following account approaches the subject chronologically. After a brief overview of the events that led to the outbreak of war in 1914, Part 1 of this volume will analyse the debates during and immediately after the war, before the reactions of so-called revisionists and anti-revisionists to the Treaty of Versailles are highlighted in Part 2. In Part 3, the consensus following the Second World War, and the challenges posed to that new orthodoxy by the German historian Fritz Fischer are considered. Finally, Part 4 examines the last decades of scholarship on the topic, and introduces some recent debates. At the end of nearly ninety years of scholarship, and at the end of this investigation into a debate that has spanned almost the entire twentieth century, it will be asked what consensus, if any, now exists among historians regarding the origins of the First World War. Before we turn to interpretations, however, we need briefly to consider the events themselves.

Long- and short-term causes of the First World War[5]

Some investigations into the origins of the war begin as early as 1870/71, the time of the founding of the German Empire.

German unification occurred as a result of three wars between 1864 and 1871, against Denmark, Austria and France. Following the foundation of the new German Empire, Chancellor Otto von Bismarck was concerned to avoid further conflict with Germany's neighbours. His complicated alliance system served to ensure that what he considered a 'nightmare of coalitions' against Germany could not threaten the new status quo. He declared that Germany was 'saturated' following her recent unification and the annexation of Alsace-Lorraine, and that she sought no further conflict with her neighbours. During his time in office, the alliance system that he created aimed at preserving peace and preventing Germany's neighbours from drawing up alliances against her. Germany was allied to Austria-Hungary in the Dual Alliance of 1879, which became *de facto* a Triple Alliance when Italy was included in 1882. A few years later, in 1887, Germany concluded the secret 'Reinsurance Treaty' with Russia, guaranteeing neutrality in the event of a future war (in contradiction with the alliance agreement with Austria-Hungary). With the accession to the throne of Kaiser Wilhelm II, however, and particularly following Bismarck's dismissal in 1890, this carefully constructed system of alliances began to be dismantled by his successors who entertained different political ideas and were less concerned than Bismarck to guarantee and preserve the current status quo in Europe. German foreign policy under Wilhelm II became more erratic and began to threaten the European balance of power that had developed since 1871.[6]

Under Wilhelm II, Imperial Germany entered a new era in which it was thought that its newly gained position of economic might should be reflected in achieving a position of world power. It was alleged that the country had missed out when other European nations had acquired their colonial empires, because a unified German state had only come into existence in 1871. Germany's leaders, and in particular the new German Kaiser Wilhelm II, who acceded to the throne in 1888, wanted for Germany a 'place in the sun' which would reflect its economic predominance on the continent and its population's size. Under Wilhelm II's erratic leadership and in pursuit of the goal of becoming a *Weltmacht* (world power), the powerful new Germany at the centre of Europe soon began to challenge its neighbours, who were quick to react to the perceived threat emanating from Imperial Germany by forming defensive alliances. France (which still begrudged Germany the annexation of Alsace-Lorraine in 1871) and Russia made the start in negotiations between 1892 and 1894 which led to the conclusion of a military alliance which, in turn, gave rise to a feeling of 'encirclement' in Germany. Given its geographic situation, Germany now faced potential enemies both in the west and the east, and felt 'encircled' by envious and potentially dangerous neighbours who were forming alliances against it.

Germany's foreign policy following Bismarck's dismissal led to the establishment of two competing alliances.[7] On the one hand, Germany, Austria-Hungary and Italy formed the Triple Alliance. On the other hand, the Franco-Russian alliance of 1894 was followed by the conclusion of the Entente Cordiale between France and Britain in 1904; the loose arrangement of the two powers that was strengthened as a result of the first Moroccan Crisis in 1905–6, during which Germany reacted to French colonial aspirations in the region by attempting to break up the new allies Britain and France. Britain had given up its position of 'splendid isolation' in 1902 when it had become allied to Japan, but it was the conclusion of the Entente with France that indicated to perceptive Germans that Britain would be found on the side of Germany's enemies in any future European conflict. In effect, this Entente allied Britain and Russia, too, via their shared ally France. This friendship was given more permanence when Britain and Russia concluded an entente agreement in 1907. Now the Triple Entente stood in opposition to the Central Powers' Triple Alliance, and any conflict between an Entente and an Alliance country would in future threaten to escalate and embroil all the major European powers.

Germany had stirred Britain into a position of hostility towards it by deliberately and openly challenging British supremacy at sea with the programme, begun in 1897/98 under Admiral Alfred von Tirpitz, to build a great navy which would, in time, be able to hold its own against the British. Britain took up the challenge and responded in 1906 with the construction of the first *Dreadnought*. The introduction of this 'all gun ship' levelled the playing field and ruined Tirpitz's grand design. The main result of this Anglo-German naval race was enmity and suspicion in the governments and populations of both countries.[8] In Britain, Germany's expanding navy was regarded as one of the ways in which Germany was attempting to improve its international position and challenge its rivals, while in Germany it was felt that the country deserved to play a greater international role and to have 'a place in the sun', for which a powerful navy was portrayed as an essential prerequisite.

Some historians would argue that it was to a large extent Germany's aggressive posturing in the years before 1914 that poisoned the international climate and seemed to bring war ever closer, while others would maintain that it was British and French inflexibility that helped to exacerbate international tensions. The worsening of Anglo-German relations has often been stressed as playing a major part in leading to a general deterioration of the relations between the great powers, and thus as a contributing factor leading to an increasingly warlike mood before 1914. Although there were some attempts to come to amicable agreements between Berlin and London (for example the 1912 'Haldane mission'), none came to fruition.[9] Among the reasons for this failure were German insistence on a formal alliance with Britain and Germany's unwillingness to cease building a strong navy, as well as the threat that German foreign policy seemed to pose to the European status quo, and to Britain's own foreign policy ambitions. In Britain the government faced crucial decisions: who would be the more useful future ally, and who the more worrying future enemy among the continental great powers? To British statesmen, the price

Germany seemed to be demanding for an understanding with Britain was the freedom to attack France and Russia at will without fear of a British involvement – a price that they believed to be too high to pay, particularly in view of their concerns for the safety of the British Empire. It has therefore been argued that in addition to the existing Anglo-German antagonism, British policy in the prewar years and Britain's decision to join the war in August 1914 were motivated by fears of an overly powerful Russian Empire, and the threat that a victorious Russia would pose to the British Empire, particularly in India. In the British Foreign Office, it was believed that an unfriendly France and Russia would be a much greater threat to the Empire than an unfriendly Germany.[10]

In the years preceding the outbreak of war, a number of international crises and localized wars endangered the peace of Europe, and threatened to escalate into a European war.[11] The Russo-Japanese War of 1904–5 involved land battles of almost unprecedented scale, and provided a taste of things to come. It was a great surprise that a European 'white' country was being defeated by a 'non-white' race – this is how the events appeared to many contemporary commentators. The most important result was a significant change of the balance of power in Europe. Following Russia's defeat and the revolution of 1905, Japan had emerged as a force to be reckoned with, and the renewal and extension of the Anglo-Japanese Alliance just before the peace agreement of Portsmouth has to be seen in this light. Russia, however, was for the time being so weakened that it could almost be discounted as a great power. The lost war spelt the end of Russia's imperialist aspirations in the Far East for the foreseeable future. Any future expansion would have to look towards Europe. France had been spared the possibility of having to take sides if a conflict between Russia and Great Britain had resulted from the Russo-Japanese war.

However, France was also adversely affected by Russia's lost war in the Far East, for, in the aftermath of its defeat, Russia could be of no support to its French ally, as was the case in the First Moroccan Crisis. Moreover, it was Russia's weakened state which encouraged Germany to challenge France's Moroccan policy, based on the assumption that Russia would be unable to come to its ally's aid, thus heightening Germany's chances of achieving a diplomatic victory. At the same time Germany's military planners developed a new and daring deployment plan (the so-called Schlieffen Plan), based on the assumption that the recently defeated Russia would not pose a real threat to Germany in the east in the near future.

While Russia and Japan were fighting in the east, Germany provoked an international crisis over the Anglo-French agreement regarding the territory of Morocco. Germany's policy in 1905 was really only superficially about Morocco. Aside from the concerns of some German companies established in the region, Germany had little actual interests in Morocco, but felt slighted by not having been consulted by France and Britain, and wanted to demonstrate that a great power such as Germany could not simply be passed over when such important colonial decisions were made. Germany primarily objected for reasons of prestige. Friedrich von Holstein, a senior figure in the German Foreign Office at the time, feared that if Germany allowed its 'toes to be trodden on silently' in Morocco, this would amount to allowing a 'repetition elsewhere'.[12] German policy also aimed at demonstrating that France could not rely on its Entente partner Britain, and that Russia was too weak to support it in an international crisis. At the heart of the Moroccan Crisis was Germany's desire to show up the newly formed Entente Cordiale between Britain and France as useless, to split the Entente partners before they had a chance to consolidate their bond, and to intimidate the French. Rather than a war, Germany's leaders aimed at a diplomatic victory that would demonstrate to its European neighbours the importance of the German Empire and the desirability of being allied with Germany. However, these bullying tactics did not succeed. On the contrary, the newly formed Entente between Britain and France emerged strengthened from the crisis, with both countries realizing the benefits to be had from such a coalition, while the international conference at Algeciras, which was the result of Germany's demands, amounted only to a Pyrrhic victory for Germany. Germany found herself isolated, with support only from its ally Austria-Hungary, and had revealed itself to the rest of Europe as an aggressive bully.

Just as it was no great surprise that a European war would eventually result from these tensions, it was equally no surprise that a Balkan crisis would provide the trigger for such a conflict. The years before 1914 saw frequent crises in the Balkans which threatened to escalate, and a European war was only narrowly avoided on several occasions. It was with the disintegration of the Ottoman Empire that the status quo in the Balkans changed fundamentally. The smaller Balkan states were keen to expand their area of influence into former Turkish lands, thus posing a direct threat to Austro-Hungarian ambitions. Austria-Hungary had as much interest in preventing the area from being taken over by Serbs as Russia had in supporting Serbian ambitions in the region. Serbia, Austria-Hungary's main Balkan rival, received moral support from Russia, who considered itself the guardian of the pan-Slav movement. There were disputes over access to the sea, over control of the Straits of Constantinople, providing vital access to the Black Sea, and simply over territorial possessions. For Austria-Hungary, the matter was made worse by the fact that the Dual Monarchy united many disparate nationalities in one empire, some of which wanted to establish their independence. In many ways the Balkans, then as now, were an area of conflict for which no easy solutions could be found, as nationalist aspirations and the desire for territorial expansion resulted in repeated conflict. The Bosnian Annexation Crisis was one such serious dispute, which threatened to bring war to Europe as early as 1908.

Following the Austro-Russian Entente of 1897, when the two powers had come to an agreement over the Balkans, relations between the countries had been amicable. The

Balkan issue only reappeared after Russia's disastrous experience in the Far East, when her interest in the Balkans was reawakened. Revolution in Turkey by the 'Young Turks'[13] in 1908 led to a change of government and policy, and the previously assumed disintegration of the Ottoman Empire seemed to be halted – a threatening development for those European countries that had an interest in Turkey's decline and had welcomed it. The multi-national empire of Austria-Hungary faced numerous internal threats due to the nationalist aspirations of its many national minorities, and Austria-Hungary's Foreign Minister Count Alois Aehrenthal aimed at diverting domestic discontent with the help of an aggressive foreign policy. On the back of the Young Turk revolution, Aehrenthal decided to annex the provinces of Bosnia and Herzegovina, which Austria had occupied following the Treaty of Berlin in 1878, but which had formally remained under Turkish suzerainty.[14]

Russia, too, hoped to gain from the instability in the Balkans, and the Russian Foreign Minister Izvolsky and Aehrenthal came to a secret agreement in 1908. Austria would be allowed to go ahead with the annexation, and in return was expected to support Russian interests in the Bosphorus and Dardanelles. However, Aehrenthal proceeded with the annexation on 5 October 1908 before Izvolsky had time to secure diplomatic support from other European capitals. Izvolsky felt betrayed by Aehrenthal, and denounced the secret agreement. Serbia was ready to go to war over the annexation, but in the event was not supported by Russia, who was still militarily weak following the war against Japan. Given the fact that Germany gave unconditional support to Austria-Hungary over this Balkan matter, it was primarily Russia's mediating influence on Serbia that prevented a war on this occasion.

Germany's open and unconditional support of its ally had significantly changed what had so far been a purely defensive alliance agreement between it and Austria-Hungary. From now on, Austria's leaders believed they would be able to count on Germany even if an international crisis resulted from their own actions. The Bosnian Annexation Crisis marked an important juncture in this respect. In future, Serbia, humiliated in 1909, would be keen to redress its status in the Balkans, while Russia was now suspicious of German interests in that region, and more determined than ever to regain its military power. The European armaments race which followed was started by Russia's desire to increase its military potential, and soon led to army increases by all major European powers.[15] Russia and Serbia had been forced to back down on this occasion, but they were unlikely to do so again in future.

In 1911 Germany tried again to assert its claim as a great power who could not simply be ignored in colonial affairs. When the French sent troops to Morocco to suppress a revolt (and thus, by implication, to extend their influence over Morocco), Germany considered this to be a move contrary to the international agreements which had been concluded following the First Moroccan Crisis. Germany intervened in reaction to French oppression of Morocco. After failing to find a diplomatic solution, Germany's political leaders decided to dispatch the gunboat *Panther* to the port of Agadir to intimidate the French. Germany demanded the French Congo as compensation for the extension of French influence in Morocco. However, as during the First Moroccan Crisis, France received support from Britain, and the links between the two Entente partners were only further strengthened as a consequence of German intervention. Britain let Germany know in no uncertain terms that it intended to stand by France, and David Lloyd George's famous 'Mansion House Speech' of 21 July 1911, threatening to fight on France's side against Germany if the need arose, caused great indignation in Germany. Although the crisis was resolved peacefully, and Germany was given a small part of the French Congo as compensation, the affair was in fact another diplomatic defeat for Germany, whose leaders were becoming increasingly worried that their foreign policy adventures were not leading to the breaking-up of the hostile alliances. Moreover, Austria's lukewarm support suggested that the ally could only be definitely counted on if an international crisis directly affected its own interests. Germany's decision-makers arrived at the important realization that only a crisis in the Balkans would guarantee the all-important Austro-Hungarian support.

Soon after the Agadir Crisis, the Balkans once again demanded the attention of Europe's statesmen. Following the humiliation of 1909, Russia had encouraged the creation of a coalition of Balkan states, and in 1912 Bulgaria, Greece, Montenegro and Serbia formed the Balkan League. In October 1912 the League declared war on Turkey. The latter was quickly defeated and driven out of most of the Balkans, but in the aftermath of the war the victors fell out over the spoils, and ended up fighting each other in the Second Balkan War of 1913. As a result of the wars, Serbia doubled its territory, and now posed an even greater threat to Austria-Hungary, both externally, and by encouraging the sizeable Serbian minority within the Dual Monarchy to demand its independence. This background is essential for understanding Austria's reaction to the Serbian-supported assassination of the heir to the Austro-Hungarian throne on 28 June 1914. Given the long-standing Balkan instability, and Serbia's many provocations, this was a threat to the Empire's international reputation that Vienna's statesmen felt they could not ignore. With the moral right seemingly on their side, the assassination seemed to provide an opportunity to dispose of the Serbian threat once and for all.

The July Crisis and the outbreak of war

In view of these tensions and underlying hostilities of the prewar years, it is perhaps not surprising that war would eventually result from such international rivalries, although that is not to say that such a turn of events was inevitable, given, for example, the existence of an increasingly vociferous peace movement in all the major powers. A reason was needed that would trigger such a final conflict, and it was provided by the murder of the Austrian heir to the throne, Archduke Franz Ferdinand and his wife in Sarajevo on 28 June 1914. The assassination has often been described as the spark that would set light to a continent that was riddled with international tensions. With hindsight, it appears almost as if war could not have been avoided. However, even in July 1914 a European war was not inevitable. Right until the last moment, some were desperately trying to avoid the outbreak of war and to resolve the crisis at the conference table, while others did everything in their power to make it happen. That war finally broke out was less the product of fate or bad fortune than the result of intention. In order to understand why the crisis escalated into full-scale war, we must look at Vienna and Berlin, for it was here that war (at least a war between Austria-Hungary and Serbia) was consciously risked and planned. France, Russia and Britain entered the stage much later in July 1914, when most decisions had already been taken.[16]

In Vienna, the reaction to the assassination was officially one of outrage, although behind the scenes many voices were secretly pleased, because Franz Ferdinand had not been universally popular. It is ironic that the Archduke's assassination should have provided the reason for a declaration of war on Serbia, given that Franz Ferdinand had been opposed to war during his lifetime, and had been a powerful opponent to the bellicose Chief of the Austrian General Staff, Franz Conrad von Hötzendorf. Conrad welcomed an excuse for a war with Serbia. He still regretted what he (as well as his German counterpart Helmuth von Moltke) had considered the 'missed opportunity' for a 'reckoning with Serbia' in 1909.[17] In Berlin, the possibility of a Balkan crisis was greeted favourably, for such a crisis would ensure that Austria would definitely become involved in a resulting conflict. Most historians would today agree that Berlin's decision-makers put substantial pressure on Vienna to demand retribution from Serbia, and that they were happy to take the risk that an Austro-Serbian conflict might escalate into a European war. When the

Austrian envoy Count Hoyos arrived in Berlin to ascertain the powerful ally's position in case Austria demanded recompense from Serbia, he was assured that Germany would support Austria all the way, even if it chose to go to war over the assassination, and even if such a war would turn into a European war. This was Germany's so-called 'blank cheque' to Vienna. In a strictly confidential telegram of 5 July to the Austro-Hungarian Foreign Minister Count Berchtold, the Austrian ambassador to Berlin, Count Szögyény, reported the following account of his meeting with the German Kaiser.

> The Kaiser authorised me to inform our Gracious Majesty that we might in this case, as in all others, rely upon Germany's full support. [...] He did not doubt in the least that Herr von Bethmann Hollweg [the German Chancellor] would agree with him. Especially as far as our action against Serbia was concerned. But it was his (Kaiser Wilhelm's) opinion that this action must not be delayed. Russia's attitude will no doubt be hostile, but for this he had for years prepared, and should a war between Austria-Hungary and Russia be unavoidable, we might be convinced that Germany, our old faithful ally, would stand on our side. Russia at the present time was in no way prepared for war, and would think twice before it appealed to arms. [...] If we had really recognised the necessity of warlike action against Serbia, he (Kaiser Wilhelm) would regret if we did not make use of the present moment, which is all in our favour.[18]

The Kaiser spoke without having consulted the Chancellor, Theobald von Bethmann Hollweg, whose approval he simply took for granted. Wilhelm II not only actively encouraged Austria to take action against Serbia, but even insisted that such action must not be delayed, and that it would be regrettable if the opportunity were not seized. He clearly expected Russia to adopt a hostile attitude, but felt that it was ill-prepared for war 'at the present time' and might therefore perhaps not take up arms. The Kaiser urged Austria to 'make use of the present moment', which he considered to be very favourable.

While most political and military decision-makers in Berlin did not actually want a *European* war, they were certainly willing to risk it. They had been encouraged to do so by Germany's leading military advisers, who had advocated war 'the sooner the better' on many occasions and had assured the politicians that Germany stood a good chance of defeating its enemies. Germany's military leaders had been conjuring up the image of a Russia that could still be defeated by Germany at this time, but that in future would be too strong to be taken on successfully.[19]

Armed with such reassurances from Germany, the Austro-Hungarian ministerial council decided on 7 July to issue an ultimatum to Serbia. This was to be deliberately unacceptable, so that Serbian non-compliance would lead to the outbreak of war with the 'moral high ground' on Austria's side. However, much time would pass before the ultimatum was finally delivered to Belgrade: first the harvest had to be completed, since most soldiers of the Dual Monarchy were away on harvest leave. Moreover, it was decided to wait until the state visit of Raymond Poincaré, the French president, to Russia was over, so that the two allies would not have a chance to coordinate their response to Austria's ultimatum. While all this was being plotted behind the scenes, both Vienna and Berlin gave the impression of calm to the outside world, even sending their main decision-makers on holiday to keep up this illusion. It is due to this deception that the other major powers did not play a role in the July Crisis until 23 July, the day when the ultimatum was finally delivered to Belgrade. They were largely unaware of the secret plotting in Vienna and Berlin.

The Serbian response to the 'unacceptable' ultimatum astonished everyone. In all but one point they agreed to accept it, making Austria's predetermined decision to turn down Belgrade's response look suspicious in the eyes of those European powers who wanted to try to preserve the peace. Even Kaiser Wilhelm II now decided that there was no longer any reason to go to war, much to the dismay of his military advisers. Britain suggested that the issue could be resolved at the conference table, but its mediation proposals and attempts to preserve the peace were not taken up by Vienna or Berlin. Some historians would argue that Britain could have played a more decisive role by declaring its intentions to support France earlier, rather than trying to be non-committal until the last possible moment. It is alleged that if Germany's decision-makers had known earlier and with certainty that Britain would be involved in a war on the side of the Entente, they would have accepted mediation proposals and would have counselled peace in Vienna.[20] It certainly is worth speculating that Bethmann Hollweg's mediation proposal to Vienna late in the crisis would have been delivered sooner, and more forcefully, if the Chancellor had known earlier of Britain's definite resolve to come to France's aid in a European war. However, the British Cabinet objected to a British involvement in a European war, and no definite decision to support France was made until Germany's violation of neutral Belgium. In the crucial last days of July, Britain's decision-makers were divided on how to deal with the threat of war on the continent. Nonetheless, the ambivalence of Sir Edward Grey's policy should not be seen as a cause of the war. After all, this hesitant attitude was motivated by the desire to *avoid* an escalation of the crisis (Grey feared that a definite promise of support might have led France or Russia to accept the risk of war more willingly), while German and Austro-Hungarian decisions were based on the explicit desire to *provoke* a conflict. As the former ambassador to London, Prince Lichnowsky, summed up in January 1915:

> On our side nothing, absolutely nothing, was done to preserve peace, and when we at last decided to do what I had advocated from the first, it was too late. By then Russia, as a result of our harsh attitude and that of Count Berchtold [the Austrian Prime Minister], had lost all confidence and mobilised. The war party gained the upper hand. [...] Such a policy is comprehensible only if war was our aim, not otherwise.[21]

Only at the very last minute, when it was clear that Britain, too, would become involved if war broke out, did the German Chancellor try to restrain the Austrians – but his mediation proposals arrived far too late and were in any case not forceful enough. Austria declared war on Serbia on 28 July, and thus set in motion a domino effect of mobilization orders and declarations of war by Europe's major powers. By the time Britain had declared war on Germany on 4 August, following Germany's invasion of neutral Luxembourg and Belgium (necessitated by the Schlieffen Plan), the Alliance powers (without Italy, which had decided to stay neutral) faced the Entente powers in the 'great fight' that had been anticipated for such a long time. However, the war, which was commonly expected to be 'over by Christmas', did not go to plan.[22] The longer it lasted, the more victims it took, and the worse it went for the Central Powers, the more important did it become to construct an apologetic version of the events that had led to the war's outbreak. On the other hand, for those countries who felt they were suffering due to the aggression of the Central Powers, attributing blame and – eventually – demanding retribution became a prime concern. Not surprisingly, even before the fighting had ended, the debate on the war's origins had already begun.

This brief outline of prewar diplomatic and political events has to be supplemented by a word of warning. Just like all the other accounts examined in this volume, this version of events might be regarded as highly contentious by some historians. There is no interpretation, no 'factual' account of the events that led to war that could not be criticized or rejected by historians who favour a different explanation of the origins of the war – after all, this is precisely why this debate has occupied historians for nearly a century. Moreover, it is an account based on hindsight, and on decades of scholarship on the topic. Some of the information it contains would not have been available to historians writing in the immediate post- and interwar years, whose work will be introduced and discussed here. Historians today have a considerable advantage over those who began to investigate the causes of the conflict almost as soon as the war had started. We have more evidence at our disposal (although this has not resulted in a general agreement on the topic), and we are not personally affected by the horrors of the war in the same way that contemporaries inevitably were. To historians writing during and immediately after the war, the origins of the conflict were not yet history, and settling the question of responsibility was of immediate political and economic concern, as well as a question of pride and national honour. It is to those early views on the origins of the war that this examination of the debate on the origins of the First World War will turn first of all.

Notes

1 George P. Gooch, *Before the War: Studies in Diplomacy*, vol. 2: *The Coming of the Storm*, London 1938, p. v.

2 Philip Bell, 'Origins of the War of 1914', in Paul Hayes (ed.), *Themes in Modern European History 1890–1945*, London and New York 1992, p. 106.

3 A phrase coined much later by George F. Kennan, *The Decline of Bismarck's European Order: Franco-Russian Relations, 1875–1890*, Princeton 1979, p. 3.

4 John W. Langdon, *July 1914: The Long Debate 1918–1990*, New York and Oxford 1991.

5 A thorough account of the diplomatic developments that led to war in 1914 is beyond the scope of this volume whose emphasis is on the debate on the origins of the war, rather than the events themselves. The following is only a brief chronological overview of European political history in the prewar years. It is intended as background for the analysis of the debates which follow. References to further reading are provided. In addition, readers are referred to Hew Strachan's account of the origins of the war in *The First World War*, vol. I: *To Arms*, Oxford 2001, pp. 1–102 and Holger H. Herwig's summary 'Origins: Now or Never', in *The First World War: Germany and Austria–Hungary 1914–1918*, London 1997, pp. 6–42. An essential introduction to the subject is James Joll, *The Origins of the First World War*, 2nd edn, London 1992.

6 For a recent overview see Matthew S. Seligmann and Roderick R. McLean, *Germany from Reich to Republic 1871–1918*, London 2000.

7 See Map 1: European alliances before the First World War.

8 See, for example, Volker Berghahn, *Der Tirpitz-Plan: Genesis und Verfall einer innenpolitischen Krisenstrategie unter Wilhelm II*, Düsseldorf 1971; Berghahn, *Germany and the Approach of War*, 2nd

edn, London 1993; Paul M. Kennedy, 'The Development of German Naval Operations Plans against England, 1896–1914', in idem (ed.), *The War Plans of the Great Powers, 1880–1914*, London 1979; idem, *The Rise of the Anglo-German Antagonism*, London 1980; Michael Epkenhans, *Die wilhelminische Flottenrüstung 1908–1914: Weltmachtstreben, industrieller Fortschritt, soziale Integration*, Munich 1991. A brief English account can be found in Berghahn, *Imperial Germany 1871–1914: Economy, Society, Culture and Politics*, Oxford 1994.

9 For details, see e.g. R.T.B. Langhorne, 'Great Britain and Germany, 1911–1914', in F.H. Hinsley (ed.), *British Foreign Policy under Sir Edward Grey*, London 1997, pp. 288–611; R.J. Crampton, *The Hollow Détente: Anglo-German Relations in the Balkans, 1911–1914*, London 1980; Kennedy, *Rise of Anglo-German Antagonism*. On the construction of Admiral Tirpitz's battle fleet, see Berghahn, *Der Tirpitz-Plan*.

10 See, for example, Keith M. Wilson, *The Policy of the Entente: Essays on the Determinants of British Foreign Policy 1904–1914*, Cambridge 1985; Rainer Lahme, 'Das Ende der Pax Britannica: England und die europäischen Mächte 1890–1914', *Archiv für Kulturgeschichte*, vol. 73, No. 1, 1991, pp. 169–92.

11 For the following see, for example, Joll, *The Origins of the First World War*; Berghahn, *Germany and the Approach of War*; Seligmann and McLean, *Germany from Reich to Republic*; Strachan, *The First World War*.

12 Holstein, minutes of 3 June 1904, *Die Grosse Politik*, 20/I, No. 6521, cited in Gregor Schöllgen, 'Germany's Foreign Policy in the Age of Imperialism: A Vicious Circle?', in idem (ed.), *Escape into War? The Foreign Policy of Imperial Germany*, Oxford 1990, p. 125.

13 'Young Turks' was the name given to a liberal reform movement in Turkey. The revolution of 1908 led to the establishment of constitutional rule in Turkey.

14 For more information, see Samuel R. Williamson, Jr., *Austria-Hungary and the Origins of the First World War*, London 1991.

15 On the armaments race see David Stevenson, *Armaments and the Coming of War: Europe 1904–1914*, Oxford 1996; David G. Herrmann, *The Arming of Europe and the Making of the First World War*, Princeton, 1997.

16 For further information on the diplomatic events of the July Crisis see in particular Imanuel Geiss (ed.), *July 1914: The Outbreak of the First World War. Selected Documents*, London and New York 1967; as well as Luigi Albertini, *The Origins of the War of 1914*, 3 vols, Engl. transl., Oxford 1952–57; Fritz Fischer, *War of Illusions: German Policies from 1911–1914*, London 1975; Joll, *Origins of the First World War*; Keith M. Wilson (ed.), *Decisions for War, 1914*, London 1995; Stevenson, *Armaments and the Coming of War*, pp. 366ff.; Langdon,

July 1914; David Stevenson, *The Outbreak of the First World War*, London 1997. Further references can be found in Annika Mombauer, *Helmuth von Moltke and the Origins of the First World War*, Cambridge 2001, ch. 4.

17 Franz Conrad von Hötzendorf, *Aus meiner Dienstzeit* 1906–1918, 5 vols, Vienna, Leipzig and Munich 1921–25, vol. I, p. 165.

18 Geiss, *July 1914: Selected Documents*, p. 77.

19 See Mombauer, *Helmuth von Moltke*, pp. 121ff.

20 These arguments can be found in Part 3 below.

21 Lichnowsky's memorandum cited in John C.G. Röhl (ed.), *1914: Delusion or Design? The Testimony of Two German Diplomats*, London 1973, pp. 79ff.

22 Stig Förster has recently argued that Germany's leading military decision-makers did not believe in a short war: 'Der deutsche Generalstab und die Illusion des kurzen Krieges, 1871–1914: Metakritik eines Mythos', *Militärgeschichtliche Mitteilungen*, 54, 1/1995, pp. 61–98.

Part 1

The Question of War Guilt during the War and at the Versailles Peace Negotiations

Introduction

Should all our attempts [for peace] be in vain, should the sword be forced into our hand, we shall go into the field of battle with a clear conscience and the knowledge that we did not desire this war. Theobald von Bethmann Hollweg, August 1914[1]

The debate on the origins of the First World War, which had begun as early as 1914, was intensified by the impact of the Versailles Peace Settlement following Germany's defeat. During and immediately after the war, each combatant power was convinced of the enemy's war guilt and belligerence, and after the Treaty of Versailles, victors and vanquished were at loggerheads over attributing blame for the outbreak of the war. After 1919, 'revisionists' (those who objected to the war guilt allegation of the victors and wanted to revise it) and their opponents ('anti-revisionists') battled over what they considered the right interpretation of the events that had led to war.

In the following section it will be asked why was it deemed necessary to allocate blame and responsibility for the outbreak of war, and how those accused of causing the war, particularly in Germany, reacted to this apportioning of guilt. What were the motives behind the denial of war guilt by some commentators, and behind its attribution by others? How did Germany react to the war guilt accusation, and who came to Germany's defence abroad in asserting a more general responsibility?

This part also examines the influence of governments on shaping official views on the outbreak of the war, both during the war itself, when all leaders understandably engaged in propaganda which made their own policy appear in a positive light, and in the postwar years, when successive German governments ensured that the official innocence view was supported by numerous official and semi-official German publications.

The beginning of the debate on the War's origins

Clio was, in fact, deceived in Germany as early as 1914. Holger Herwig[2]

Attempts to allocate blame for the outbreak of war in 1914 began even before the fighting had started. Understandably, all governments emphasized the defensive nature of their actions. For all combatant nations, it was imperative that their own population felt they were fighting a just and justified war, in which they were defending their country against an aggressive enemy. 'Ordinary' men and women would not have fought in their millions in a war of aggression, as the governments of Europe knew only too well.

In Vienna the 'disguise' of an ultimatum to the government in Belgrade, worded to be deliberately unacceptable, attempted to put the blame for the outbreak of the war on Serbia. In Britain, France, Belgium and Russia, people were in no doubt that the aggressors had been located in Berlin and Vienna, while their own nations were either defending themselves, as in the case of Russia, France and Belgium, or were coming to the rescue of a weaker neighbour and the defence of their alliance partners, as in the case of Britain. For Germany's enemies, the violation of its neutral neighbouring states Luxembourg and Belgium seemed ample proof of German belligerence in 1914. However, Germans and Austro-Hungarians equally believed that they were defending themselves against hostile Entente powers. In Germany, the so-called *Burgfrieden* (political truce between the anti-war

Socialist Party (SPD) and the government) could only be achieved on the basis that the German government was innocent in the events that had led to war. Therefore it was claimed in Germany that the war was a result of Tsarist aggression (for example, in Chancellor Theobald von Bethmann Hollweg's Reichstag speech of 4 August, and in the German White Book, compiled in the early days of August). Germany's 'innocence complex' was thus not solely a product of the Treaty of Versailles (which will be examined below), but was 'an integral component of German policy since the July Crisis of 1914 itself'.[3] Stating and proving one's innocence in bringing about the war was of crucial importance both before and during the war, and not just a product of the postwar peace agreement.

Conscious efforts were made in Berlin to make Germany appear threatened and ultimately attacked, with Chancellor Bethmann Hollweg blaming Russia for the escalation of the crisis. Germany's Chancellor had, for example, encouraged Kaiser Wilhelm II on 28 July to send a conciliatory telegram to Tsar Nicholas II, which claimed that it was in the Tsar's hands to avert 'the misfortune which now threatens the entire civilized world'. As Bethmann Hollweg callously explained to the Kaiser, should war nonetheless result from the crisis, the existence of such a telegram would point clearly to Russia's guilt and would make it appear as if Germany had wanted to preserve peace in July 1914.[4] When war had become a reality, the chief of the Kaiser's navy cabinet, Admiral Georg Alexander von Müller, recorded in his diary: 'Brilliant mood. The government has succeeded very well in making us appear as the attacked.'[5]

Soon after the outbreak of war, all major powers involved in the fighting published official documents in so-called 'coloured books', designed to prove their own innocence in the events that led to war (the German White Book, the British Blue Book, the Russian Orange Book, the Austro-Hungarian Red Book, the French Yellow Book, etc.). These very selective collections were justificatory, but their official nature gave them an air of objectivity. It is not difficult to see the motivation behind such publications – no government wanted to appear guilty of causing the war, neither to the outside world, nor to their own people, whose will to fight depended to a large extent on the notion that they were involved in fighting a just war.

As part of its attempt to downplay Germany's role in the outbreak of the war, the German government published its White Book (*Deutsches Weissbuch*) as early as 3 August 1914. Like all the 'coloured books' published by the belligerent powers just after the outbreak of war, Germany's White Book, compiled by the Chancellor's private secretary Kurt Riezler, aimed to prove Germany's innocence in the events that led to war. Hence it was subtitled: 'How Russia and her Ruler betrayed Germany's confidence and thereby made the European War.' Hermann Kantorowicz, who in the 1920s came to doubt the official German innocence interpretation, called it 'the most falsified coloured book on the outbreak of the war'.[6] Such critical views were not, however, made public either during or after the war, leaving the German population understandably aggrieved that their enemies should attempt to place blame for the war's outbreak on Germany, when the official evidence available to them so clearly stated the opposite.

Of course, the Berlin government could not have known just how important it would become for Germany to be able to demonstrate to the world its own innocence in the events that led to war. In the summer of 1914 Germany's leaders still confidently expected a victory for the Central Powers. However, it was nonetheless deemed necessary to collate and publish suitable material, not least because there were some critical voices within Germany that needed to be countered. Among those who failed to be convinced by the thesis that Germany had been attacked by its enemies was the socialist and pacifist Karl Liebknecht, who had led a small group of deputies demanding that the Socialist Party vote against war credits as early as 3 August 1914, and who on 2 December

1914 was the only deputy to vote openly against further such credits in the Reichstag. He explained his decision thus:

> This war which none of the participant nations itself has wanted was not started for the welfare of the German or any other people. It is an imperialist war, a war for capitalist control of important settlement areas for industrial and banking capital. From the point of view of the armaments race it is a preventive war brought about by the German and the Austrian war party together in the darkness of semi-absolutism and secret diplomacy.[7]

Given such openly voiced criticism, and in the light of the perceived urgency to appear attacked, Foreign Secretary Gottlieb von Jagow instructed his subordinate Arthur Zimmermann at the end of August to prepare 'for the imminent battle of opinions the publication of a comprehensive edition on the prehistory of the war', and in particular to compile suitable material for such a larger publication 'so that we can publish within a few days if necessary'.[8] In Holger Herwig's words, 'Clio was, in fact, deceived in Germany as early as 1914.'[9]

In the first weeks of the war, the question of war guilt had been understandably high on the political agenda. Not only was it deemed important to convince the general public that they were being asked to fight for the right reasons, but other political considerations also existed. In an angry response to a German publication of September 1914 entitled *Truth about Germany: Facts about the War*, written by a committee of German authors which included former Chancellor Bernhard von Bülow and the industrialist Albert Ballin, the British commentator Douglas Sladen outlined his overriding concerns at the time. He suspected that the German publication had been conceived with the aim of 'deceiving Americans as to the true causes of the outbreak of the war'. For much the same reason, or rather for that of educating the United States about what he considered the truth, Sladen prepared a reprint of the German text, and annotated it to highlight 'all its misstatements'. As the edition makes clear, the concern of both the German publication and the British commentator was to warn America of the consequences of becoming involved on the 'wrong' side, or even of not becoming involved at all in the war in Europe. The German text warned in no uncertain terms about the likely consequences of American non-intervention.

> The war, provoked by Russia because of an outrageous desire for revenge, supported by England and France, has no other motive than envy of Germany's position in economic life, and of her people, who are fighting for a place in the sun. [. . .] One can easily imagine the feelings of these peoples when they observe the rapid and successful growth of Germany, and one wonders if these same feelings will not one day be directed against the youthful North American giant.[10]

Ultimately, America's statesmen were not convinced by such arguments, and entered the war on the side of Germany's enemies in 1917. United States' troops played a decisive part in defeating the Central Powers, and President Woodrow Wilson's 'Fourteen Points', promising a new European diplomatic order, formed the basis on which the defeated Germans based their hopes for a relatively fair, if not lenient, peace treaty.[11]

Given the general conviction on all sides that the opponents had caused the war, and given the length and severity of the conflict, it was naturally becoming increasingly difficult, if not impossible, to have a dispassionate debate about its origins. There were no attempts at a serious analysis of the events during the war, or of the reasons why each side was under the impression it was fighting a defensive war. As Hartmut Pogge von Strandmann has argued: 'Such a study would have demanded a knowledge of the political, military, and economic establishments, their plans, ambitions and assumptions. Clearly, this was beyond the inclination of diplomats and publicists as well as historians at the time.'[12] Moreover, any argument against the official line would have been considered treacherous and disloyal, and the increasing loss of life and suffering diminished what little chance there might have been of an objective assessment.

And yet, crucially for the further development of the debate on the outbreak of the war, there did exist some accounts which were based on such knowledge of political, military and economic circumstances, and their publication during the war was both embarrassing to the German government and enlightening to those of its enemies. The Berlin lawyer Richard Grelling was among those who left Germany in protest after the beginning of the war. From his exile in Switzerland he studied the available literature, including the 'coloured books', and came to the conclusion that the German government had wanted war more than Austria-Hungary's leaders. Not surprisingly, given such 'disloyal' findings, his book, *J'accuse . . .*, which he published in France, was banned in Germany, although, in private, a leading German general, Count Max von Montgelas, agreed in a letter to Grelling with his general conclusions and spoke of 'Germany's triple guilt':

> 1. Before the war it tried to preserve peace with the antiquated and unsuitable means of constantly increased armaments. 2. It consciously brought about the war as a *preventive war*. 3. It had war aims which no reasonably honour-loving opponent *could* accept.

Moreover, Montgelas admitted that 'the preventive war decided upon on 5th July became a war of conquest in September 1914'.[13] Despite this conviction during the war, Count Montgelas would strongly refute this point of view following Germany's defeat, as will be seen below.

Another critical and informed account was the lengthy memorandum written by Germany's former Imperial ambassador to London, Prince Karl Max von Lichnowsky, about his experiences in the prewar years. As a diplomat and German aristocrat, his connections with Germany's leading decision-makers ensured that he had enjoyed more insight than most into German politics in the years prior to the outbreak of war.

During July 1914 he had worked ceaselessly in London to avoid an escalation of the crisis into war. When he returned to Berlin at the beginning of August, he realized that he 'was to be made the scapegoat for the catastrophe which our government had brought upon itself against my counsels and warnings'. In the German press, he was accused of having been responsible for Britain's decision to enter the war on the side of Germany's enemies. His memorandum 'My London Mission' was written against this background in the summer of 1916, designed as a private justification against such claims. Lichnowsky had not intended a publication – rather, the text had been the basis of an address he gave privately in late July 1916, printed and passed from hand to hand. He had shown it to 'very few political friends', as he explained in a letter to the Chancellor in March 1918, but a copy was leaked to the government in Berlin by a captain in the German General Staff, and another found its way to neutral Sweden, where it was published in the socialist newspaper *Politiken*.[14] By the end of 1917, the document circulated widely in Germany, and played a part in the left-wing Spartacus League's agitation to end the war. Lichnowsky was subjected to severe criticism from the government, and was expelled from the Prussian House of Lords in April 1918.[15]

In 1918, before the war had come to an end, Munroe Smith, an American commentator and translator of the memorandum, summed up the account's 'chief value' as residing 'in the fact that [Lichnowsky] rejects and helps to disprove every plea in justification of Germany's conduct that has been advanced since the outbreak of the World War by Germany's official apologists'. Moreover, the account demonstrated that 'Germany was not isolated by the wiles of its neighbours; it had isolated itself by its own conduct'.[16] Indeed, this astonishing and revealing document portrayed Germany's prewar policy in a very negative light, and placed the responsibility for the escalation of the crisis firmly on Berlin. Little wonder that the Entente partners focused on this account in blaming Germany for the outbreak of war, or that the memorandum would again serve as evidence against Germany more than fifty years after the outbreak of war, during the Fischer controversy of the 1960s and 1970s.[17]

Munroe Smith even hoped that after the war evidence such as Lichnowsky's would be accepted by the German public: 'In a Germany sobered by defeat, the Lichnowsky memorandum, with the Muehlon letters and many other pieces of evidence that demonstrate the guilt of Berlin, will doubtless attract increasing attention, and it may be anticipated that the truth will slowly filter into the German mind.'[18] Wilhelm Muehlon, member of the Board of Directors of the Krupp Works at Essen, had published a pamphlet consisting of extracts from his diaries and letters, entitled *Die Verheerung Europas* (The Devastation of Europe) in Switzerland in 1918. He was, in Munroe Smith's opinion, 'one of the relatively few Germans who knew, from the outset, that the Central Empires had forced an unnecessary and unjustifiable war upon Europe; and he was one of the far smaller number of Germans whom the conduct of their government stirred into indignation and revolt'.[19] Muehlon's material claimed, for example, that the German Kaiser and his military advisers had wanted war in 1914, that Wilhelm II had only gone on his cruise during July 1914 to keep up appearances and that he had expressed his determination not to 'fall down' again during the current crisis at meetings in Berlin with the industrialist von Bohlen und Halbach. However, while Muehlon's evidence was to some extent based on hearsay, Lichnowsky's account seemed to be more reliable proof for the Allies, if proof were needed, of Germany's guilt in 1914, especially given the fact that Lichnowsky tried to suppress his memorandum after it had been leaked, and given that the German government was at such pains to suppress it, and to make the Prince appear as somewhat deranged, or a pathological fool.[20] Such evidence from the enemy could be used for propaganda purposes in Britain while the war lasted, as a commentator put it in the *Daily News* in 1918:

> It blows to the winds the last fragment of the case of those who have opposed this war – who for three years and more have said that we were guilty too, who have taught the unthinking the mischievous cant about a fight between this group of capitalists and that, and encouraged them to doubt and ask 'What are we fighting about?' Lichnowsky knows what we are fighting about. Thousands in Germany know what we are fighting about, and millions soon will know.[21]

The following extract from Lichnowsky's writings demonstrates the nature of his allegations:

> It is shown by all official publications and is not disproved by our White Book, which, owing to the poverty of its contents and to its omissions, constitutes a grave indictment against ourselves, that:
>
> 1. We encouraged Count Berchtold to attack Serbia, although no German interest was involved and the danger of a World War must have been known to us. Whether we were acquainted with the wording of the ultimatum is completely immaterial.
> 2. During the period between the 2nd and the 30th of July, 1914, when M. Sazonof emphatically declared that he could not tolerate an attack on Serbia, we rejected the British proposal of mediation, although Serbia, under Russian and British pressure, had accepted almost the whole of the ultimatum, and although an agreement about the two points at issue could easily have been reached and Count Berchtold was even prepared to content himself with the Serbian reply.
> 3. On the 30th of July, when Count Berchtold showed a disposition to change his course, we sent an ultimatum to St Petersburg merely because of the Russian mobilization and though Austria had not been attacked; and on the 31st of July we declared war against the Russians, although the Czar pledged his word that he would not permit a single man to march as long as negotiations were still going on. Thus we deliberately destroyed the possibility of a peaceful settlement.

> In view of these incontestable facts, it is no wonder that the whole civilized world outside of Germany places the sole responsibility for the World War upon our shoulders.[22]

Outside of Germany, early investigations into the origins of the war tended to adhere to the national line and emphasized the guilt of the Central Powers. In Britain, six Oxford historians published an account based on Germany's and Britain's 'coloured books' entitled *Why We Are at War: Great Britain's Case* in September 1914. German militarism and a quest for power were cited here as the reason for the outbreak of the war, and Britain's entry into the war was justified by the country's need to uphold international law.[23] The authors described it as 'England's duty' to come to the aid of smaller nations like Belgium and Serbia. 'In fighting for Belgium we fight for the law of nations; that is, ultimately, for the peace of all nations and for the right of the weaker to exist.' For Britons engaged in fighting the war, such arguments provided reassurance that theirs was a legitimate and even honourable quest. The authors provided a lengthy history of Belgium and Luxembourg, and explained how Belgium had acquired its special status as an independent state. By introducing their readers to The Hague Peace Convention of 1907, according to which 'belligerents are forbidden to move across the territory of a neutral power troops or convoys, either of munitions of war or supplies', and the Treaty of London of 1839 in which Britain, among other countries, had agreed that 'Belgium shall form an independent and perpetually neutral state', the professors ensured that their audience was in no doubt as to why Britain was embroiled in the war, and that they were fighting for a just cause. 'If treaties count for nothing, no nation is secure so long as any imaginable combination of Powers can meet in battle or diplomacy on equal terms', they asserted.[24] Similarly, E. Barker argued in a short pamphlet of 1915 that 'England' had needed to support Belgium for moral and political reasons: 'the security of England depends, and has depended for centuries, on the integrity and independence of

Belgium', he asserted in this patriotic publication, written by 'one Englishman speaking for England'.[25]

The historian and politician James W. Headlam-Morley also studied the 'coloured books' and other available evidence during the war, and he, too, found Germany to blame for the escalation of the July Crisis. He concluded after 'long and careful study of all that has been put forward by the German Government that it is impossible to put any reliance on anything that they say either with regard to their own motives or intentions or in regard to the simplest facts'. According to Headlam-Morley, the German government

> have been successful in persuading the German nation to believe that Russian mobilisation was aggressive; but this has only been done by themselves publishing a version of what happened which is throughout misleading, and by excluding from general circulation in Germany the British diplomatic correspondence.

This was a fairly typical point of view in Britain during the war. There was no doubt in the author's mind that Germany was guilty of unleashing the war, and that its government had something to hide. Rather self-righteously, Headlam-Morley considered what he would have done if he had found himself in a similar situation to German authors, having studied his government's actions: 'Had I found in the course of the work that the result would be unfavourable to the justice and honesty of the British cause, I should have adopted the only possible course and kept silent till the war was over.'[26] Given that he was not keeping silent, the implication for his readers was that they could feel assured of the truth of his account.

However, there were also some dissenting voices who doubted Headlam-Morley's truth, and who refused to keep silent until the war was over. In Britain, Edmund D. Morel was an outspoken opponent of the view that Germany was to blame for the outbreak of war. In his 1916 publication *Truth and the War*, he argued instead that secret diplomacy was the real culprit, and he made a passionate plea for the truth to be

suffering among soldiers and civilians alike, the war had come to an end. Thirty-six countries had participated in the fighting and had mobilized some 70 million men, at least 10 million people lost their lives, and a further 20 million soldiers were left crippled. Accurate figures for the millions of civilian casualties do not exist.[30] The German Empire and its allies were finally defeated and an armistice was declared on 11 November 1918. Kaiser Wilhelm II had abdicated and fled his country on 9 November, and Philipp Scheidemann had proclaimed a Republic to replace the monarchy that had gone to war in 1914 – visible signs that Germany had been defeated, and that the future would spell a decisive break from the past. The fate of the defeated Germans now depended on the will of the Allies. Following years of fighting, the victorious Entente partners were keen to ensure that German aggression would be curbed, that the country would not be able to unleash another war, and they wanted to hold Germany accountable for the war that they believed its leaders had caused. Throughout the conflict, they had been convinced that Germany had been guilty of starting the war, that it had encouraged Austria-Hungary to pursue its bellicose policy *vis-à-vis* Serbia, that it had refused mediation proposals designed to defuse the situation, and that it had wanted war to realize its own expansionist aims. Now that the war was over, the black-and-white war guilt interpretations continued as they had during the war, only with different aims in mind.[31]

More was at stake now than simply establishing the responsibility for the outbreak of war. Public opinion in France and Britain demanded revenge for the alleged and actual atrocities committed by German troops, particularly against Belgian and French civilians, and Germany was to be made to pay for the damage caused as a result of the war.[32] 'Le boche payera' had been a French rallying cry both during the war and during the French election campaign in 1919, while in Britain during the November elections of 1918, all political parties had to address the anti-German feelings in the country, and many even tried to stir up popular hatred of the former enemy. As one commentator, Leo Amery, noted: 'The great British people are not in the least interested in Social Reform or Reconstruction, but only in making the Germans pay for the war and punishing the Kaiser.'[33] Although Lloyd George had tried to stay outside of such anti-German agitation, and tried initially to focus on domestic issues in his speeches (Britain was to become 'a fit country for heroes to live in'), his audiences wanted to hear about his plans for punishing Germany. One MP even launched the slogan 'I am for hanging the Kaiser.'[34]

During and immediately after the war, the Kaiser's culpability seemed without question among French and British commentators. 'When all is said and done the German Emperor [. . .] is the responsible author of the misfortunes that afflict the world', judged a French critic.[35] It was not only the victorious Allies who blamed Wilhelm II for the outbreak of war. In Germany, too, he was seen by many as responsible for the disastrous foreign policy that had led to war. In a somewhat simplistic way many critics focused on his personality and his alleged psychological disturbance. Following his abdication, a number of supposedly scientific studies appeared in Germany which found reasons for the Kaiser's bellicosity in his assumed madness. 'For the experienced physician and psychiatrist there can be no doubt that Wilhelm II already as a youth was mentally ill. [. . .] The blame for the war that can be attributed to him was the result of his illness', judged the psychiatrist Paul Tesdorpf in 1919. As Thomas Kohut suspects, while such authors were no doubt genuinely trying to understand such a 'puzzling and to them historically decisive personality, it seems clear that a diagnosis of inherent "degeneracy", like the veiled imputation of the German defeat to Wilhelm's psychopathology generally, suited the need of Germans to distance themselves from their Kaiser after 1918'.[36] In many ways, it was easier to come to terms with the defeat, and with the allegation of war guilt, if both could be blamed on the 'insane' and now departed former Kaiser.

It was almost a foregone conclusion that the peace

agreement would be harsh, given the conviction among Germany's enemies that it, and its rulers, had deliberately unleashed war in 1914. Nonetheless, many Germans hoped for a moderate treaty based on Woodrow Wilson's 'Fourteen Points'.[37] After all, it was not only the victors who felt that they had fought a justified, defensive – and thus legitimized – war. Most Germans had believed their Kaiser's proclamation to the German people in August 1914, in which he had exclaimed: 'In the midst of peace the enemy attacks us!', while the Chancellor, as noted above, had similarly conjured up the image of Germany defending itself against hostile neighbours. The German people did not know how important 'appearing attacked' had been in the scheme of German decision-makers during the July Crisis of 1914, and to what extent they had been victims of a calculated propaganda manoeuvre in which the war guilt question had been an issue even before hostilities had begun.[38] During the course of the war, such propaganda had continually ensured a patriotic conviction among the German people. Little wonder that they were aggrieved at the thought of having to shoulder the burden for a war they had neither wanted nor felt responsible for.

What is more, Germans did not really 'feel' defeated. Since August 1914, they had been led to believe that peace would come in the shape of German victory. Little news of defeats and setbacks on the various fronts had ever reached them during the war. Germany had even defeated Russia, and in the Treaty of Brest-Litovsk in March 1918 had imposed harsh peace conditions on the enemy. It had come close to winning the war in the spring and summer of 1918, or so the official propaganda had made the German people believe. Now, almost out of the blue, they were expected to accept defeat. In November 1918, aside from the Kaiser's abdication and the declaration of the Republic, there were few obvious outward signs of a defeat. There were no foreign soldiers on German soil, and German troops returned seemingly 'undefeated from the front' in an orderly fashion that did not seem to suggest they had just lost the war. The myth of the undefeated

German army, stabbed in the back by traitors from within, could easily develop in such conditions, and it made the harsh peace conditions that the victors imposed on Germany at the Paris Peace Conference even harder to come to terms with. German opposition to the peace treaty was almost a foregone conclusion, and it united almost the entire political spectrum of the new German Republic on one important issue: to fight against the Versailles settlement.[39]

Given that Germans thought they had fought a defensive (and reasonably successful) war, the outrage with which the defeated Germans greeted the Treaty of Versailles, the victors' decisions on the future of Germany, on reparations and on war guilt, taken without any consultation of the German government, was all the greater. Among the victors, President Woodrow Wilson had battled with the British Prime Minister David Lloyd George and French Prime Minister Georges Clemenceau over the nature of the treaty. While Wilson insisted on a peace treaty that took account of some of the principles he had laid down in his 'Fourteen Points', and in particular on the establishment of a League of Nations, Lloyd George and Clemenceau were adamant on a German acknowledgement of liability, rather than merely an Allied assertion, and they consequently demanded a harsh peace treaty. In the end, 'Wilson obtained his League of Nations – Clemenceau and Lloyd George their war-guilt clause.'[40] Within Germany, Wilson's 'Fourteen Points' had initially received little support, and were only adopted for pragmatic reasons when things were beginning to look desperate for the country and a defeat seemed unavoidable. The outrage with which Germany's apparent betrayal at Versailles was greeted, where Wilson's Points did not come to bear, is not difficult to comprehend, given that German hopes for a lenient peace treaty were based on Wilson's alleged promises.[41] And yet, Germany itself had dealt harshly with Russia in the peace agreement of Brest-Litovsk, a fact that was conveniently overlooked now that Germany was on the receiving end of a victor's peace.

The Allies' allegation that Germany was to blame for the outbreak of the war was a sensitive matter of honour and was considered even more intolerable than the harsh economic sanctions which Germany suffered as a result of the lost war.[42] Because the allegation of war guilt justified these sanctions, Germany's alleged sole responsibility for the outbreak of war had to be disproved in order to put an end to them. The full extent of the damages Germany was to repay was not yet settled in the summer of 1919, when the German delegation reluctantly signed the treaty, and the decision on the amount of reparations was postponed. The question of 'war guilt' had been decided, however. Germany's new government had been excluded from the negotiations and the German peace delegation, consisting of six German politicians led by the Minister of Foreign Affairs Count Ulrich Brockdorff-Rantzau, was simply presented with a draft of the peace conditions on 7 May 1919 and told that they were obliged to comment in writing on the treaty within fifteen days. Oral negotiations were ruled out.[43]

Given that Brockdorff-Rantzau had only accepted the appointment to lead the peace delegation under the condition that he could refuse to sign the treaty if it were of a nature 'such as to deprive the German people of a decent livelihood', the harsh treaty on which the victorious Allies had agreed was bound to cause upset and objection among the peace delegation.[44] When Brockdorff-Rantzau was finally presented with the draft treaty proposal at the Trianon Palace Hotel in Versailles, he reacted with a passionate and defiant speech, during which he broke diplomatic etiquette by refusing to stand up to address Clemenceau, the chair of the proceedings. He commented on the question of war guilt in particular:

> We are under no illusions as to the extent of our defeat and the degree of our powerlessness. We know that the strength of the German arms is broken. We know the intensity of the hatred which meets us, and we have heard the victor's passionate demand that as the vanquished we shall be made to pay, and

> that as the guilty we shall be punished. The demand is made that we shall acknowledge that we alone are guilty of having caused the war. Such a confession in my mouth would be a lie.

While not denying that atrocities had been committed, for example in Belgium, Brockdorff-Rantzau insisted that 'Germany was not the only one that erred' in this respect, calling attention in particular to the Allied blockade and reminding delegates that the 'hundreds of thousands of non-combatants who have perished since November 11, because of the blockade, were destroyed coolly and deliberately after our opponents had won a certain and assured victory. Remember that, when you speak of guilt and atonement'.[45] While this unrepentant style of address was bound not to make the best impression at Versailles, such public statements only helped to underline further the conviction within Germany that the agreement was a victor's peace. Germany's 'innocence complex' was able to continue unabated in such conditions.

Not surprisingly, given the nature of the Treaty and the way in which it was presented to the German delegation, and given Brockdorff-Rantzau's defiance, there ensued 'a brisk paper warfare' before the Treaty was signed, as Harold W.V. Temperley describes in his *History of the Peace Conference of Paris*. In an indignant note to Clemenceau of 13 May 1919, Brockdorff-Rantzau explained how Germany viewed the proposed peace treaty, and in particular the offending article detailing Germany's war guilt. While the delegation had accepted the demand for reparations, Brockdorff-Rantzau pointed out this had been done independently of the question of war guilt, and it certainly had not amounted to any admission of responsibility or guilt on the part of Germany. The German delegation could not accept that the assumed guilt of a former German government would result in claims from the victorious allies against the new government, or worse, against the German people. Brockdorff-Rantzau summed up the current thinking in Germany: 'The German people did not will the war and would never have undertaken a war of aggression. They have always remained convinced that this war was for them a defensive war.' Moreover, he could not accept that the former German government should bear the sole, or even the main, responsibility for causing the war, and he pointed out that the draft of the peace treaty did not offer any evidence for such a claim. He repeated his demands for an impartial tribunal to establish the real cause of the war which he had first raised at his initial address to the conference.[46]

In his reply of 20 May, Clemenceau rejected Brockdorff-Rantzau's objections to the peace treaty. He contended that simply changing the political system, and replacing the men who had been in charge when war broke out, did not remove Germany's responsibility for the war. Germany herself, he pointed out, had not treated France differently when she became a Republic in 1871, following the Franco-Prussian War, or Russia when the Tsar was removed following the Russian Revolution. In 1871, as in March 1918, the victorious Germans had imposed very harsh peace treaties on their defeated enemies. Clemenceau was not prepared to accept Brockdorff's objections, nor was he prepared to allow Germany access to the evidence the commission had gathered, which he described as 'documents of an internal character which cannot be transmitted to you'.[47]

In order to settle the question of war guilt, a special 'Allied Commission on the Responsibility of the Authors of the War and on Enforcements of Penalties' inquired into the responsibilities relating to the war. In its report, the Commission concluded

> that the responsibility for [the war] lies wholly upon the Powers which declared war in pursuance of a policy of aggression, the concealment of which gives to the origin of this war the character of a dark conspiracy against the peace of Europe. This responsibility rests first on Germany and Austria, secondly on Turkey and Bulgaria. The responsibility is made all the graver by reason of the violation by Germany and Austria

> of the neutrality of Belgium and Luxembourg, which they themselves had guaranteed. It is increased, with regard to both France and Serbia, by the violation of their frontiers before the declaration of war.

In conclusion, the document stated:

> 1. The war was premeditated by the Central Powers together with their Allies, Turkey and Bulgaria, and was the result of acts deliberately committed in order to make it unavoidable.
> 2. Germany, in agreement with Austria-Hungary, deliberately worked to defeat all the many conciliatory proposals made by the Entente Powers and their repeated efforts to avoid war.[48]

Given such certainty among the delegates, it is worth asking which documents of an allegedly 'internal character' the peace-makers had at their disposal. It would seem as if their actual evidence was somewhat sparse, and that their decision depended in no small part on their general assumption of German war guilt, as it had existed throughout the war, together with the fact that German troops had violated the neutrality of neighbouring states. Among the documents used by the Commission were the German White Book, the French Yellow Book, the Serbian Blue Book, Lichnowsky's memorandum, and Wilhelm Muehlon's letters. Additional evidence was the German Chancellor's Reichstag speech of 4 August 1914, in which Bethmann Hollweg had admitted that the violation of Belgian neutrality had been contrary to international agreements and had constituted an injustice. This amounted to relatively little actual proof of German guilt from reliable sources, given that Lichnowsky's and Muehlon's accounts were only personal opinions and hardly hard and fast evidence, and that the German White Book contained nothing that could incriminate Germany, while the French Yellow Book contained many falsified documents. Clemenceau's reluctance to disclose to the German delegation what evidence they had available may have been due to the fact that documentary verification of Germany's war guilt was limited.

Following these exchanges, the German peace delegation

sent a Counter-Proposal of more than 400 pages to the Allies. In it, Germany again made the claim already raised by Brockdorff-Rantzau that its government represented the new democracy, and protested in particular against the territorial clauses of the Treaty, against the proposed Polish border and against reparations. The covering letter that accompanied the Allies' reply to this proposal sums up strikingly the mood at Versailles, and goes some way towards explaining the harsh nature of the Treaty. Temperley, who had been present at the negotiations, summed up the most important points:

> The attitude taken up is of great consequence, for it explains the severity of some terms of the Treaty. Germany, being responsible for the war and for the 'savage and inhumane manner in which it was conducted', had committed 'the greatest crime against humanity and the freedom of peoples that any nation, calling itself civilized, has ever consciously committed'. Seven million dead lie buried in Europe, more than twenty millions bear wounds and sufferings 'because Germany saw fit to gratify her lust for tyranny by resort to war!' Justice was indeed to be the basis of the peace, which Germany had asked [for] and was to receive. 'But it must be justice for all. There must be justice for the dead and wounded and for those who have been orphaned and bereaved that Europe might be freed from Prussian despotism ... There must be justice for those millions whose homes and land, ships and property German savagery has spoliated and destroyed.' That was the reason for reparation, for punishment of criminals, and for the economic disabilities and arrangements to which Germany must temporarily submit.[49]

Clearly, there was no doubt in the minds of those who ruled at Versailles that their assumption of war guilt was correct, and no question in Temperley's mind that Germany was to blame. However, given that there was little actual evidence available at Versailles to substantiate such claims, and given that Germans felt unfairly blamed, the German peace delegation continued to deny responsibility.

In May 1919, as part of Germany's bid to put her case to the delegates at Versailles, the German government published a second German White Book which addressed the war guilt question, entitled *Deutschland Schuldig?* (Germany Guilty?).[50] It included a memorandum composed by several eminent German professors, the so-called *Professoren-Denkschrift*, in which the authors protested against the Versailles verdict, demanded an impartial inquiry and blamed the policy of the Entente powers for the outbreak of war.[51] Despite the evidence they presented, and despite the German peace delegation's protests and initial refusal to sign, the Allies issued an ultimatum and insisted that Germany sign the Peace Treaty under the threat of renewed hostilities in case they refused to comply.

On 22 June 1919, one day before the ultimatum was due to expire, Germany was finally prepared to accept most of the Treaty. In a note of acceptance, Gustav Bauer, who had taken over as Chancellor following Philipp Scheidemann's resignation on 20 June, outlined that the Treaty had been agreed to because 'the German people does not wish for the resumption of the bloody war'. He listed many reservations against the signing of the Treaty, such as the loss of German territory and German nationals, and he pointed out that the German government would not sign the peace treaty 'of its free will'.[52]

> The Government of the German Republic solemnly declares that its attitude is to be understood in the sense that it yields to force, being resolved to spare the German people, whose sufferings are unspeakable, a new war, the shattering of its national unity by further occupation of German territories, terrible famine for women and children, and merciless prolonged retention of the prisoners of war.

However, Bauer declared that Germany could not accept Article 231 of the Peace Treaty 'which demands Germany to admit herself to be the sole and only author of the war, and does not cover this article by her signature'. Similarly, Germany could not accept Articles 227 to 230, requiring Germany to give up its control over war-trials, and to deliver war criminals, including the exiled Kaiser, to the Allied and Associated Powers for trial.[53]

As far as the Allied Powers were concerned, however, the question of responsibility was settled, and they would not accept a mere partial signing. Despite their reservations and protests, the German delegates were forced to sign at Versailles, including the offending article that alleged Germany's war guilt. In a note of unconditional acceptance of the Allies' peace stipulations, the German government made no secret of the fact that it regarded the Treaty as a grave injustice:

> The government of the German Republic is overwhelmed to learn [. . .] that the Allies are resolved to enforce, with all the power at their command, the acceptance even of those provisions in the treaty which, without having any material significance, are designed to deprive the German people of their honor. The honor of the German people cannot be injured by an act of violence. The German people, after their terrible sufferings during these last years, are wholly without the means of defending their honor against the outside world. Yielding to overpowering might, the government of the German Republic declares itself ready to accept and to sign the peace treaty imposed by the Allied and Associated governments. But in so doing, the government of the German Republic in no wise [*sic*] abandons its conviction that these conditions of peace represent injustice without example.[54]

In Germany, a treaty signed under such conditions was regarded as a *Diktat*, forced upon a defeated nation by unreasonable and vindictive victors. In an appeal to the German people of 24 June 1919, the government asked for Germans to preserve peace and accept the Treaty, while admitting that the decision for a signature had been taken 'with heavy hearts, under the pressure of the most unrelenting power, and with only one thought: to save our defenceless people from having to make further sacrifices and endure added pains of hunger'.[55]

The Allies had dealt harshly with Germany in their desire to ensure that Germany would never again be an aggressor, by reducing its size and its military potential, and by removing the country's 'great power' status. Germany's territorial losses amounted to one-seventh of the Reich's prewar territory, and one-tenth of its population, in addition to its colonial possessions. The Saarland was placed under French administration, the Rhineland was partly occupied and demilitarized, Germany's armed forces were reduced to 100,000 troops and the German General Staff was dissolved.[56] This 'victor's peace' was difficult to accept, but reparations and the war guilt allegation made the Treaty even harder to endure. Such a *Diktat* was irreconcilable with German national pride. As Marshall Lee and Wolfgang Michalka point out, opposition to the peace treaty in Germany helped prolong the animosities between the former enemies:

> At virtually every political level, Germans considered the treaty a searing wound to their national pride and a deep affront to the German character. The unanimous condemnation of the treaty in Germany as a *Diktat* obscured the possibility of political understanding and cooperation between victors and vanquished, which could have reduced international tensions left by the war.[57]

Moreover, the peace treaty sparked a renewed and more urgent interest in examining the origins of the war with an even more pressing agenda. What was at stake now was not just convincing the German people that theirs had been a just war, but convincing the former enemies that their war guilt decision had been wrong. Not surprisingly, it was with the publication of the Peace Treaty that the debate on the origins of the First World War began in earnest.

The German 'innocence campaign'

Essentially German historians studied the outbreak of war in order to absolve their country from guilt; the French and British – at first anyway – in order to justify the peace terms. **R.J.W. Evans and H. Pogge von Strandmann[58]**

Of the Treaty's many unpopular components, none proved more controversial in Germany than the famous 'war guilt clause', Article 231 of the Treaty of Versailles. Germans were united in the desire to fight the article, which was considered unacceptable on moral as well as economic grounds. The enormous reparation payments which Germany was burdened with were to a large extent justified by the war guilt dictum. Therefore, proving that Article 231 was wrong had to be the first step towards unburdening Germany of reparations. The controversial war guilt section read as follows:

> The Allied and Associated Governments affirm and Germany accepts the responsibility of Germany and her allies for causing all the loss and damage to which the Allied and Associated Governments and their nationals have been subjected as a consequence of the war imposed upon them by the aggression of Germany and her allies.[59]

Allocating war guilt in this way was unprecedented. Prior to the First World War, the question of guilt had never really featured in connection with wars. War had always been a fact of life for people and states, an acceptable means of solving international conflicts which diplomacy failed to settle. However, following this world war of such proportion, public opinion, particularly in France and Britain, demanded that the guilty parties be identified and punished. 'Prussian militarism' was seen as responsible for the outbreak of war, and the victors intended to stamp it out. The harsh reparations which were demanded by the victors were a reflection of this desire. Germany was not only supposed to pay for the damage it had caused, but for the entire cost of the war, a sum that had not yet been agreed when the Treaty was signed. Although the Allies had devised the war guilt paragraph essentially as a legal measure, designed to make Germany legally accountable for the war damage its former enemies had sustained, the one-sided war guilt ruling was understood in Germany as a moral judgement, and as such passionately rejected.[60]

As this perceived 'victor's peace' was considered unacceptable in Germany, it became the mission of successive German governments to prove to the world that the 'war guilt paragraph' was unjustified. The Weimar years witnessed a concerted effort by successive governments to whitewash German policy in and before 1914. As Holger Herwig argues, 'from June 1919 through the Third Reich, key elements of the German bureaucracy mounted a massive and successful campaign of disinformation that purveyed false propaganda through a wide range of channels'.[61] The war guilt question became a 'national fetish', and German revisionists had everything to gain and nothing to lose in their attempts to prove the Allies wrong. They turned the historical question of the responsibility for the outbreak of war into a political issue.[62]

At the same time, the lost war and the inglorious peace agreement led to a flood of justificatory accounts from leading statesmen who had been in charge of German policy in the immediate prewar period. Their agenda tended to be twofold: to exonerate themselves from any responsibility for the events that had led to war, and to blame Germany's enemies in an attempt to prove their war guilt assumptions wrong. They had good reasons for doing so, as John Röhl explains:

> Given the scale of the disaster, it is hardly surprising that those few men who held power in Berlin in 1914 should afterwards deny responsibility and seek to shift the blame, at least in public, particularly when the punitive peace terms imposed at Versailles were predicated on the guilt of Germany and its allies, and there existed a real possibility of extradition to face trial before an international tribunal.[63]

Gottlieb von Jagow, who had been in charge of Imperial Germany's foreign policy in 1914, criticized the validity of even speaking of guilt in connection with the outbreak of war. In his memoirs he asserted that only those who deny the experience of history can speak of 'guilt' regarding the war. 'As long as there has been politics – that is, history – the *ultima ratio* in the differences between the peoples has been an appeal to the decision of weapons. The heroes of all times and all countries would then also be merely "guilty", half of the statues of the world would have to be torn down', he claimed. According to Jagow, the responsibility for the war lay with the Slavs, as well as with Britain for failing to contain them, and with France which had wanted revenge for the war of 1870/71. The former State Secretary firmly maintained that 'Germany, the Kaiser, the Chancellor and all responsible leaders did not wish for the war'. It goes without saying that Jagow himself was included in the last category. His disapproval of the victors' peace agreement is plain:

> The use of the terms guilt and punishment amount to disgusting hypocrisy. Does the Entente want to justify in front of its own peoples the exorbitant demands which it makes of its defeated opponents in blind hatred or coolly calculating desire to destroy?[64]

Former Chancellor Bethmann Hollweg also felt the need to defend himself after the war. According to his memoirs *Betrachtungen zum Weltkrieg,* which were a passionate indictment of Versailles and its consequences for Germany, the decision for war had been taken by Germany's enemies, primarily Russia which failed to control Serbia and bring about a peaceful solution. 'Today we know that Mr Sasonov was practically bent on the disruption of European peace, because he wanted Constantinople and needed a European war for that aim', Bethmann claimed. However, France also got its share of the blame. France's role had been determined 'through her alliance with Russia and the newly launched revanche idea under Poincaré'.[65] Bethmann also maintained, as he had done ever since the July Crisis, that Britain had to some extent been responsible for the outbreak of war, because Britain's leaders had not made their intentions of supporting France and Belgium clear from early in the crisis. In an emotional scene, the Chancellor had told the British ambassador Sir Edward Goschen on the eve of the war:

> It was in London's hand to curb French revanchism and Pan-Slav chauvinism. It has not done so, but has, rather, repeatedly

> egged them on. And now England has actively helped them. Germany, the emperor, and the government were peace-loving; that, the Ambassador knew as well as I. We entered the war with a clear conscience, but England's responsibility was monumental.[66]

Bethmann claimed in his memoirs that Britain had not gone to war because of Germany's violation of Belgian neutrality, but because it felt morally bound to France and wanted to protect its ally.[67] Not surprisingly, Bethmann's interpretation shaped the official propaganda during the war and became widely accepted in Germany in the interwar years.

Another contemporary reflecting on the events that had led to war concluded in his memoirs that Britain was to blame above everyone else. The former State Secretary of the Reich Treasury Karl Helfferich reminded his readers of the mood of 1914, the feeling in Germany that the war was forced upon the country from the outside, and he exonerated the Kaiser who had 'preserved peace for his people for 26 years'. Helfferich confidently forecast that history writing of the future would not be fooled by the lies of the victors and would demonstrate that Britain had wanted the war for its own imperialist aims: 'Britain has once again reached her goal. The strongest continental power, her strongest competitor on the world's markets lies on the ground, as did previously Spain, the Netherlands and France.'[68]

Despite such public claims, however, in private these men sometimes admitted that their own actions had been at the root of the origins of the conflict, albeit as blunders, rather than any intentional desire for a war. Already during the war, Chancellor Bethmann Hollweg had admitted to the journalist Theodor Wolff that he felt oppressed by the thought that Germany bore a share of the responsibility for the outbreak of war (something that he would vehemently deny in his memoirs), while Jagow admitted to a friend that he could no longer sleep at night because Germany 'had wanted the war'. Even as early as August 1914, in the light of the horrors of the war that was only a few weeks old, and given what Wolff knew of its origins, he noted in his diary: 'If only the many dead don't finally rise and ask: why?'[69]

However, it was only during the continuing debate after the Second World War, as will be seen, that evidence such as the diaries of Theodor Wolff emerged. Wolff's numerous conversations with important decision-makers during the war gave him the distinct impression that German policy had contributed significantly to the outbreak of war. During and immediately after the war, few voices deviated from the official line which was confirmed by the many memoirs published once the war was lost.

Such private accounts were useful additional ammunition against Versailles, but successive Weimar governments went further by setting up several official and semi-official bodies in Germany to investigate the origins of the war. The first was the Parliamentary Committee of Inquiry (*Parlamentarischer Untersuchungsausschuss*). During the revolutionary period immediately after the Armistice, such a committee had been demanded by the Independent Socialists in the Reichstag, who wanted the truth about the origins of the war to be established. It was formally constituted in August 1919, consisting of 28 members, but it was never able to function properly, as the government (no longer as revolutionary as the one which had demanded the inquiry in the first place) had the final say over which documents the Committee members were allowed access to. Moreover, the Committee's work, and its conclusions, were ultimately vetoed by another government organization charged with the task of investigating the war's origins, as will be seen below. In contrast with the other official war guilt organizations, the Committee at least aimed at a fair and objective enquiry into the origins of the war when it was first established. However, during the course of the 1920s, as the composition of the Reichstag shifted increasingly to the right, more conservative and nationalist members made up the subcommittees of inquiry, taking away the initial driving force behind the parliamentary investigation.[70]

The German 'innocence campaign' was directed by the

German Foreign Office, the *Auswärtiges Amt*, which established a powerful propaganda organization for this very purpose, the War Guilt Section (*Kriegsschuldreferat*), in 1919. The existence and effectiveness of this 'General Staff of the war guilt struggle'[71] can be regarded as 'one of the best-kept state secrets of the Weimar Republic',[72] and according to a contemporary critic, it was 'a massive and successful undertaking, fired by patriotic love of the country, but careless regarding any other moral demands'.[73] Its sole purpose was to refute the Allies' war guilt accusation. The War Guilt Section was first headed by Legation Secretary Bernhard Wilhelm von Bülow, the man who had previously been appointed by Brockdorff-Rantzau to lead the War Guilt Section's predecessor, the so-called 'Special Bureau von Bülow' (*Spezialbüro von Bülow*). The Bureau had been set up following the Armistice, and its task had been to collect documents from various offices, primarily the *Auswärtiges Amt*, as well as examining the Russian documents that had been made available by the Bolshevik government (the Bosheviks had blamed the Tsarist government for the outbreak of war and had made documents available for public scrutiny as early as 1917[74]). The Bureau was to prepare them for foreign policy use, mainly with a view to countering the Allies' war guilt allegations at Versailles. For this purpose, the documents were sorted into 'defence' and 'offence' categories.[75] The documents collected by this Bureau served as the basis for an attempt by the German delegation to Paris to refute the war guilt allegation: the so-called 'Professors' memorandum', which amounted to a substantial report on the war guilt question, and which was given to the Allies on 27 May 1919. It was based on Bülow's findings, and probably also written by him, while the four eminent professors who signed it did so 'for patriotic reasons', rather than necessarily out of conviction.[76]

Bülow's attitude towards such a collection of evidence set the tone for the whole revisionist campaign of the German Foreign Office. The name 'revisionist' in this context stems from the explicit intention to revise the ruling of Versailles which was the basis of the entire innocence campaign of the *Auswärtiges Amt*. Bülow explained rather disparagingly to his subordinate Hans Freytag that, based on documents, 'any nation can be charged successfully' with the responsibility for the outbreak of war. 'I would undertake "to prove" conclusively from the archives of any nation that it, and it alone, is responsible for the war – or for whatever else you like.'[77] Clearly this is evidence that the war guilt campaign in Germany was not concerned to establish the truth about 1914. While such cynicism may seem deplorable, it is nonetheless important to realize that one reason why the debate has continued to divide historians to this day is precisely because it is indeed possible, with selective use of available evidence, to make a case for any of the major powers being responsible for war in 1914. As will be seen during this study, historians have come to differing, and often even opposing conclusions, based on the same documentary evidence.

Public outrage in Germany over the Peace Treaty subsided relatively quickly, although the initial shock was exacerbated when a list with names of alleged war criminals was delivered to the German government in February 1920.[78] It did not take long, however, until concerns about the severe domestic problems in the new and volatile Republic superseded feelings of hurt pride. This situation changed in January 1921, when the victors met in Paris to announce the amount that Germany had to pay in reparations to its former enemies. If the Allies' peace conditions had already been hard to swallow, the campaign against the 'victor's peace' became even more purposeful in the light of the unimaginable sum of 269 billion gold marks that Germany was to pay over 42 years (a sum that was reduced at the London Reparations Conference in May 1921 to 132 billion (132,000,000,000, an almost equally fantastic sum).[79] Again, Germany was forced to accept the demands of the Allies under threat of military action. As a result, the government's anti-Versailles propaganda machine increased its efforts drastically.

While the *Auswärtiges Amt* had initially hoped that it could conduct its own propaganda with the help of the War Guilt Section, it soon seemed politic to hand this task to seemingly independent bodies, so that the information distributed did not appear to originate from the German government. For this purpose, two further organizations were founded in April 1921, which were financed and controlled by the *Auswärtiges Amt*, but gave the impression of being independent bodies. One was the Centre for the Study of the Causes of the War (*Zentralstelle für die Erforschung der Kriegsursachen*), a 'pseudo-scholarly bureau' which had among its staff some of the main proponents of revisionist history writing, such as Max Montgelas, Bernhard W. von Bülow, Hans Delbrück and Hermann Lutz.[80] Its main task was the 'enlightenment' of public opinion in neutral and former enemy countries, which the government considered 'a basic task for the assertion of a revision of the Peace Treaty', as Chancellor Joseph Wirth put it in November 1921.[81] At the same time, the second organization, the Working Committee of German Associations (*Arbeitsausschuss Deutscher Verbände*), was founded. Its tasks were similar, but it focused on propaganda within Germany, and was hugely successful in popularizing the official view of German innocence. The *Arbeitsausschuss* incorporated no less than between 1,700 and 2,000 different organizations by 1930, which had in some way striven to undermine the Versailles war guilt decision, and which had been encouraged by the War Guilt Section to unite with the aim of advancing the official German innocence thesis. The *Arbeitsausschuss* was an 'overt mass propaganda distribution center', in Holger Herwig's words, lavishly funded and able to spread its message by way of seminars, conventions, exhibitions and rallies. It had contacts with about 1,500 newspapers in Germany, ensuring that hundreds of articles on the topic of the war guilt question were published.[82] As well as producing a popular journal entitled *Der Weg zur Freiheit* (The Path to Liberty), it also made printed propaganda material available to schools and universities, and even used the new medium of the radio to reach the public.

The German government tried to extricate itself from the reparations payments almost as soon as the London ultimatum had been accepted. It attempted to demonstrate to the Allies that Germany was unable to meet the repayments that had been arranged. Britain did not oppose Germany in this, leaving France isolated with its hard-line reparation demands. The French Prime Minister Raymond Poincaré and his government were under severe public pressure to maintain their tough stance with Germany, while in Germany, extreme inflation resulted in an inability to pay reparations in 1922. By the end of that year, Germany was in arrears with its payments, and in response to German non-payment French and Belgian troops occupied the industrial Ruhr area. The Ruhr conflict has been regarded by some as 'the climax of a decade of warfare' which had been continued by economic means long after the physical fighting had ended.

> The struggle between Germany and her antagonists, whose military phase ended on 11 November, continued unabated for the next five years. Despite Versailles, or perhaps because of it, the Great War was extended by political and economic means, until political, economic and military warfare came together in the Ruhr conflict to bring the war to an end.[83]

As we shall see, these international conflicts shaped and influenced the debate on the origins of the war. The argument over war guilt and responsibility for the war was at all times closely linked to the foreign and domestic policy concerns of the nations involved.

The reparations demands rested on the question of war guilt, and if national pride had not been ample reason to want to prove to the world that Germany had not desired or started the war, then the need eventually to put an end to the reparations payments ensured that the innocence campaign continued with renewed vigour. The founding of the *Zentralstelle* and the 'Working Committee' in April 1921 was doubtless motivated by this new impetus for war guilt publications which amounted to a 'propaganda offensive'.[84] The

Zentralstelle published not only countless studies and documents but even, from 1923, a journal dedicated solely to the question of war guilt, entitled *Die Kriegsschuldfrage* (The War Guilt Question).[85] Even at the height of the inflation in the autumn of 1923, the necessary financial means for the launch of this publication were made available in gold marks, a fact that emphasized the importance the *Auswärtiges Amt* attached to it.[86] This periodical published revisionist writings from all over the world; apart from German authors, it frequently featured texts from French, British, Italian and American revisionists. The War Guilt Section also funded and encouraged foreign authors who were arguing against German war guilt. By supplying them with documents and already published revisionist studies, by financing foreign publications and enabling foreign researchers to travel to Germany, and by providing a forum in which their findings could be published, the War Guilt Section and its journal did much to advance the revisionist cause abroad. Apart from this periodical, and its more 'common' cousin, *Der Weg zur Freiheit*, the government contracted work to several scholars and politicians, such as Bülow, Mendelssohn-Bartholdy, Montgelas, Schücking, Schwertfeger, Stieve and Thimme.[87]

The output of the *Auswärtiges Amt* regarding the war guilt question was particularly numerous for special occasions, and the *New York Times* suspected in May 1924 that it was no coincidence that Germany released important source material just when its reparations payments to the Allies were due.[88] The propaganda campaign had two immediate aims. The first was to convince public opinion at home and abroad that Germany was not responsible for the war, and to raise understanding for revisionist demands. The other aim was to censor publications that might suggest otherwise, particularly any by the Parliamentary Committee of Inquiry, which investigated the causes of the war independently from the *Auswärtiges Amt*. The first objective was particularly the domain of the *Zentralstelle*, which concentrated on publishing works that sought to prove 'scientifically', i.e. on the basis of documentary evidence, the 'innocence-thesis', and which prepared document collections with this aim in mind. It was also keen to get support from abroad and to demonstrate the validity of its case. The second aim was achieved by delaying or even forbidding publications that advanced a different, anti-revisionist argument. As a result, 'the thesis of Germany's relative or complete innocence regarding the outbreak of war in 1914' was advanced in the majority of interwar publications.[89] Various German societies, such as the League of German Patriots and, of course, the Working Committee of German Associations, joined in the anti-Versailles chorus, making it difficult for Germans 'to keep a judicial balance on the subject'.[90] Holger Herwig is more blunt in his assessment of this propaganda:

> By selectively editing documentary collections, suppressing honest scholarship, subsidising pseudoscholarship, underwriting mass propaganda, and overseeing the export of this propaganda, especially to Britain, France and the United States, the patriotic self-censors in Berlin exerted a powerful influence on public and elite opinion in German and, to a lesser extent, outside Germany. Their efforts polluted historical understanding both at home and abroad well into the post-1945 period.[91]

At the same time, any criticism of the previous political system became almost impossible. Instead, the Kaiserreich was overvalued and idealized, leading to an additional weakening of the political self-confidence of the new German state.[92] Born out of defeat, the new Republic was unloved by many Germans, who hankered either for the 'glorious' imperial past before the World War, or longed for a future in which Germany no longer had to carry the burden of war guilt and could be a proud nation and a 'great power' again. The inability of most Germans to accept the country's responsibility for the outbreak of war, and consequently to accept the Versailles Treaty, burdened the new state as much as the myth that an undefeated Germany had been stabbed in the back.

Official document collections

The war guilt question must be treated objectively by all. Any other method is suspect. The partisan polemics are beginning to nauseate the public.

Theobald von Bethmann Hollweg, 1920[93]

A significant part of the early debate on the origins of the First World War was the unprecedented publication of official documents by the belligerent powers. In Russia, the Bolshevik Party had led the way in November 1917 by announcing that they would abolish all secret diplomacy and, in an attempt to discredit the Tsarist government, would be opening the state archives to the public. The first documents were published in *Pravda* in November and December 1917, and the publications continued in other newspapers until February 1918.[94] A special journal entitled *Krasnyi Arkhiv* was published from 1922 onwards, whose basic task was 'to expose the secrets of imperialist policy and diplomacy'.[95] The difference to similar publications in other countries was that the new Russian government was at pains to prove that the former Tsarist regime, as well as all other imperialist powers, were to blame for the outbreak of war, whereas the official publications of other governments aimed at denying any responsibility for the outbreak of war. In its desire to hold imperialism accountable for the war, the Bolshevik Party was motivated by ideological concerns, rather than the patriotism that inspired their German, British or French counterparts. Moreover, if it could be shown that the Tsarist regime had collaborated with its French alliance partner and that both were jointly responsible for the outbreak of war, the new government could, in John Keiger's words, 'kill two birds with one stone: discredit tsarist Russia and partly justify not repaying to France the massive pre-war loans'.[96]

In Germany, the establishment of the Parliamentary Committee of Inquiry in the revolutionary period immediately after the war was an attempt to investigate the origins of the war without patriotic concerns, but it soon gave way to a more apologetic agenda. A significant part of the effort to disprove the war guilt ruling was given to the publication of documents to prove German innocence. Just a week after the war had ended, on 18 November 1918, the 'Council of People's Commissars' had made a public promise to open Germany's archives, and Karl Kautsky, a member of the USPD (the Independent Social Democratic Party), was given the task of preparing an edition of official documents. Kautsky's collection was ready in March 1919, but it threw 'an unfavourable light' on German policy in the immediate weeks before the outbreak of the war. The *Auswärtiges Amt* asked an internal consultant, Count Oberndorff, to vet the planned edition. Oberndorff decided that it would be preferable to suppress the whole collection, because the documents were so incriminating for German policy prior to the outbreak of war that Germany would be best served if they did not appear.[97] Although Kautsky's collection did not demonstrate that Germany had planned the war, he came to the conclusion that Germany's rulers had acted 'unspeakably carelessly and unthinkingly', and that they were mainly responsible for the outbreak of war.[98] While Kautsky had been working on his edition, the socialist movement in Germany had split in December 1918, and the USPD, Kautsky's party, left the cabinet. The most radical socialists formed the Communist Party (KPD), and Kautsky was left 'politically isolated'. When his collection was completed, his critical work carried with it the 'stigma of treasonable socialism'.[99] The *Auswärtiges Amt*, as well as the cabinet, decided to delay its publication; Brockdorff-Rantzau was, as might be expected, a particular opponent.[100] It was feared that a publication at this stage of the Versailles proceedings might have unfavourable repercussions for the Allies' assessment of German foreign policy in the prewar months. Kautsky was asked to postpone publication for the duration of the peace negotiations, but the promise given in November 1918 meant that public opinion at home and abroad expected a publication at some point, and that failure to deliver might result in speculations that Germany had something to hide.[101]

Because Kautsky's findings threatened to disprove the official line, he was hindered from continuing his editorial work, and was denied access to the government archives in Berlin. For tactical reasons, however, he could not be completely excluded from the planned publication of documents, which was now continued under the auspices of two other editors, brought in to ensure that the edition conformed to the government view. Kautsky had to remain on board because it was known that he planned his own publication based on his impressions gained from the documents he had seen in the archives. The *Auswärtiges Amt* tried to influence him to delay such a publication at least until the official publication of German documents. This official edition, the so-called Kautsky documents, was published by Karl Kautsky, Maximilian Montgelas and Walther Schücking under the title *Die deutschen Dokumente zum Kriegsausbruch* (The German Documents on the Outbreak of War) in December 1919, and consisted of four volumes of carefully selected documents that were intended to prove Germany's innocence in the events of 1914.[102] Some of Kautsky's own thoughts and findings had, however, been previously published in newspapers in Britain and Holland just prior to the publication of the *Dokumente*, apparently arranged by Kautsky's editor against his will. Thus *The Times* published an article entitled 'The Kaiser's Guilt. New Evidence from Vienna' on 26 November, and followed it up with 'ample extracts' of Kautsky's documents three days later.[103] When the documents were published in December, they did not have the favourable reception that the *Auswärtiges Amt* had hoped for. Even in neutral countries, there was a hostile reaction to them, as their propaganda purpose seemed obvious, and they failed to achieve the *Auswärtiges Amt's* aim of proving Germany's innocence or having a positive impact on public opinion abroad.

With the *Deutsche Dokumente* a 'propagandistic failure,'[104] a larger edition of documents was quickly planned. Under the auspices of the *Auswärtiges Amt*, the official document collection *Die Grosse Politik der Europäischen Kabinette* (The High

Policies of the European Cabinets) was edited from 1922 onwards. The War Guilt Section reserved the right to censor the volumes and had the final say over the contents of the edition; following the Kautsky débâcle, it did not want to be in a position again where it could not prevent potentially damaging material from being published. After all, one of its main tasks was to control and select the documentary evidence which was to be made available to the public, while ensuring that only 'politically reliable' historians had access to secret documents.[105]

The collection aimed to add substantial evidence to the Kautsky documents, in particular documents which threw light on the actions of other European governments, and to prove to the world that Germany's prewar policy had not led to war. The documents in this collection reach back as far as 1871, the year of the founding of the German Empire. It aimed to place the blame for the outbreak of war on collective responsibility, but in particular on the policy of the Entente. The purpose of the publication of *Die Grosse Politik* was to educate scholars, and by implication the general public, about Germany's role in the events that led to war and, as a memorandum of May 1921 stated, the collection was not prepared 'so that its volumes [. . .] might only gather dust in archives or be studied by isolated historians with effects which will be apparent only after years'.[106] Rather, as Chancellor Wilhelm Marx told the British Prime Minister Ramsay MacDonald in 1924, Germany would use *Die Grosse Politik* to challenge the victors of 1918 to allow an international court of arbitration to investigate the causes of the First World War. For the German government, as Foreign Minister Gustav Stresemann explained in 1925, the publication was an act of self-defence.[107]

Die Grosse Politik was published in forty volumes by the German government between 1922 and 1927, and to this day they remain an important, if selective, collection for historians. The volumes were received favourably by some foreign commentators, such as the American historian Bernadotte E.

Schmitt and Michail N. Pokrovsky, the editor of Imperial Russian documents, who considered them one of the greatest achievements in this area.[108] The editors (Friedrich Thimme, Johannes Lepsius and Albrecht Mendelssohn Bartholdy) guaranteed that no important documents had been omitted from the collection, and that with this publication Germany was putting its cards on the table.[109] While Friedrich Thimme publicly declared the edition 'free of every apologetic tendency, whether nationalist or of another kind', and of 'any consideration for individuals whether dead or alive', in private he felt confident of being able to achieve 'a substantial rehabilitation of the old regime and, morally at least, of the Kaiser'. As Peter Lambert points out in his study of Thimme's role as editor of *Die Grosse Politik*, Thimme expressed this aim 'before he could conceivably have looked at the evidence in detail'.[110]

Given such public assurances, and the sheer volume and speed of the publication, the flaws in the collection were perhaps not immediately apparent to contemporary commentators. After the Second World War, A.J.P. Taylor was less complimentary of the documents than Schmitt and Pokrovsky had been. He criticized, for example, the arrangement of documents in thematic, rather than chronological order in the volumes of *Die Grosse Politik*, an arrangement that might serve to allow German prewar policy to appear in a better light:

> the *Grosse Politik*, by its selection of documents and still more by arrangement of them, gave a false impression of the harmlessness of German policy and of the malignancy of Germany's opponents. For instance, the documents relating to the Morocco Crisis of 1905 are in one volume; the documents concerning the abortive Russo-German alliance of 1905 (the Treaty of Björkö) are in another.[111]

As a result, it remained obscure how these two international events were connected, and that the object of Germany's policy behind both events at the time had been to alter the current balance of power in its favour.

However, the massive edition had more serious shortcomings. Crucially, the volumes were based entirely on Foreign Office files, omitting documents from the Reich-Chancellery, and military and naval institutions, such as the General Staff, the Ministry of War and the Navy Office, the inclusion of which would have presented a different picture of prewar decision-making. Moreover, potentially damaging documents, as well as Kaiser's revealing and incriminating marginal comments, were sometimes omitted or were relativized by apologetic commentaries from the editors. An investigation undertaken by Fritz Klein in the 1950s revealed the apologist intentions behind the edition and the methodology with which this was achieved.[112] In pursuit of the aim of revision of the Treaty of Versailles, the editors of the German documents deliberately omitted uncomfortable facts and crucial documents, such as the 'blank cheque' issued by Berlin to Vienna in the early days of July 1914 or details about the discussions at Potsdam on 5 and 6 July 1914 between the Kaiser and his political and military advisers and with the Austrians, as well as other important evidence in connection with German decision-making during the July Crisis.[113] In 1930, when commenting on the recently completed Austrian document collection, Friedrich Thimme, one of the editors of *Die Grosse Politik*, revealed the deliberately obscure way in which his edition had been compiled, and the intentions behind this strategy. 'In the German publication, of course, I had above all to keep in mind the objective that through the method of publication the enemy States would be forced to make public their material, too.' This aim, Thimme thought, 'would not have been possible if we had presented our publication purely chronologically', or without the footnote commentary that alerted the reader to evidence which incriminated the enemies.[114]

Despite these shortcomings, many of which were not immediately apparent, Germany had led the way in publishing official documents with this voluminous edition. The other European nations soon felt the need to follow suit and publish documents that would likewise prove their own innocence in the events that led to war, much as they had all published their 'coloured books' in the first weeks after the outbreak of the war. However, the victorious Entente powers were initially slow to release any documents, a reluctance which had negative consequences for their own war guilt propaganda. Once Germany had made its documents public, the delay made it look increasingly as if Britain and France might have had something to hide.[115]

Britain was the first Entente power to rise to Germany's challenge of making secret documents available for scrutiny. *The British Documents on the Origins of the War* were published between 1926 and 1938 by George P. Gooch and Harold W.V. Temperley and consisted of eleven volumes. The editors followed the German model of *Die Grosse Politik* and organized the British documents by subject, rather than in chronological order and, like the German example, this publication also omitted some potentially damaging documents, for example relating to France and friendly neutral powers, which were either left out at the behest of governments or suppressed by anxious civil servants who were determined to conceal certain evidence from the editors.[116] The British Foreign Office found it much more uncomfortable to allow outsiders access to its files than the *Auswärtiges Amt* had in Germany. After all, in Germany and Russia it had required defeat and revolution to achieve such relative openness. However, British politicians felt the need to react not just in the light of official document publications in Germany, but also, for example, because of accounts such as Freiherr von Eckardstein's memoirs from his time as First Secretary of the German embassy in London, which seemed to suggest that the Anglo-German antagonism of the prewar years had not been solely Berlin's fault.[117]

Great scrutiny was exercised over the choice of the editors and the published documents. Previously, there had been objections within the Foreign Office to Gooch being one of the contributors to *The Cambridge History of British Foreign Policy*, for which he was to write on British foreign policy

Gooch

between 1907 and 1914, because the Germanophile historian was regarded as politically unreliable. Permanent Under-Secretary Sir Eyre Crowe and fellow historian James W. Headlam-Morley were uncertain about his political judgement. In 1920 Headlam-Morley complained after a conversation with Gooch that he had 'no real grasp of the nature of the responsibilities which fall upon a man of action' (i.e. a politician), and was 'therefore constitutionally unable to understand or sympathise with a statesman who may have deliberately to do a minor injustice or adopt a course of action which obviously has many inconveniences attending on it in order not to sacrifice greater and more important objects'. Gooch's second alleged failing was that he had been critical of Sir Edward Grey's policies in the run-up to the outbreak of war. What was more, 'he reads everything – especially everything which appears in Germany – and I know by experience how difficult it is to keep one's mind unbiased if one is constantly studying German political literature'. The great danger was of course that Gooch might be critical in his evaluation of Grey's policy, and that his writings might create the impression 'that after all it was errors of judgement made by Sir Edward Grey that were very largely responsible for the state of things out of which the war inevitably arose'.[118] Gooch and Temperley put up more resistance to the attempts at censorship from successive governments than did their German counterparts, even threatening to resign over such disputes. It is indicative of the importance of the question of the origins of the war in the 1920s that even a country like Britain, which had not been burdened by war guilt allegations, was so keen to avoid any possible accusations concerning its government's own policy in the run-up to the war.

Other countries soon began to publish their own collections of primary sources. Following the early Bolshevik policy of publishing documents, the German and British example provided the incentive for a comprehensive Soviet edition of documents. The first five volumes of the Soviet Union's official document collection *International Relations in the Age of*

Imperialism were published between 1931 and 1934, a project that was begun under the leadership of Pokrovsky, but which remained unfinished.[119]

In France, Germany's document publications of the 1920s were regarded as propaganda, and French diplomats asked the French Foreign Office to react to this perceived provocation with a publication of French documents. Given that French decision-makers, and the Lorrainer Poincaré in particular, were accused in Germany of having been motivated by a desire for revenge (*revanche*) for the war of 1870/71 and of having been responsible for the war, there was a particular need in France to refute such allegations. However, the French government was concerned not to do anything that might hamper reparations payments from Germany, including the publication of potentially incriminating evidence from French archives. Poincaré had underlined this concern as early as February 1922, when he declared that the French government would do nothing that might lead to 'a weakening of the acknowledgement of German responsibilities'.[120] The Quai d'Orsay was not impressed with Britain's efforts in publishing documents either, objecting to some of the contents of the volumes of the *British Documents,* which 'remain[ed] silent about some of the most notorious facts establishing the responsibility of Germany and its allies in regard to the world war'.[121]

However, France's politicians realized that nothing could be gained from allowing Germany to publish its own version of events without reacting with a French publication, especially given German criticisms of the falsifications contained in the French Yellow Book. Pierre de Margerie, the French ambassador in Berlin, warned Foreign Minister Aristide Briand in 1926:

> There can be no doubt that under the influence of the enormous quantity of documents that the Wilhelmstrasse has thrown on to the historical market, world opinion has already begun to change to our disadvantage. The rapid publication of

> the documents in our archives relating to the events of 1914, thus demonstrating, particularly to Anglo-Saxon opinion, that we have nothing to fear from the judgement of posterity, would be desirable.[122]

For France, there was thus much at stake in the question of the origins of the war, resulting in a desire to prove that French *revanche* had not been a cause of the conflict. In fact, as John Keiger argues, 'the war guilt debate became all the more impassioned for the fact that in the postwar period Poincaré was still in power and pursuing a strict application of the Versailles Treaty and the payment of reparations'.[123] In the light of criticism raised against the Quai d'Orsay's foreign policy in 1914, France was just as keen as Germany to prove its innocence in the events that had led to the war and the government refused to accept arguments that deviated from the official view that France had been threatened by Germany for years and had been attacked by the brutal neighbour under a pretext.[124]

Germany's intentions behind the official document publications to put foreign governments on the defensive, as well as changing international opinion in its favour, seem to have been largely achieved. The other belligerent powers could not afford to hold back on their publications. However, it was not until 1928, when the final volume of *Die Grosse Politik* had already appeared, that Aristide Briand established the *Commission de Publication des Documents relatifs aux Origines de la Guerre de 1914–1918*, whose task it was to oversee the publication of French documents.[125] The first volume of the official French collection, *Documents Diplomatiques Français 1871–1914*, appeared in 1930, too late to make much of an impact on the developing revisionist consensus. The last of the 32 volumes only appeared in 1953.

Italy did not join in the publication race. Having only entered the war in May 1915, it was not at pains to demonstrate its innocence in the events that led to war in 1914 (although it bears the sole responsibility for entering the war in 1915 in an attempt to secure territorial aggrandizement), and following the Peace Settlement, its concern was in any case less with the outbreak of the war than with its results for Italy. The country felt cheated by the Peace Treaty and let down by its allies. The origins of the war were of no immediate concern given Italy's grievances about its outcome.[126] The government refused to publish prewar documents and, as a result, the publication of Italian documents of the pre-1914 period, *I Documenti Diplomatici Italiani,* was only begun after the Second World War and is still ongoing. Similarly, the most important memoirs of Italian statesmen were only published after 1945.[127]

Austria's peace negotiations had taken place at St Germain outside Paris, and the country had unwillingly accepted its peace treaty. Unlike in Germany, the war guilt question, dealt with in Article 177 of the Treaty of St Germain, was only of secondary importance to Austrians. Much more controversy was aroused by the *Anschluss* question (the question of a union with Germany) throughout the interwar years. The Austrian government's policy regarding war guilt was influenced by its very limited bargaining position, as it feared that any extensive discussion of war guilt might lead to Allied demands for reparations. Therefore the government in Vienna admitted to some responsibility of the Austro-Hungarian monarchy for the ultimatum to Serbia, but it blamed Hungary in particular, and alleged that a Magyar clique had been controlling the Foreign Office at the time. The Austrian government had also considered an early publication of official documents, and had given Roderich Gooss the task of publishing them. However, they held back with the publication while negotiations at Versailles were still ongoing, for fear of harming German interests. Gooss's work, *Das Wiener Kabinett und die Entstehung des Weltkrieges,* was published in 1919 after the Treaty of Versailles had been signed. It was not a document collection, but rather an apologetic account based on documentary evidence. The Austrian Foreign Ministry published selected documents as early as 1919, but it would be some time before a major edition was under way, not least due to lack of funds for such a project. [128]

After much deliberating and planning, Austria published nine volumes of official documents in 1930, entitled *Österreich-Ungarns Aussenpolitik von der Bosnischen Krise 1908 bis zum Kriegsausbruch 1914* (Austria-Hungary's Foreign Policy from the Bosnian Crisis 1908 until the Outbreak of War 1914). Germany had put some pressure on the Austrian government to do so. During a visit to Berlin in 1926, the Austrian Chancellor Ramek was encouraged by the German Secretary of State Schubert to publish Austrian documents. The *Auswärtiges Amt* advised Ramek how pleased the German government would be if Austria were to publish the documents relevant to the prewar events, as it was hoped that this would help disprove the war guilt allegations against Germany and Austria. Work on a publication began in May 1926, under strict guidelines regarding the secrecy of the operation.[129] Ludwig Bittner, one of the men in charge of the Austrian edition, travelled to Berlin to meet Friedrich Thimme for advice on how to compile the work. But there was more concrete help from Germany, too, in the shape of financial support of the Austrian project by Berlin. The German *Auswärtiges Amt* not only helped finance Austria's edition, but also controlled it with the help of members of its staff.[130] Before the edition was officially published, the German government had already ordered 300 copies which it wanted to distribute to various newspapers.[131]

All these document collections and official publications were necessarily selective and reflected their editors' apologetic intentions, but nonetheless they made available a large number of documents at a time when government archives were mostly still closed to researchers. Revisionists and anti-revisionists were able to draw on this evidence for their accounts of the origins of the war. The selection of documents was less influenced by the criteria a historian would have applied than it was guided by current political concerns. Thus British Foreign Secretary Austen Chamberlain told the editor of the British documents, G.P. Gooch, in 1926 that it was his 'first duty [. . .] to preserve peace now and in the future. I cannot sacrifice *that* even to historical accuracy.'[132] In fact, Keith Wilson suspects that this was not just a trend of the 1920s and 1930s, and that, whatever the circumstances, 'in the forging, or shaping of the collective memory, the role of governments has always been greater than that of historians, and is likely to remain so'.[133] If there was indeed a conflict between historians on the one hand, and the government on the other, this was less the case in Germany, where most historians adopted the official line regarding the question of war guilt. Armed with official document publications from several countries, two schools of thought set to work to prove to the rest of the world that their interpretation of the events that led to the outbreak of the First World War was correct. The arguments between revisionists and anti-revisionists are the subject of the next part of this book.

Notes

1 Cited in Konrad Jarausch, *The Enigmatic Chancellor: Bethmann Hollweg and the Hubris of Imperial Germany*, New Haven, 1973, p. 177.
2 Holger Herwig, 'Clio Deceived: Patriotic Self-Censorship in Germany after the War', first published in *International Security*, 12, 1987, reprinted in Keith M. Wilson (ed.), *Forging the Collective Memory: Government and International Historians through Two World Wars*, Providence and Oxford 1996, pp. 87–127, p. 90 (all citations from the reprint).
3 Imanuel Geiss, *Studien über Geschichte und Geschichtswissenschaft*, Frankfurt/M. 1972, p. 113.
4 Imanuel Geiss (ed.), *Julikrise und Kriegsausbruch: Eine Dokumentensammlung*, 2 vols, Hanover 1963/64, vol. II, No. 587.
5 Quoted in John C.G. Röhl, 'Admiral von Müller and the Approach of War, 1911–1914', *Historical Journal*, XII, 4, 1969, p.670.
6 Cited in Imanuel Geiss, 'Die manipulierte Kriegsschuldfrage, Deutsche Reichspolitik in der Julikrise 1914 und Deutsche Kriegsziele im Spiegel des Schuldreferats des Auswärtigen Amts, 1919–1939', *Militärgeschichtliche Mitteilungen*, 34, 2/1983, p. 34. For a discussion of the relative merits of the different 'coloured books', see S.B. Fay, *The Origins of the World War*, 2nd revised edn, New York 1930, pp. 3ff. On the controversy around Kurt Riezler's diaries see also below, pp. 155ff.
7 Cited in Fischer, *Illusions*, p. 463.

8 Geiss, *Studien*, pp. 113–4. See also Herwig, 'Clio Deceived', p. 90, for early attempts to prove German innocence, including Jagow's instruction to Zimmermann at the end of August 1914 to think about a larger publication along the lines of 'The ring of entente politics encircled us ever more tightly'.

9 Ibid., p. 90.

10 Douglas Sladen, *Germany's Great Lie: The Official German Justification of the War*, London 1914, p. vii.

11 The American president had outlined peace aims in a speech to Congress on 8 January 1918, which contained fourteen points for a future peace programme, and which specified, among others, the right of autonomous development for minority nationalities within the Habsburg and Ottoman Empires, the plan of a league of nations, and a peace based on the principles of democracy, justice and equality. Although the German press had initially reacted scathingly and attacked the programme as a plan to achieve 'Anglo-Saxon world hegemony', and the German government had only sent a non-committal reply, when defeat was on the cards, Germany's leaders began to realize the potential protection against punishment from Britain and France that the peace programme seemed to offer. On 3 October 1918, the German government asked Wilson for an armistice and subsequent peace settlement on the basis of his 'Fourteen Points'. See Alma Luckau, *The German Delegation at the Paris Peace Conference*, New York 1941, pp. 1ff.; Klaus Schwabe, *Woodrow Wilson, Revolutionary Germany and Peacemaking, 1918–1919: Missionary Diplomacy and the Realities of Power*, Chapel Hill and London 1985; Ruth Henig, *Versailles and After: 1919–1933*, London 1984, 2nd edn 1995, pp. 10–11.

12 Hartmut Pogge von Strandmann, 'Germany and the Coming of War' in R.J.W. Evans and Hartmut Pogge von Strandmann (eds), *The Coming of the First World War*, Oxford 1988, p. 94.

13 Grelling and Montgelas are discussed in Fischer, *Illusions*, p. 464. Citations from Richard Grelling, *La Campagne innocentiste et le traité de Versailles*, Paris 1925, ibid. Because Montgelas denied his concurring with Grelling after the war, Grelling published a facsimile of the letter in *La Campagne innocentiste*. For details of the events of 5 July, see above, Introduction.

14 *Die Denkschrift des Fürsten Lichnowsky*, edited by 'a group of peace lovers', Bern 1918. Lichnowsky's letter on pp. 4–5.

15 Röhl, *1914: Delusion or Design*, pp. 46–9.

16 Munroe Smith (ed.), *The Disclosures from Germany*, New York 1918, p. 9; Prince Lichnowsky, 'My London Mission, 1912–1914' (1916), reprinted ibid., pp. 24ff. Citations on p. 117 and p. 11.

17 See below, Part 3.

18 Smith, *The Disclosures from Germany*, p. 22.

19 Ibid., p. 185. On Muehlon, see also Fischer, *Illusions*, p. 464.
20 An argument made by the anonymous Swiss editors (a group of peace lovers) of the memorandum in 1918. Smith, *The Disclosures from Germany*, pp. 7–8.
21 A.G. Gardiner cited in C.A. McCurdy, *Guilty! Prince Lichnowsky's Disclosures*, National War Aims Committee, London, no date [1918], p. 12.
22 Lichnowsky, 'My Mission to London', in Smith, *The Disclosures from Germany*, pp. 119ff.
23 E. Barker, H.W.C. Davis, C.R.L. Fletcher, A. Hassal, L.G. Wickham Legg and F. Morgan, *Why We Are at War: Great Britain's Case*, Oxford 1914. See also Hartmut Pogge von Strandmann, 'Germany and the Coming of War', pp. 91ff.
24 Barker et al., *Why We Are at War*, pp. 14–15; 19–20.
25 E. Barker, *Britain's Reasons for Going to War*, London 1915.
26 Citations from J.W. Headlam-Morley, *The History of Twelve Days*, London 1915, pp.xi, xii–xiii, viii. Headlam-Morley also published *The German Chancellor and the Outbreak of War*, London 1917.
27 For E.D. Morel, see also pp. 91f. below.
28 Gerd Krumeich, 'Vergleichende Aspekte der "Kriegsschulddebatte" nach dem Ersten Weltkrieg' in Wolfgang Michalka (ed.), *Der Erste Weltkrieg: Wirkung, Wahrnehmung,* Analyse, Munich and Zurich 1994, pp. 913–28, p. 922.
29 Count Brockdorff-Rantzau to Clemenceau, 13 May 1919, quoted in Fritz Berber, *Das Diktat von Versailles. Enstehung – Inhalt – Zerfall. Eine Darstellung in Dokumenten*, 2 vols, Essen 1939.
30 Stig Förster, Introduction, in Roger Chickering and Stig Förster (eds), *Great War, Total War: Combat and Mobilization on the Western Front, 1914–1918*, Cambridge 2000, p. 6.
31 Winfried Baumgart (ed.), *Die Julikrise 1914 und der Ausbruch des Ersten Weltkriegs 1914*, Darmstadt 1983, p. xii.
32 Demands were also made at Versailles for the restitution of the destroyed library at Louvain, among others, which had become a symbol of German atrocities on enemy territory. The 'Oxford of Belgium' was to be restored out of Germany libraries. See Wolfgang Schivelbusch, *Eine Ruine im Krieg der Geister: Die Bibliothek von Löwen, August 1914 bis Mai 1940*, Frankfurt/M. 1993. On the German occupation of Belgium, see, for example, Mark Derez, 'The Experience of Occupation: Belgium', in John Bourne, Peter Liddle and Ian Whitehead (eds), *The Great World War, 1914-1945*, vol. I: *Lightning Strikes Twice*, London 2000, pp. 511–32. On the war against non-combatants, see e.g. John Horne and Alan Kramer, 'War between Soldiers and Enemy Civilians, 1914–1915', in Chickering and Förster (eds), *Great War, Total War*, pp. 153–68.
33 Cited in Erik Goldstein, 'Great Britain: The Home Front', in

M.F. Boemke, G.D. Feldmann and E. Glaser (eds), *The Treaty of Versailles: A Reassessment after 75 Years*, Cambridge 1998, pp. 147–66, p. 152. For France see Krumeich, 'Vergleichende Aspekte', p. 920.

34 Goldstein, 'Great Britain: The Home Front', p. 155. See also Joll, *Origins of the First World War*, p. 2.

35 M. Muret, *L'Evolution belliqueuse de Guillaume II*, Paris 1919, cited in Christopher Clark, *Kaiser Wilhelm II*, London 2000, p. 257.

36 Thomas A. Kohut, *Wilhelm II and the Germans: A Study in Leadership*, New York and Oxford 1991, p. 226; Paul Tesdorpf, *Die Krankheit Wilhelms II*, Munich 1919, cited ibid., p. 225.

37 See above, p. 26.

38 Geiss, 'Die manipulierte Kriegsschuldfrage', pp. 33–4.

39 The Paris Peace Settlement consisted of several different treaties. The Treaty of Versailles of 28 June 1919 dealt with Germany, Austria's agreement with the Allies was settled at St Germain on 10 September, on 27 November 1919 Bulgaria's peace treaty was signed at Neuilly, the Treaty of Trianon of 4 June 1920 dealt with Hungary, and the Treaty of Sèvres on 10 August 1920 decided the peace agreement with Turkey. Not only Germany, but all her allies were made to accept responsibility for the outbreak of war, but for Germany the war guilt allegation had the most serious consequences, and thus led to the most outspoken protest against it.

40 Antony Lentin, *Lloyd George, Woodrow Wilson and the Guilt of Germany*, Leicester 1984, pp. 66, 72. Britain also insisted on the principle of freedom of the seas. For initial objections from British and French governments to Wilson's peace programme, see Luckau, *The German Delegation at the Paris Peace Conference*, p. 24.

41 Fritz Klein, 'Between Compiègne and Versailles: The Germans on the Way from a Misunderstood Defeat to an Unwanted Peace', in M.F. Boemke, G.D. Feldmann and E. Glaser (eds), *The Treaty of Versailles*, pp. 217–18.

42 Wolfgang J. Mommsen, 'Max Weber and the Peace Treaty of Versailles', ibid., p. 535.

43 The prior events are described in detail in Luckau, *The German Delegation at the Paris Peace Conference*, pp. 54ff.

44 Cited ibid., p. 55.

45 Brockdorff-Rantzau's speech, ibid., pp. 220ff.

46 Text of the letter in Fritz Berber, *Das Diktat von Versailles*, vol. 2, pp. 1226f. English text in *The German White Book Concerning the Responsibility of the Authors of the War*, edited by the *Auswärtiges Amt*, English translation New York 1924, p. 6. Also reprinted in Luckau, *The German Delegation at the Paris Peace Conference*, pp. 241–2.

47 The text of Clemenceau's letter in Berber, *Das Diktat von Versailles*, vol. 2, p. 1227ff.; Luckau, *The German Delegation at the Paris Peace Conference*, p. 254.

48 Report of the Allied Commission on the Responsibility of the Authors of the War and on Enforcements of Penalties, ibid., pp. 272ff., citations on p. 272 and p. 279.
49 H.W.V. Temperley, *A History of the Peace Conference of Paris*, 5 vols, London 1920, vol. 2: *The Settlement with Germany*, p. 11.
50 *Deutschland Schuldig? Deutsches Weissbuch über die Verantwortlichkeit der Urheber des Krieges*, Berlin 1919 (Germany Guilty? German White Book on the Responsibility of the Creators of the War).
51 See also below, p. 51, for the 'Professors' memorandum'.
52 See Map 2: German territorial losses following the Treaty of Versailles.
53 Text of the note in Luckau, T*he German Delegation at the Paris Peace Conference*, pp. 478ff.
54 German Note of 23 June 1919, cited ibid., p. 482.
55 Appeal of the German government to the German people, 24 June 1919, ibid., p. 496.
56 See Marshall Lee and Wolfgang Michalka, *German Foreign Policy 1917–1933: Continuity or Break?*, Leamington Spa 1987, p. 26, for a summary of the Allies' demands.
57 Ibid., pp. 28–9.
58 Evans and Pogge von Strandmann, *The Coming of the First World War*, p. vi.
59 The text of the Treaty can be found in Anton Kaes, Martin Jay and Edward Dimenberg (eds), *The Weimar Republic Sourcebook*, Berkeley and London 1994, pp. 819ff.
60 Baumgart, *Julikrise und der Ausbruch des Ersten Weltkrieges 1914*, p. xii. See also Fritz Dickmann, 'Die Kriegsschuldfrage auf der Friedenskonferenz von Paris 1919', *Historische Zeitschrift*, 197, 1963, pp. 1–100.
61 Herwig, 'Clio Deceived', p. 88.
62 See Selig Adler, 'The War-Guilt Question and American Disillusionment, 1918–1928', *Journal of Modern History*, xxiii, No. 1, March 1951, pp.1–28, p. 5.
63 John Röhl, 'Germany', in Keith Wilson (ed.), *Decisions for War, 1914*, London 1995, p. 27.
64 Gottlieb von Jagow, *Ursachen und Ausbruch des Weltkrieges*, Berlin 1919, pp. 179–80, 8–9.
65 Theobald von Bethmann Hollweg, *Betrachtungen zum Weltkrieg*, 2 vols, Berlin 1919, vol. I: *Vor dem Kriege*, pp. 119–20, 159.
66 Bethmann Hollweg's note of the events, dated 13 November 1914, cited in Jarausch, *The Enigmatic Chancellor*, pp. 176/177.
67 Bethmann Hollweg, *Betrachtungen zum Weltkrieg*, vol. I, pp. 174–5.
68 Karl Helfferich, *Die Vorgeschichte des Weltkrieges*, Berlin 1919, pp. 225, 230.
69 Bernd Sösemann (ed.), *Theodor Wolff. Tagebücher 1914–1919. Der*

Erste Weltkrieg und die Entstehung der Weimarer Republik in Tagebüchern, Leitartikeln und Briefen des Chefredakteurs am 'Berliner Tageblatt' und Mitbegründer der 'Deutschen Demokratischen Partei', 2 vols, Boppard am Rhein 1984, pp. 156, 665, 92. See also Röhl, 'Germany', p. 28.

70 For details see Herwig, 'Clio Deceived', pp. 108–9.

71 Wolfgang Jäger, *Historische Forschung und politische Kultur in Deutschland*, Göttingen 1984, p. 47.

72 Geiss, 'Die manipulierte Kriegsschuldfrage', p. 31.

73 Hermann Kantorowicz, cited ibid., p. 32. For details on the War Guilt Section see e.g. Jäger, *Historische Forschung*, pp. 44ff.; Herwig, 'Clio Deceived', p. 88.

74 See also below, p. 57.

75 Ulrich Heinemann, *Die Verdrängte Niederlage: Politische Öffentlichkeit und Kriegsschuldfrage in der Weimarer Republik*, Göttingen 1983, p. 38; Herwig, 'Clio Deceived', p. 92.

76 The 'Professors' memorandum' was signed by Hans Delbrück, Maximilian von Montgelas, Albrecht Mendelssohn-Bartholdy and Max Weber. See Heinemann, *Verdrängte Niederlage*, p. 45; Herwig, 'Clio Deceived', pp. 93–4. As we have seen above, the memorandum formed part of the second German White Book.

77 Cited in Herwig, 'Clio Deceived', p. 93.

78 The list contained 853 names of Germans, accused of war crimes, including leading military and political figures such as Hindenburg, Ludendorff, Bethmann Hollweg and the Prussian and Bavarian Crown Prince. In response, the *Reichswehrministerium* conducted its own innocence campaign to prove that allegations of war crimes were unjust. In addition to the debate of war guilt in terms of causing the war, another disputed matter was thus the question of war guilt during the war. See Alan Kramer, 'Der Umgang mit der Schuld: Die "Schuld im Kriege" und die Republik von Weimar', in Dietrich Papenfuss und Wolfgang Schieder (eds), *Deutsche Umbrüche im 20. Jahrhundert*, Cologne 2000.

79 Detlef Peukert, *The Weimar Republic: The Crisis of Classical Modernity*, New York 1992, p. 53; Heinemann, *Verdrängte Niederlage*, p. 62; Lee and Michalka, *German Foreign Policy*, p. 40. On the actual sum paid (21,448,475,148.75 marks) and on the struggle on Germany's part to reduce the payment and finally put an end to the reparations, see Sally Marks, 'Smoke and Mirrors: In Smoke-Filled Rooms and the Galerie des Glaces', in Boemke et al. (eds), *The Treaty of Versailles*, pp. 337–70.

80 Herwig, 'Clio Deceived', p. 101.

81 Cited in Geiss, 'Die manipulierte Kriegsschuldfrage', p. 34.

82 Herwig, 'Clio Deceived', p. 103; Geiss, 'Die manipulierte Kriegsschuldfrage', p. 36.

83 Ibid., pp. 43ff.; quote on p. 47. On the Ruhr struggle, see e.g. Bruce Kent, *The Spoils of War: The Politics, Economics, and Diplomacy of Reparations 1918–1932*, Oxford, 1989, pp. 169ff.
84 Jäger, *Historische Forschung*, p. 46.
85 *Die Kriegsschuldfrage: Monatshefte für Internationale Aufklärung*. In 1929, the journal's title was changed to *Berliner Monatshefte*.
86 Geiss, 'Die manipulierte Kriegsschuldfrage', p. 37.
87 Herwig, 'Clio Deceived', p. 101.
88 See Adler, 'The War-Guilt Question', p. 20, note 143.
89 See Jäger, *Historische Forschung*, p. 46.
90 Adler, 'The War-Guilt Question', p. 7.
91 Herwig, 'Clio Deceived', pp. 88–9.
92 See Jäger, *Historische Forschung*, p. 45.
93 Bethmann Hollweg in private conversation, 1920, cited in Konrad Jarausch, 'The Illusion of Limited War: Chancellor Bethmann Hollweg's Calculated Risk, July 1914', *Central European History*, vol. II, 1969, pp. 48–76, p. 49.
94 Details on Russian document collections in Derek Spring, 'The Unfinished Collection: Russian Documents on the Origins of the First World War', in Wilson (ed.), *Forging the Collective Memory*, pp. 63ff.
95 Cited ibid., p. 67.
96 John Keiger, *Raymond Poincaré*, Cambridge 1997, p. 194.
97 Geiss, 'Die manipulierte Kriegsschuldfrage', pp. 41–2.
98 Heinemann, *Verdrängte Niederlage*, p. 40.
99 Herwig, 'Clio Deceived', p. 91.
100 Heinemann, *Verdrängte Niederlage*, p. 41.
101 See ibid., pp. 75ff. for this and the following.
102 Karl Kautsky, Max Montgelas and Walter Schücking (eds), *Die deutschen Dokumente zum Kriegsausbruch*, 4 vols, Berlin 1919 (Engl. trans. *The Outbreak of the World War*, London 1924).
103 *The Times*, 'The Kaiser's Guilt: New Evidence from Vienna', 26 Nov. 1919; 'The Potsdam War Conspiracy: New Wilhelmstrasse Documents', 29 Nov. 1919.
104 Heinemann, *Verdrängte Niederlage*, p. 78.
105 Geiss, 'Die manipulierte Kriegsschuldfrage', pp. 40–1.
106 Cited in Keith M. Wilson, 'Introduction: Governments, Historians, and "Historical Engineering"', in Wilson (ed.), *Forging the Collective Memory*, p. 11.
107 These statements, ibid., pp. 11–12.
108 Jäger, *Historische Forschung*, p. 52.
109 Adler, 'The War Guilt Question', pp. 4–5; J. Lepsius, A. Mendelssohn Bartholdy, F. Thimme (eds), *Die Grosse Politik der Europäischen Kabinette, 1871–1914: Sammlung der Diplomatischen Akten des Auswärtigen Amtes*, 40 vols, Berlin 1922–27.

110 Peter Lambert, 'Friedrich Thimme, G.P. Gooch and the Publication of Documents on the Origins of the First World War: Patriotism, Academic Liberty and a Search for Anglo-German Understanding, 1920–1938', in Stefan Berger, Peter Lambert and Peter Schumann (eds), *A Dialogue of the Deaf? Historiographical Connections between Britain and Germany, c. 1750–2000*, Göttingen 2002 (my thanks to Dr Lambert for making this forthcoming piece available to me).

111 Cited in Wilson, 'Introduction', in Wilson (ed.), *Forging the Collective Memory*, p. 11, note 45.

112 Heinemann, *Verdrängte Niederlage*, p. 82; Herwig, 'Clio Deceived', pp. 96–7; Fritz Klein, 'Über die Verfälschung der historischen Wahrheit in der Aktenpublikation "Die Grosse Politik der Europäischen Kabinette 1871–1914"', *Zeitschrift für Geschichtswissenschaft*, 7, 1950, pp. 318–330. See, for example, Konrad Canis, *Von Bismarck zur Weltpolitik: Deutsche Aussenpolitik 1890 bis 1902*, Berlin 1997, pp. 121–122, who exposes the difference between an original document (in this case Crown Council minutes from 1894) and its version in *Die Grosse Politik*, and shows that important sections of the document have been omitted by the editors.

113 See Geiss, *Julikrise*, vol. I, pp. 33–34; Herwig, 'Clio Deceived', p. 97. For details of these events, see above, Introduction.

114 Quoted in Ulfried Burz, 'Austria and the Great War: Official Publications in the 1920s and 1930s', in Wilson (ed.), *Forging the Collective Memory*, p. 187.

115 Adler, 'War-Guilt', p. 4.

116 Lambert, 'Friedrich Thimme, G.P. Gooch', unpublished MS, p. 19; Wilson, 'Introduction', in Wilson (ed.), *Forging the Collective Memory*, pp. 1–23.

117 Keith Hamilton, 'The Pursuit of Enlightened Patriotism: The British Foreign Office and Historical Researchers During the Great War and its Aftermath', ibid., p. 207; Hermann Freiherr von Eckardstein, *Lebenserinnerungen und politische Denkwürdigkeiten*, 3 vols, Leipzig 1919.

118 Cited in Hamilton, 'The Pursuit of Enlightened Patriotism', p. 204. On G.P. Gooch see also Lambert, 'Friedrich Thimme, G.P. Gooch', in Berger et al (eds), *A Dialogue of the Deaf*, forthcoming.

119 *Mezhdunarodnye Otnosheniya v Epokhu Imperializma: Dokumenty iz arkhivov tsarskogo I vremennogo pravitel'stv* (International Relations in the Age of Imperialism: Documents from the Archives of the Tsarist and Provisional Government); Spring, 'The Unfinished Collection', pp. 71ff. The third series, covering July 1914–March 1916, was translated and published in German as *Die internationalen Beziehungen im Zeitalter des Imperialismus*, Berlin 1931–34. Outside of the Soviet Union, some Russian documents were published in Germany, such as Friedrich Stieve's edition of Izvolsky's dispatches from Paris, *Der*

diplomatische Schriftwechsel Iswolskis 1911–1914, 4 vols, Berlin 1925; and in France by René Marchand, *Un livre noir*, 3 vols, Paris 1921–22.

120 Keith Hamilton, 'The Historical Diplomacy of the Third Republic', in Wilson (ed.), *Forging the Collective Memory*, pp. 43–4, citation on p. 44.

121 Ibid.

122 Cited ibid., p. 44.

123 Keiger, *Poincaré*, p. 194.

124 See Krumeich, 'Vergleichende Aspekte', p. 920.

125 For details, see Hamilton, 'The Historical Diplomacy of the Third Republic', pp. 44–5.

126 For Italy's frustration about the Peace Settlement, see M. Clark, *Modern Italy 1971–1995*, 2nd edn, London and New York 1996; Denis Mack Smith, *Modern Italy: A Political History*, New Haven and London 1997; Holger Afflerbach, '"... nearly a case of Italy contra mundum?" Italien als Siegermacht in Versailles 1919', in Gerd Krumeich (ed.), *Versailles 1919. Ziele – Wirkung – Wahrnehmung*, Essen 2001, pp. 159–73.

127 Giorgio Rochat, 'Die italienische Historiographie zum Ersten Weltkrieg' in Wolfgang Michalka (ed.), *Der Erste Weltkrieg*, pp. 972–90, p. 974. See Afflerbach, 'Italien als Siegermacht', in ibid, pp. 159–60, for a discussion of Italian memoirs and documents, and for further references.

128 Burz, 'Austria and the Great War', pp. 181ff.; Rudolf Jerábek, 'Die österreichische Weltkriegsforschung', in Wolfgang Michalka (ed), *Der Erste Weltkrieg*, pp. 953–71, p. 961. The Foreign Ministry published *Die österreichisch-ungarischen Dokumente zum Kriegsausbruch: Diplomatische Aktenstücke zur Vorgeschichte des Krieges 1914*, which were reprinted in Germany in 1923.

129 Quoted in Burz, 'Austria and the Great War', p. 186. L. Bittner and H. Übersberger (eds), *Österreich-Ungarns Aussenpolitik von der Bosnischen Krise bis zum Kriegsausbruch 1914*, 9 vols, Vienna 1930.

130 Jäger, *Historische Forschung*, p. 52; Heinemann, *Verdrängte Niederlage*, pp. 90–1.

131 Quoted in Burz, 'Austria and the Great War', p. 186.

132 Cited in Wilson, 'Introduction', in Wilson (ed.), *Forging the Collective Memory*, p. 2.

133 Ibid.

Part 2

Revisionists and Anti-Revisionists

Introduction

In the middle twenties, sources and monographs on the war appeared in such abundance that, by making the proper selection, one could build almost any 'frame of reference' and fortify it with enough facts to make it plausible. **Selig Adler[1]**

In the interwar years, a variety of views were advocated as to why war had broken out in 1914, ranging from blaming Germany (Article 231, Treaty of Versailles), to blaming fate (B.E. Schmitt). Arguments were advanced that Europe slithered into war as a result of blunders and accidents (Lloyd George), that France and Russia were primarily to blame (H.E. Barnes), or that no one was ultimately responsible for the escalation of the July Crisis into war (S.B. Fay).[2] By the 1930s, a new war guilt consensus had been established in most of Europe, following the transition from 'Germany was solely responsible' to 'the nations slithered into war'. When Hitler came to power in Germany, the war guilt question was officially declared resolved in Germany's favour. As far as Germans were concerned, the war of 1914 had not been their country's responsibility or intention. They no longer felt they had to live with the blame for its outbreak, and with the concomitant economic sanctions and constraints. The following section charts the development of the debate from contested war guilt allegations to the more comfortable consensus (for Germans, at least) of the 1930s.

The German quest for a revision of Versailles

We will be destroyed. The cities [. . .] half dead blocks of stone, still partly inhabited by wretched people, the roads are run down, the forests cut down, a miserable harvest growing in the fields. Harbors, railways, canals in ruins, and everywhere the sad reminders standing, the high, weather-worn buildings from the time of greatness. [. . .] A folk lives and is dead.
Walter Rathenau, 1919[3]

Given the war guilt allegations against it, Germany felt the need to prove its innocence. Consequently, as we have seen, particular effort was devoted to the official document collections, and much use was made of the available publications. On the basis of this documentary evidence, German politicians continued to petition their former enemies with requests for a revision of the war guilt dictum. In an article entitled 'The Responsibility for the War' published in the American journal *Foreign Affairs* in January 1926 and widely discussed in America, former German Chancellor Wilhelm Marx reviewed the available documentary evidence in an attempt to disprove the allegation that Germany was responsible for the war. He based his argument on Russian and German documents, for no others were then available, as he pointed out with scarcely hidden criticism. 'The British Government has, it is true, promised to make such a publication, but this promise still remains to be fulfilled', he complained, while France had so far only published a narrow range of documents which allowed 'no conclusions as to the general policy of France prior to 1914'.[4] Such statements illustrate the international pressure on the belligerent countries to make their documents available, if they wanted to avoid the criticism that they might have something to hide and, indeed, Selig Adler has argued that 'one of the major blunders of Anglo-French policy after 1918 was the delay in releasing their war material'.[5] Marx warned against the widely held assumption that only 'Nationalist Die-hards' in Germany demanded a revision of Versailles, and pointed out that 'ever since Germany was forced to subscribe to the dictates of Versailles, the entire German people have not ceased to protest against the imputation'. He made quite clear that the quest for a revision of the Versailles' war guilt decision transcended all party divisions in Germany:

> Ministers of every party have joined in the protest – Bauer, the Social Democrat; Rathenau, the Democrat; Dr. Wirth, of the Centre Party; Stresemann, the leader of the German People's Party; and men like Baron von Rosenberg, Cuno and Luther – all have unanimously stressed Germany's disclaimer of the terrible reproach of having disturbed the peace of the world.

Having reviewed the documentary evidence, Marx concluded that only a revision of the Treaty of Versailles, meaning both an end to reparations and a reassessment of the war guilt allegations, could ensure the future happiness of humanity. 'Reconciliation among the nations is only possible if spite and hatred yield to calmness and discernment', he warned, painting a gloomy picture of conditions in Europe several years after the end of the war: 'military disarmament will only become possible when moral disarmament has made sufficient headway, above all only when the moral condemnation of Versailles has been cancelled, when that mutual hatred has subsided which, though seven years have passed since the World War ended, still cankers the minds of men.'[6]

Despite Marx's claim that by way of the official document collection *Die Grosse Politik* 'Germany is presenting to the world an unvarnished and ungarnished view of her past and is making it possible for anyone who chooses to examine matters for himself',[7] the German documents were far from complete and presented a very one-sided picture, as we have seen. It was up to later historians, such as Luigi Albertini and Fritz Fischer, to uncover some of the more incriminating evidence that such editions had deliberately excluded. Since the Second World War, many more documents have come to light to inform historians about the events leading up to war in 1914. The almost continuous interest in the origins of the First World War has led to an abundance of documentary evidence being available on the subject.[8]

In the early postwar years, however, the published evidence was initially limited to that from Russia and Germany. Based on the carefully selected documents that the official publications provided, each European country argued the case of its own innocence, and in Germany it was maintained with particular vigour that no single nation should be made to carry the burden of responsibility for the outbreak of war. A one-volume document collection prepared by Bernhard Schwertfeger aimed to make the most important documents available to a general reader, for the many volumes of *Die Grosse Politik* exceeded what most interested members of the public could cope with. Again, the selection was made with the general revisionist agenda in mind that 'the so-called peace treaty is the harshest humiliation ever imposed on a great and proud nation'.[9]

Apart from the official government voices, and those directed and financed by the *Auswärtiges Amt*, historians, politicians, and public figures from a variety of backgrounds and political persuasions joined in the revisionist campaign, as indeed opposition to the Treaty of Versailles helped to unite even the most disjointed and disparate groups in Weimar society. For all their differences, nothing proved a more uniting quest than the opposition to the Treaty of Versailles in those volatile years, although, unlike in America, eminent historians tended to keep out of the debate, which they considered to be 'current events' rather than history. Whereas Germany's leading historians would shape the debate post-1945, in the interwar years 'they left the debate by default in the hands of the Foreign Ministry and its minions'.[10]

Alfred von Wegerer in many ways epitomized the Weimar revisionist attempts and its views. As leader of the *Zentralstelle* and editor of the journal *Die Kriegsschuldfrage* from 1923 until December 1936, he had encouraged the founding of the *Gesellschaft für die Erforschung der Kriegsursachen* (Society for Research into the Causes of the War) in 1923, under the leadership of the historian Ludwig Raschdau. Under Wegerer's auspices, the *Zentralstelle* had 'fought the scientific and moral fight against the war guilt lie', as he put it in 1939.[11] In 1928 he had published *Die Widerlegung der Versailler Kriegsschuldthese*, which was later translated into French and English, and he published over 300 articles during the inter-war years in which he attempted to demonstrate 'the truth' behind the war guilt allegations.[12] Count Max Montgelas, the co-editor of the *Deutsche Dokumente*, also published his own thoughts on the war guilt question in 1923 with his *Leitfaden zur Kriegsschuldfrage*. His account on the origins of the war was revisionist, but he aimed at a more balanced portrayal of events than Wegerer and the *Zentralstelle*, perhaps because he was himself uncertain as to Germany's actual role in the events that had led to war.[13]

Such publications aside, the Weimar governments made many official and semi-official declarations against the war guilt allegation. In February 1921, for example, Foreign Minister Dr Simons declared in a speech that 'we do not accept this penal judgement as the final decision of world history', to which Lloyd George replied in March of the same year that it should be accepted once and for all that Germany's responsibility for the war should be treated as a 'cause jugée'.[14] In 1924, against the background of negotiations regarding Germany's entry into the League of Nations, Chancellor Wilhelm Marx declared in the Reichstag that Germany did not accept the war guilt decision of the Allies. Britain and France responded by lodging a formal complaint. Germany's attempts to have the war guilt clause revoked both during negotiations regarding the League of Nations and the Locarno Treaty also failed.[15]

In September 1927, during the opening speech at the memorial for the Battle of Tannenberg, President von Hindenburg publicly denied German war guilt. 'We refute, the German people in all its classes refute, the accusation that Germany was to blame for this greatest of all wars!', he declared, and he re-emphasized the notion that the war of 1914 had not been a war of aggression, but rather one in which Germans had fought in defence of their fatherland. He repeated the earlier demand for an impartial tribunal to investigate the causes of the war.[16] Moreover, Hindenburg publicly declared the tenth anniversary of the signing of the Treaty of Versailles 'a day of mourning', and he again emphasized that 'Germany signed the treaty without acknowledging herewith that the German people are the cause of the war. This accusation does not allow our people to rest and disturbs the trust among the nations'.[17] Even ten years after its signing, Germany's politicians and statesmen still refused to accept the Treaty of Versailles and continued to fight against it openly.

However, it is important to realize that not only Germans were revisionists, and that the available evidence suggested to other commentators, too, that Germany might not have been solely responsible for the outbreak of war and that it had been unfairly blamed in 1919. In fact, support from abroad played a decisive part in the success of the revisionist argument in Germany. Such revisionist accounts were motivated as much by the current political concerns of their authors as by any sense that Germany had been unfairly treated, as the example of prominent American revisionists demonstrates.

American revisionists

In America, a 'gigantic shift of opinion' took place after 11 November 1918.[18] Revisionist interpretations dominated the interwar years, in an attempt to convince the American people that their views on the origins of the war were wrong. Revisionism became part of a wider revolt against nineteenth-century values and, as Selig Adler points out, 'regardless of what a defence of Germany connoted after 1933, in the twenties it was the revisionists who were the "liberals" '.[19]

The desire to correct the war guilt assumptions was motivated by condemnation of the Treaty of Versailles, which had been rejected as too harsh by the United States Senate. Moreover, there were political reasons why Americans paid particular attention to examining the outbreak of the war. The controversy over the origins of the First World War was intertwined with the debate about American intervention in the European war in 1917. In Warren Cohen's words,

> the war-guilt question [...] had a special significance for Americans. Many believed that the United States had intervened in a war in which American security had not been threatened, in which American interests had not been at stake. [...] The United States fought, some may have recalled, not out of self-interest, not in answer to a threat, but to defend the forces of light and goodness against the forces of darkness and evil. If this was not the case, why had the United States intervened?[20]

An important additional reason for 'the kaleidoscopic changes in interpretation after 1920' was the availability of documentary source material.[21] The primary evidence from Russia and Germany was used by American revisionists, who were disillusioned by the harsh nature of the Versailles settlement, to investigate the actions of the Entente powers in order to prove their responsibility for the outbreak of war. It did not work in Britain's or France's favour that their own documents were only published with a substantial delay, while Germany seemed to be delivering all important documents for the benefit of international scrutiny. To the American revisionists, it appeared as if the Entente powers had something to hide, while Germany was able to allege that it had put all its cards on the table.[22]

Among the most influential American revisionists of the 1920s and 1930s were the historians Sidney Bradshaw Fay and Harry Elmer Barnes. After the war, Fay claimed that in 1914 he had 'refused to join in the chorus' of American public opinion, 'soon under the influence of propaganda and war prejudice', which denounced Germany and the Kaiser as being guilty of causing the war.[23] John E. Moser analyses the nature of that propaganda, and its influence on the American revisionist tradition in the interwar period. During the years 1914–19, 'British speakers, authors and diplomats [...] expended a great deal of money and effort to convince

Americans that the war was Germany's fault, and that it was being fought to make the world "safe for democracy"'. After the war, revisionists like Fay would maintain that British propaganda 'had lured the U.S. into a war in which it had no vital interest'.[24]

With a view to proving such propaganda wrong, Fay began to analyse the documentary evidence as soon as it became available, and his first articles on the origins of the war were published in the *American Historical Review* in 1920/21. Based on a careful examination of the evidence, he came to the conclusion that no European country had actually wanted war in 1914, that the war had been an accident, and that all major European powers shared the blame for the escalation of the crisis. 'No one country and no one man was solely, or probably even mainly, to blame', he argued in his two-volume study *The Origins of the World War*, published in 1929. In contrast with much of the writing of his contemporaries, his account was sober and attempted to be fair. 'None of the Powers wanted a European War', Fay concluded from his findings, and 'one must abandon the dictum of the Versailles Treaty that Germany and her allies were solely responsible'.[25] In summary, Fay's volumes asserted that 'Austria was more responsible for the immediate origins of the war than any other Power', although it acted, from its point of view, in self-defence; Germany did not plot a European war and 'made genuine, though too belated efforts, to avert one'; France's part was 'less clear', as it had not yet published any official documents, Italy and Belgium played no decisive part and, in Britain, Sir Edward Grey had made genuine mediation proposals. From his detailed study, based on the official documents available to him, Fay concluded that 'the verdict of the Treaty of Versailles that Germany and her allies were responsible for the war, in view of the evidence now available, is historically unsound. It should therefore be revised'. He doubted, however, that such a 'formal and legal revision' was practicable at the present moment, 'because of the popular feeling widespread in some of the Entente countries'. First, public opinion would need to be revised, a process that depended on further revision by historians.[26]

The political agenda of the American revisionists, such as their opposition to America's intervention in the war, did much to motivate their history writing, although Fay denied that he had any 'political motive, either to justify the Treaty of Versailles or to demand its revision but simply to carry out what a great master has defined as the proper task of the historian – to tell how it really came about'.[27] However, with hindsight we can see that with an emotionally charged topic like the origins of the First World War, this was becoming an increasingly difficult task, if it had indeed ever been possible.

If Fay's moderate revisionist publications were already welcome in Germany, H.E. Barnes went even further and completely turned the tables by blaming the Entente powers, particularly Russia and France, for the escalation of the crisis in 1914, whilst being an apologist for the Central Powers.[28] Barnes, who had favoured American intervention before 1917, came to regret his attitude after Versailles, when he became convinced that America had intervened on the wrong side. Revisionism was for Barnes a means to discredit economic imperialism and, as a professional historian, he quickly became a leader among the American revisionists.[29] In 1922 he argued that the responsibility for the war was divided between the Entente and Central powers. By 1924 he considered Austria primarily responsible, but France and Russia more guilty than Germany, and finally he arrived at the conclusion that they, rather than Germany, were solely responsible for the outbreak of war.[30]

Barnes summarized and expanded his work in his 1926 publication *The Genesis of the World War*, the first American book to be written from the available documentary sources. During two visits to Europe in 1926 and 1927, Barnes had been able to interview many of the leading German and Austrian decision-makers of 1914 and, perhaps not surprisingly, their statements confirmed Barnes's opinion about the origins of the war. His speeches on the war guilt question were, of course, favourably received in Germany.[31] According to Barnes, Germany was the victim of an Entente plot. Barnes rejected any challenge to his thesis from his American colleagues with reference to 'five thousand documents' to prove his case, leading Alfred von Wegerer to comment that for Germany's revisionist cause it would be 'scarcely possible to provide a better book than this one'.[32] For Barnes, more was at stake than simply proving that the war guilt settlement had been wrong. He was also attacking the concept of a 'just war' and the idea that America had been right to get involved in a conflict with the alleged aim of creating a better world. Thus he wrote in 1925:

> If we can but understand how totally and terribly we were 'taken in' between 1914 and 1918 by the salesmen of this most holy and idealistic world conflict, we shall be the better prepared to be on our guard against the seductive lies and deceptions which will be put forward by similar groups when urging the necessity of another world catastrophe in order to 'crush militarism', 'make the world safe for democracy', 'put an end to all further wars', etc.[33]

Consequently, in his preface to *Genesis of the World War*, Barnes put forward the idea that the last war had been an 'unjust war', and that studying the war guilt question might help in preventing future wars. He further believed

> that the truth about the causes of the World War is one of the livest [*sic*] and most important practical issues of the present day. It is basic in the whole matter of the present European and world situation, resting as it does upon an unfair and unjust Peace Treaty, which was itself erected upon a most uncritical and complete acceptance of the grossest forms of war-time illusions concerning war guilt.[34]

His motivation in writing his revisionist history was, in his own words, his 'hatred of war in general and an ardent desire to execute an adequate exposure of the authors of the late World War in particular'.[35] Barnes's conclusions were damning for the Entente powers, and welcome clarification for Germany of its position:

> In estimating the order of guilt of the various countries we may safely say that the only direct and immediate responsibility for the World War falls upon Serbia, France and Russia, with the guilt about equally distributed. Next in order – far below France and Russia – would come Austria, though she never desired a general European war. Finally, we should place Germany and England as tied for last place, both being opposed to war in the 1914 crisis. Probably the German public was somewhat more favorable to military activity than the English people, but [. . .] the Kaiser made much more strenuous efforts to preserve the peace of Europe in 1914 than did Sir Edward Grey.[36]

As this extract demonstrates, this extreme revisionism could not have been further removed from the conclusions reached at Versailles regarding the question of war guilt.

As a result of their work, the American revisionists advocated that the war guilt accusation should be revoked. They received support for their cause from official quarters, too, in the shape of Senator Robert Latham Owen, who raised the war guilt question in the Senate, and who became convinced that the Allies 'had greatly deceived the people of the United States [. . . and that] the theory that the war was waged in defence of American ideals was untrue'.[37] Owen was a Democratic senator from 1907 until 1925. In 1917 he had supported Woodrow Wilson and had approved of the United States' entry into the war, and in 1919 he had been in favour of forcing Germany to accept the Treaty of Versailles. The war, he had thought then, had been 'an offensive war of the completely prepared German and Austrian military autocracies against the unsuspecting and inadequately prepared democracies of the world'.[38] Towards the end of his career as a senator, following a trip to Europe in the summer of 1923, where he read a number of revisionist works, he changed his mind and converted to the revisionist camp. The German State Secretary of the *Auswärtiges Amt,* Ago von Maltzan, convinced Owen to speak on behalf of Germany in the American Senate on the war guilt question. Owen, who now believed that the United States had been deceived by the Entente powers in 1917, and who considered himself partially responsible for this deception, felt obliged to champion Germany's cause. His aim was an eventual revision of the war guilt allegation and of German reparation payments, which he considered unfair as they rested on the assumptions of Article 231.

Owen 'burst into prominence' on 18 December 1923 with his speech entitled 'The Inner Secrets of European Diplomacy Disclosed for the First Time to the American Public'.[39] His speech, in which he based his argument largely on the works of German, English and French revisionists, maintained that the Germans had a right to be bitter about Article 231. It was well received by other revisionists, and not only in Germany. In Britain, E.D. Morel, for example, noted in response to Owen's speech that this was 'the first time since that war ended [that] a member of one of the world's legislatures has broken through this conspiracy of silence [. . .]. German militarism is a bogey of the heated fancy. French militarism is a reality and sets its iron heel on Europe at this hour'.[40] The French militarism that Morel had in mind had, after all, recently been demonstrated during the Ruhr occupation, France's answer to Germany's refusal to comply with the reparations payments.[41]

For the German War Guilt Section, Owen's speech represented a triumph, and it ensured that the text was widely available in translation in German, as well as French, Spanish and Italian, and discussed in the neutral press. Moreover, in America the speech marked 'a revolution [. . .] in how the war guilt question was judged in the political world of the United States'.[42] Demands for an official investigation into the war guilt question were raised and would be discussed over the next few years. The Senate commissioned the Legislative Reference Service of the Library of Congress to compile 'an impartial abstract and index of all authentic important evidence, heretofore made in printed form or otherwise readily accessible, bearing on the origin and causes of the World War'. During their investigation, they had received much practical support from the German War Guilt Section. Alfred von

Wegerer himself had travelled to Washington and discussed the available literature with the men of the Legislative Reference Service, ensuring that all the relevant revisionist publications were readily available to them. The officials working on this understaffed project eventually reached the conclusion that, due to the overwhelming amount of documentation, only future historians would be able to determine the war guilt question, and that the time was not right for an enquiry of this nature.[43]

In the second half of the 1920s, the focus of the debate in the United States shifted from concerns over war guilt to the question of why America had intervened in the war in 1917, and by the end of the decade, the Great Depression and subsequent economic slump determined American attitudes towards foreign policy.[44] As Selig Adler shows, revisionism was one of the factors that greatly influenced the 'marked increase in isolationist sentiments in the twenties. By 1929 it would have been difficult to believe that, a decade before, a historian had written that isolationism conflicted with the realities of modern life and had vanished forever'.[45] As a result of the passionate debate on the origins of the First World War, America would need much convincing before she would become involved again in European affairs, and much of America's foreign policy was based on the impression that the country 'had been "taken in" before'.[46] It was in no small part due to the accounts of the revisionists that many Americans felt that their country had been manipulated into the war by the Entente and that the conflict had been the result of secret diplomacy. As a result, they were going to be much more careful before committing themselves again in the future.

European revisionists

Germany and America were not the only places where historians advocated a revision of the war guilt question. Other commentators critical of the Versailles war guilt allegation included Edmund D. Morel in Britain, Georges Demartial in

France and Mathias Morhardt in Switzerland. They were motivated by pacifist ideas, and by their desire to demonstrate the perils of secret diplomacy.[47] Their influence on American views was particularly pronounced, perhaps, as Selig Adler speculates, because anything 'Made in Germany' on the origins of the war was somewhat suspect, whereas French or British assertions of their own war guilt, and of German innocence, seemed more convincing.[48]

In Britain, Edmund Dene Morel had been among those MPs who had resigned from the Liberal Party in protest when Britain had gone to war in 1914, 'under the influence of the profoundest conviction' that to do so was wrong, as he wrote after the war.[49] His opposition to the fighting continued throughout the conflict. Before the war, he had opposed Britain's Entente with France and had worked for an Anglo-German *rapprochement*. Against the background of the Second Moroccan Crisis he had published *Morocco in Diplomacy*, arguing for 'the establishment and maintenance of friendly relations' between Britain and Germany. In 1915, under the influence of the horrors of the war, he summed up where he saw the reasons for its outbreak: 'It has become evident that Secret Diplomacy and the "Balance of Power", with their alliances and commitments, have not saved Europe from a universal loss of life, of wealth, or international goodwill far surpassing the most frightful examples and the most frightful forecasts.'[50] Together with fellow objectors to the war, Morel founded the Union of Democratic Control (UDC) on 5 August 1914, an organization that would last for over fifty years. Its aim was to achieve a lasting postwar settlement that would avoid future wars.

Throughout the war, Morel had been a passionate and outspoken opponent of the Entente powers' desire to blame Germany for the outbreak of war. In a 1916 book entitled *Truth and the War*, he made a passionate plea for the truth about the origins of the war to be told regardless of patriotic concerns. 'My object is to assist in destroying the legend that Germany was the sole responsible author of this war, undertaken by her to "subjugate Europe".' Before and during the war, he attempted 'to be fair to our present enemies, and, in the interest of my country, to point out that the sole responsibility for the war cannot, in justice, be wholly imputed to them'.[51] Even before this publication, Morel and his fellow members of the UDC were already disliked by the government and in certain sections of the press, but this did little to change Morel's mind about the war guilt question. Following the publication of *Truth and the War*, Morel was accused of being disloyal and lacking in patriotic spirit in such difficult times. Although the government decided against censoring his publication, it was made an offence to send a copy of his book abroad.[52] Morel himself was imprisoned for five months in 1917–18 for violating the Defence of the Realm Act when he tried to send copies of his writings out of the country.[53]

After the war, Morel was outraged by the Treaty of Versailles, which did not amount to the lasting settlement that he had hoped for. In his opinion, the British people had been betrayed by the government, for they had fought for a more peaceful world. Their countless sacrifices had been in vain, because the peace was 'not constructive, but destructive. Instead of healing, it rips new wounds into the political body of Europe', he complained.[54] While such views might seem almost prescient, his biographer Catherine Cline asserts that Morel 'was not [. . .] a scholar attempting to provide a balanced picture of pre-war diplomacy, but a propagandist striving to convert the British public to acceptance of a particular programme of foreign policy'.[55]

Indeed, Morel's concern was to demonstrate that the real enemy was a different one. He believed that the secret diplomacy of the ruling classes had led to war, and that the working classes, who ended up fighting and dying in this war, were suffering in all the belligerent countries, 'victims one and all of the meaningless phrase, the empty pomp, the poisonous boast of war; victims one and all of the barbarous Statecraft, the perverted religion, the selfish exploitation of caste, and creed, and vested interest'. Equally, he felt all European governments had a share in the responsibility for the outbreak of war.

> German diplomacy has been as immoral, as short-sighted, as treacherous as any other. And it has added to those defects, habitual to Diplomacy itself, a brutality of manifestation peculiarly its own, combined with an almost phenomenal incapacity to understand, still less to appreciate, the psychology of the nations with whom it has to deal. But to each people belongs the task of purging its own Augean stables. [. . .] And if I am told that in issuing a collection of studies which establish that all the rights are not on one side and all the wrongs on the other, but that responsibility for this terrible war is much more universal than popular opinion in any of the belligerent countries is yet prepared to admit, I am injuring the 'national cause', my reply is this: – The only cause I recognise as 'national' will be helped and not injured by this.[56]

If these had been Morel's views in 1916, the outcome of the war and the peace treaty had done little to change his mind. In a confidential conversation with a member of the *Auswärtiges Amt*, Carl von Schubert, in 1922, Morel underlined that his demands for the reassessment of the war guilt question were in no way motivated by a Germanophile attitude on his part. As a member of the UDC, his aim was to achieve more control by the British people over the British parliamentary system, and his method was to show up the shortcomings of the cabinet policy of July 1914.[57] It was his conviction that secret diplomacy and statecraft were to blame for the outbreak of war, and he thought it imperative to demonstrate that this had been the case, if future wars were to be avoided, and if class solidarity were to transcend national borders.

Morel's thoughts were echoed outside of Britain, too. The Swiss historian Mathias Morhardt had already opposed French foreign policy during the war. He was a member of the 'Société d'Études Documentaires et Critiques sur la Guerre', a group that doubted the thesis of Germany's main responsibility for causing the war. Together with the Frenchmen Georges

Demartial and Alfred Fabre-Luce, he was of the opinion that the Entente powers, rather than Germany, had begun the war.[58] For most of these revisionists, simply blaming Germany seemed too easy, even dangerous, as it distracted from other important issues such as the perceived perils of secret diplomacy which, if unaddressed, increased the risk of future international conflict. French revisionists had an official publication, entitled *Évolution*, founded by Victor Margueritte and edited by Armand Charpentier, which provided a forum for revisionists like Demartial. A former director of colonial affairs, Demartial blamed France and her allies for the outbreak of war, for example in his 1922 publication *La Guerre de 1914: comment on mobilisa les consciences*. French revisionists were outspoken proponents of what has been termed 'Poincarism', stressing the alleged desire of Poincaré to prepare France for seeking revenge from Germany with the help of the Russian ally and by encouraging nationalist sentiments within France. Rumours about Poincaré's alleged responsibility for the war began to be spread as early as a month into the conflict and, according to John Keiger, seem to have been financed by Germany. The anti-Poincaré argument was taken up by French revisionists after 1919. An article by Demartial which argued along these lines, published in *Current History* in 1926, led to Demartial's suspension from the Legion of Honour for five years.[59] However, it was difficult for French revisionists to gain acceptance for their views in France, as Gerd Krumeich has demonstrated in a study on the French interwar debate. Even declared opponents of Poincaré, such as the French socialists, were unwilling to support anti-Poincaré views in Parliament. Despite public accusations, for example in the Communist journal *Humanité*, that Poincaré and the Tsarist government had collaborated in 1914 to influence the French press in favour of war, and despite revisionist publications which resulted from such new evidence, these views did not capture a mainstream audience in France. Even among outspoken anti-Poincaré agitators and among socialists who opposed French annexations and the occupation of the Ruhr area, the question whether the reparations demands had been legitimate was never raised. Accusations against Poincaré were motivated primarily by domestic policy concerns in the postwar years, rather than by a deeply felt conviction that the Treaty of Versailles had been a mistake, as was the case in Germany.[60]

Poincaré's return to government in January 1922 had provoked a hostile reaction in Germany. Opposition to Poincaré resulted in a

> lavishly funded propaganda campaign by Germany, but also the Soviet Union bent on discrediting its tsarist predecessors, [which] had a considerable effect on 'Anglo-Saxon' and neutral countries, contributing in the postwar era to the image of France, and Poincaré in particular, as Germanophobe, bellicose, militaristic and intent on restoring French hegemony to the European continent.[61]

In Britain, convinced and passionate revisionists such as Morel remained in the minority in the immediate postwar years. The majority of British historians did not follow 'that masochistic urge to blame one's own country that was so typical of many of the revisionists'.[62] Nevertheless, once the outrage and desire for revenge among the British public had subsided, the official view on the origins of the war began to change, as epitomized in David Lloyd George's famous phrase from his *War Memoirs,* where he concluded that 'the nations slithered over the brink into the boiling cauldron of war without a trace of apprehension or dismay'.[63] Lloyd George had been one of the principal creators of the Treaty of Versailles, but he came to regret his tough stance soon after the settlement was completed. Only a year after Germany had signed, he confessed to Charles Hardinge: 'If I had to go to Paris again I would conclude quite a different treaty.'[64] In his memoirs, he continued his conciliatory line by absolving the political leaders of Europe of their responsibility for the outbreak of war: 'Not even the astutest and most far-seeing statesman foresaw in the early summer of 1914 that the autumn would find the nations of the world interlocked in the most terrible conflict that has ever been witnessed in the history of mankind.'[65] Previously, the historian G.P. Gooch had already judged the Treaty of Versailles as too harsh, probably, as Hartmut Pogge von Strandmann suspects, because he did not believe that only Germany had caused the war. Of course, there were many other high-profile critics of Versailles, such as the economist John Maynard Keynes, whose critical publication *The Economic Consequences of the Peace* confirmed the worst fears of those who were opposed to the harsh treaty, and no doubt had considerable influence on the views of the revisionists.

Gooch went even further than simply considering Versailles too severe in his 1923 publication *Recent Revelations of European Diplomacy*, by claiming that no country had wanted the war. Rather than Germany bearing the sole guilt for the war, in this interpretation all countries shared a general guilt. Other revisionist historians changed their views about Germany in the postwar years – some, like Raymond Beazley and William H. Dawson, even received financial support from the German War Guilt Section to enable them to write their revisionist accounts. Conveniently for Germany, Beazley came to the conclusion that Germany 'had not plotted the great war, had not desired a war, and had made genuine, though belated and ill-organized efforts to avert it'.[66]

According to this changed and more conciliatory point of view, which quickly became the new orthodoxy of the late 1920s, the war had been an act of fate, rather than the design of any particular aggressor. As a result of more pressing domestic and foreign policy concerns, and of anti-French sentiments following the Ruhr crisis in 1923, public and official opinion, too, was transformed into a new orthodoxy. In 1926 Henry W. Nevinson, a British war correspondent, wrote in a journal that he considered Article 231 'a lie of such grossness that I wonder the hand which first wrote it did not wither', echoing a statement by the German Chancellor Philipp Scheidemann in 1919 that the hand which signed the Treaty of Versailles would have to wither.[67] In Britain, Germany was no longer blamed solely for the outbreak of the war after Lloyd George's change of heart. In order to understand the development of such a conciliatory interpretation, it is important to consider the international situation in the latter half of the 1920s, which presented Europe with new challenges and potential enemies. Bolshevism was increasingly seen as a threat to 'Western' countries, and Germany was needed as a possible ally against the Soviet Union. In view of increasing international hostility, it must have seemed politic to bury old hatchets, and Lloyd George's statement, seen in this context, seemed to offer the possibility of reconciliation. The British public would more easily accept a possible entry of Germany into the League of Nations, and perhaps even a future alliance between Britain and Germany, if that country's war guilt could be shown to have been exaggerated or untrue. In 1938 G.P. Gooch summed up the new consensus to this effect: 'That any single statesman or nation was the sole criminal is no longer seriously believed.' All the major powers had good reasons to go to war in 1914, he argued, and there could be no question of allocating blame or talking of war guilt, although 'the distribution of blame still tends to vary in some degree with the nationality of the expert'.[68]

As Holger Herwig argues, the influence of the revisionists, from Fay and Barnes in the United States, to Morel in England and Margueritte and Fabre-Luce in France, on international politics in the interwar years should not be underestimated.

> This pollution of American, British and French historical understanding of the origins of the Great War must have helped to undermine faith in the need to maintain the irenic clauses of the 1919 treaty. It remains an open question whether it also contributed to isolationism in the United States and proappeasement thinking in England in the 1930s.[69]

Pro-appeasement politicians seem to have relied to some extent on revisionism as a justification of their policy. If Germany had not been responsible for the outbreak of war, then the country had indeed been unfairly treated at Versailles, they concluded, and Hitler's foreign policy seemed justified, or more easily justifiable, in this light.

It is without a doubt that the debate was motivated by such political questions, too. For the German 'innocence campaign', these outside voices were a welcome addition to their own propaganda, regardless of the political motivations behind them, and the War Guilt Section did much to support and encourage such revisionist commentators and to provide a publishing forum for their views. German public opinion had even less of a chance of developing a realistic assessment of the war guilt question or the Treaty of Versailles, given the overt propaganda that they were exposed to from successive Weimar governments bent on revisionism. Indeed, the same could be said not just of German public opinion. Given the secrecy that was exercised by governments in Britain, France and Germany, their inhabitants stood little chance of developing a realistic assessment of the events that had led to war in 1914.

Anti-revisionists

Of course, not everyone who investigated the origins of the war in the interwar years arrived at the conclusion that the verdict of Versailles needed to be revised. Those who were convinced of Germany's war guilt, or at least believed that Germany had been mainly responsible for the events that led to the outbreak of war, are generally referred to as anti-revisionists. In Germany dissenters from the official line included, as we have already seen, Prince Lichnowsky and the former Krupp director Wilhelm Muehlon, as well as Richard Grelling, who had published *J'accuse* ... in France during the war, and whose postwar anti-revisionist publications were also published there. In Austria, Heinrich Kanner blamed the Central Powers for the outbreak of the war in two publications of 1922 and 1926.[70]

In August 1923 the German law professor Hermann Kantorowicz was asked by the Parliamentary Commission which investigated the origins of the war to prepare a report on the crisis of July 1914.[71] Kantorowicz began to examine the prewar events with the help of official documents and to evaluate the available evidence. The more he discovered, the more he revised his previous opinion, which had been along the lines of the current orthodox German view. Kantorowicz's independent enquiry into the origins of the war, based on documentary evidence, arrived at very different conclusions to the government's (and the Commission's) revisionist view, and led him to consider the Central Powers primarily responsible for the war. He became one of the few commentators of the Weimar years who did not support the official government line. In December 1923 his manuscript *Gutachten zur Kriegsschuldfrage* (Expert Report on the War Guilt Question) was completed. In it, he criticized the prewar policies of Germany and Austria-Hungary, and concluded that the Central Powers, and Austria-Hungary in particular, were primarily to blame for the outbreak of the war.

Such a heretical report could not be published in Germany at that time. As a delaying tactic the Parliamentary Commission asked Kantorowicz twice to rework and expand his report. In 1923, with the approval of Foreign Minister Stresemann, the German government postponed publication of this damaging account, and in 1927 denied Kantorowicz the right to publish his findings.[72] Until 1930 Kantorowicz fought with the War Guilt Section and the Commission, but could not effect a reversal of that decision. In an exchange with the *Auswärtiges Amt* in 1929, he summed up his views about its policies.

> I am of the certain conviction that, partially consciously, partially subconsciously, the entire official, semi-official and private innocence propaganda in the end serves no other purpose than to prepare the German people morally for the moment when, following the refutation of the 'guilt lie', the entire Versailles Treaty [. . .] is invalidated.[73]

This, he feared, would result in the 'automatic reopening of the world war', and he considered it his duty to work with his limited means against such a development. In a letter of March 1930 he expressed his fears even more strongly: he was convinced that 'the whole guilt propaganda [*sic*] is nothing but an incredible deception of the people which amounts to a moral mobilization for the next world war'.[74]

Kantorowicz's passionate efforts to publish his findings on the war guilt question had given him a reputation as a trouble-maker who was accused of 'fouling his own nest', and as a result he was even refused a chair at the University of Kiel. The decision against his promotion, and against the publication of the *Gutachten*, was made by Foreign Minister Stresemann in 1927. Stresemann feared that the publication of the text 'would render my entire Locarno policy impossible'. In other words, he knew that Germany's former enemies would be less inclined to be more lenient towards Germany on the basis of the damning evidence that Kantorowicz had assembled.[75] In 1929 the *Auswärtiges Amt* considered commissioning a 'counter-report', a decision that immediately led to Kantorowicz's resignation from the Parliamentary Commission, although not to less determination on his part to publish his findings. However, he was not even allowed to publish his report independently from the Commission.

The coming to power of the National Socialists in 1933 meant that Kantorowicz's findings would not be published at all before the Second World War or during his lifetime. The official innocence thesis could not be questioned during the 'Third Reich', and when the new regime publicly burnt the books of unwanted authors, published works by the politically uncomfortable (and Jewish) Kantorowicz were destroyed alongside those which were declared 'un-German'. This was not the political climate in which such anti-revisionism could be published. Kantorowicz's report was rediscovered by Imanuel Geiss, who published the text in 1967, forty years after its author had completed it, as a contribution to the renewed debate on the outbreak of war during the 'Fischer controversy' (see Part 3). Such had been the opposition of the *Auswärtiges Amt* to Kantorowicz's work, that even four decades after the publication had first been suppressed, former Legation Secretary Karl Schwendemann, who had been head of the War Guilt Section from 1928 to 1931, protested in a reader's letter against a positive review of Kantorowicz's work following Geiss's 1967 edition.[76]

In the late 1920s Prince Lichnowsky again made headlines, this time with his reminiscences *Heading for the Abyss*. Following its publication in November 1927, the book was greeted by a storm of hostile reviews and criticism throughout Germany. Friedrich Thimme, one of the editors of *Die Grosse Politik*, denounced Lichnowsky's book, and referred to him as the 'Ambassador who had during the war turned King's evidence against his own country'.[77] In other words, Lichnowsky's account was condemned as being that of a traitor. Thimme even went as far as to suggest that Lichnowsky himself had been behind the postwar Swiss edition of his controversial 1916 memorandum.[78] And yet, what Lichnowsky attempted to demonstrate was harmless enough and reflected the current international consensus. He explained that his intention in publishing the book had been

> to investigate the deeper causes of the catastrophe, and to do this if possible without touching on the so-called war-guilt question and without attributing the whole burden of responsibility to this or that individual in Germany or elsewhere. I have attempted to show that it was mainly the fatal system of groups and alliances inaugurated by Bismarck that led to the world war, and that the Great Powers were thereby drawn into conflicts which were quite alien to their real interests.

He hoped that his account could 'foster a spirit of reconciliation and rapprochement, while at the same time contributing to the consolidation of the peace of Europe'.[79] In fact, Lichnowsky had actually toned down his earlier accusations, formulated in 1915, stressing explicitly that blunders, rather than a desire for war, lay at the heart of Germany's decisions in 1914, and omitting what had been considered some of the most damaging passages of his wartime memorandum.

> Why had we put our finger into every pie and, even at the risk of war, meddled in matters which were no concern of ours? I am well aware that these statements will again lay me open to attack, and I am fully prepared to be reproached with having injured the German cause by publishing such comments. Can anyone do harm to our case by submitting to closest scrutiny and unsparing criticism the events that led to the great disaster? [. . .] Our cause has been injured by those who, contrary to my repeated warnings, insisted on pursuing a line of policy which, *albeit against their will*, inevitably led to war and to the collapse of the Fatherland.[80]

But even thus modified, his account was still considered damaging by the German authorities. When Lichnowsky died in February 1928, he was 'worn out with the storm of personal abuse that his work had aroused among his fellow-countrymen'.[81] For the German government at this crucial time when the war guilt question was finally being reconsidered on an international scale, his death meant there was one less vociferous and knowledgeable critic to worry about.

Outside of Germany there were, of course, also voices which warned against a revision of Versailles. The most famous American anti-revisionist was the historian Bernadotte Everly Schmitt.[82] Schmitt was Fay's most outspoken opponent, and the debate between the two scholars in the 1930s 'assumed heroic proportions' and influenced generations of Americans.[83] In the debate between Fay and Schmitt, Fay was widely regarded as the more convincing, partly, as John Langdon suspects, because his writings were more readable than Schmitt's. As a result, Fay's revisionist writings have influenced American views of the July Crisis to the present day.[84] Schmitt's own views on the war guilt question emerge, for example, from his criticism of Barnes's revisionist *Genesis of the World War*.

> It must be said that Mr. Barnes' book falls short of being [the] objective and scientific analysis of the great problem which is so urgently needed. As a protest against the old notion of unique German responsibility for the war, it will be welcomed by all honest men, but as an attempt to set up a new doctrine of unique French–Russian responsibility, it must be unhesitatingly rejected. The war was the consequence, perhaps inevitable, of the whole system of alliances and armaments, and in the origin, development and working of that system, the Central Powers, more particularly Germany, played a conspicuous part. Indeed, it was Germany who put the system to the test in July, 1914. Because the test failed, she is not entitled to claim that no responsibility attaches to her.[85]

French historians in the interwar years were in a difficult situation because Raymond Poincaré was still a prominent politician after the war. He had been French president in 1914, and was Prime Minister in the 1920s. As Bernadotte Schmitt observed in 1926, suspicions that Poincaré may have worked towards the war were first voiced in 1920, but received little attention because they were raised by socialists. Having been born in Lorraine, it was alleged that the former French president had been motivated by *revanche* ideas and had encouraged revanchist thoughts among the French people. In view of such criticisms, Poincaré issued a public defence of his actions in a publication entitled *Au Service de la France* in 1926.[86] French revisionist scholars faced the dilemma that to argue for France's culpability undermined the reparations which France needed. The alternative was to exonerate Poincaré's policy, and thus also his current leadership, even if they perhaps disagreed with his tough stance on Germany. Either way, any analysis of Poincaré's role was 'politically explosive'.[87] Poincaré had, to some extent, been 'a victim of his own success', as John Keiger explains. 'In peacetime he had prepared relentlessly for any eventuality and worked for national unity.' When the war had become a reality, 'the crisis had been well managed. Critics would not forgive a Lorrainer this coincidence'.[88] In other words, it was thought by many that Poincaré had wanted a war, and that his motivation had been revenge.

Gerd Krumeich sums up the war guilt debate in France, which has received relatively little attention from historians, thus:

> In general it can be said that it had been an exceedingly laborious process of realization [in France] that France had not only been a country that had been threatened by brutal Germany for years and that finally had been attacked under a pretext. Apart from the repercussions of wartime propaganda, official works were available, such as the Senate's report, allegedly historical and based on evidence, which had been published under the names of Emile Bourgeois and Georges Pagès and which constituted for the people at large the decisive source on the war guilt problem for more than a decade [. . .].[89]

Much like in Germany, historians had been instructed by the government to publish along the official war guilt line, and most French people believed this view on the origins of the war. Pierre Renouvin's institute at the Sorbonne had been set up by the government and given the task of providing a counter-argument to the propaganda published in Germany by the War Guilt Section. However, although Renouvin was criticized by the Left as apologetic and 'official', in fact he examined French prewar policy critically and was the first to expose the French Yellow Book for containing substantially falsified documents.[90] Rather than be affected by political concerns, Renouvin based his work on scholarly research, not an easy undertaking, as he outlined in 1929:

> Tens of thousands of diplomatic documents to read, the testimony of hundreds of witnesses to be sought out and criticized, a maze of controversy and debate to be traversed in quest of some occasional revelation of importance – this is the task of the historian who undertakes to attack as a whole the great problem of the origins of the World War.[91]

Renouvin was well equipped for this task, having been on the editorial staff of the *Documents diplomatiques français*, and he published his first account of the causes of the war, *Les Origines immédiates de la guerre,* in 1925. In this account, he did not find Germany guilty of planning the general war, but argued that because it and Austria-Hungary had been determined to risk a local war, in spite of the fact that they had 'coolly considered all the possible consequences of their actions', they therefore had to carry the main responsibility for the outbreak of war.[92]

In France and Britain, it was during the immediate postwar years that anti-revisionist voices had the most influence. The sense of outrage at the atrocities of the war, and the need to blame someone for its outbreak, led to the perceived need to identify and blame a guilty party. In France, which had suffered so heavily during the war, reparations were a political topic of particular explosiveness, especially when Poincaré ordered the French occupation of the Ruhr area over the issue of German non-payment of reparations. Any revision of the Versailles ruling would have jeopardized the reparations scheme, on which French reconstruction depended. With the passing of time, however, and as the interwar international diplomacy integrated Germany more with the Western powers, allocating blame became a less pressing concern. Other threats needed to be addressed, not only the severe economic conditions of the late 1920s, but also the fear of Bolshevism, against which Germany was needed as an ally. As time passed, revenge and punishment became less important, and the moment had come for a more conciliatory consensus regarding the war guilt question.

The comfortable consensus of the 1930s

With hindsight, as Wolfgang Jäger comments, it can be said that there were 'narrow limitations to a quiet, matter-of-fact and open discussion of the origins of the World War in the Weimar times'.[93] Given the nature of Germany's defeat, and the economic, political and social conditions of the Weimar Republic, it would always be easier to find scapegoats for the current conditions, rather than to look closely at any uncomfortable truths. Perhaps the peace treaty was too harsh for Germans to reconcile themselves to, perhaps the defeat was not total enough to allow for a complete break with the past. Too many continuities from the Second German Reich to Weimar and ultimately to the 'Third Reich' made it indeed impossible to arrive at a proper reckoning with the past.

The innocence campaign of the immediate postwar years was extremely successful within Germany, and most Germans believed that Versailles had been an unfair indictment, and that Germany was no more to blame for the outbreak of war than any other nation, or even that Russia and France had been the guilty parties. In 1930 Hermann Hesse expressed his belief to fellow writer Thomas Mann, that 'of 1,000 Germans even today 999 still know nothing of [our] war guilt'.[94] Revisionist interpretations became predominant in classrooms and in popular accounts of the origins of the war, certainly in America and Germany.[95] As a new orthodoxy developed in the late 1920s and 1930s, which emphasized collective responsibility, rather than the guilt of one nation, the efforts of the revisionists were rewarded with success. This conciliatory view became accepted in most countries. As it became less important to identify a guilty party and 'make them pay' for the war, and more important to find a *modus vivendi* with former enemies, attempts to put the responsibility for the war firmly on one country were replaced by a new orthodoxy: the European nations had slithered into war through no real fault of their own, as Lloyd George had asserted. Alliance systems and secret, 'old style diplomacy' were the real culprits. This was a consensus that Germans could also live with, and one which their own war guilt propaganda had helped formulate to a large extent.

In addition to this new consensus, prevalent Marxist interpretations saw a link between capitalism, imperialism and the outbreak of war. According to such views, the war had been an inevitable outcome of imperialist rivalries, rather than the design of any particular nation, and those rivalries in turn were regarded as the consequence of a crisis of capitalism. This view was expressed, for example, by Konne Zilliacus towards the end of the Second World War, when he summed up his study of the causes of the war of 1914:

> If there is one lesson that stands out above all the others to be learned from the history of how the first world war came, how the war ended, and what has happened since, it is the almost unbelievable blindness, tenacity, cruelty, and unscrupulousness with which the governing classes cling to their privileges and power at any cost to their suffering peoples and to the wider interests of peace and civilisation. They are so expert and cunning on details, and so blind and foolish on fundamentals.[96]

Like historians working on the topic of the origins of the First World War during the Cold War (whom we will encounter in Parts 3 and 4), Zilliacus's account addressed the worry about the prospect of a future third world war, and considered the knowledge of the origins of 'the two great catastrophes of this century' an important prerequisite for avoiding future conflicts. In 1944 he urged:

> If even today public opinion learnt the lesson of our failure to preserve peace in 1914, it might understand why we failed again in 1939. In that case we should have a better chance to win the peace after the second world war than we did after the first.[97]

In 1916 Lenin had already argued that colonial expansion and imperialist ambitions of the major combatant countries were at the heart of the origins of the war. Comparing prewar trade and production figures, he asked: 'What means other than war could there be *under capitalism* to overcome the disparity between the development of productive forces and the accumulation of capital on the one side, and the division of colonies and spheres of influence for finance-capital on the other?' In 1916, when Lenin's *Imperialism: The Highest State of*

Capitalism was written, it was aimed at proving to those socialists who had supported their country's war effort in 1914 in the belief that they were defending their country against aggressors that they had been deceived by their governments. After the war Lenin added in a preface that his study 'proved that the war of 1914–1918 was imperialist (that is, an annexationist, predatory, war of plunder) on the part of both sides; it was a war for the division of the world, for the partition and repartition of colonies and spheres of influence of finance capital etc.'[98]

Most Western historians would not have subscribed to such Marxist interpretation, but many nonetheless blamed the alliance system, the secretive diplomacy of the late nineteenth century, as well as imperial rivalries for the outbreak of war, thus confirming the general feeling of the later 1920s and 1930s that Germany was not solely to blame.

Despite the development of such a comfortable consensus, the War Guilt Section continued to censor and control German publications. In fact, it was eventually much more able to do so than in the immediate postwar years, particularly in the case of some unwanted document collections. Whereas in 1919 it could not have withheld the Kautsky documents without arousing suspicion, by the late 1920s and early 1930s it was even possible to suppress some of the official findings of the Parliamentary Committee which, as we have seen, had been established in 1918 to investigate the origins of the war. In January 1931 the Committee presented the findings of its investigation in a final report. The War Guilt Section called on an expert, Wilhelm Schaer of the Working Committee, to compile an evaluation of the Parliamentary Committee's report. As this was one of the propaganda organizations run by the *Auswärtiges Amt*, special scrutiny was assured. After all, this was hardly an independent inquiry. Schaer's report recommended that three volumes of documents which formed part of the Commission's findings, containing some previously unpublished material, should not be made public. They were too incriminating, particularly regarding German war aims, and they would throw a bad light on President von Hindenburg's role in the war. Although the debate was no longer as politically explosive as it once had been, Schaer considered the publication too dangerous. The particular threat of this report, according to him, was that it summarized a lot of evidence that had been made available over the previous years in scattered publications which scarcely anyone would look at anymore.

> It is a completely different matter if I have read bits and pieces here and there in the literature over the last ten years, which I will have forgotten by now, or if I can arrive at a complete picture today, based on such a publication, moreover an official one, of the entire German war-aim question. I do not think that anyone would go to the trouble today to check through all the publications on war aims that I have looked through [for the purpose of compiling this report].[99]

Moreover, Schaer feared that such a publication would provide Germany's former enemies with ammunition. He thought that France would only have to print those documents, 'with the less commentary, the better', and they could serve as perfect anti-German propaganda. Not surprisingly, historians investigating the origins of the war after the Second World War have concluded from Schaer's report that the evidence the *Auswärtiges Amt* censored must have contained incriminating material that would help to prove Germany's responsibility for war in 1914. The suppression of such potentially incriminating evidence has been regarded as an 'indirect admission of guilt', for why else would such documents have been censored if they did not testify to German guilt? Schaer and his colleagues of the War Guilt Section could not have known just how effective their attempts to suppress possibly incriminating evidence would be. It is particularly unfortunate for those arguing after the Second World War in favour of German war guilt in 1914 that those three volumes of documents were never published, for they are lost today and cannot be used to throw light on this debate.[100]

Imanuel Geiss points to the negative consequences of the War Guilt Section's relative success in suppressing the truth about the origins of the war. Primarily due to its efforts, the vast majority of the German people was convinced of Germany's relative innocence in 1914. The perils of this deliberate propaganda effort were more serious than merely the distortion of the truth.

> The successful manipulation of the historical truth and the 'national' consciousness of a great people also aided the victory of German National Socialism, whose favourite historical argument, next to the legend of the stab in the back, had been the aggressive protestation of German innocence during the First World War and in its outbreak. The result [. . .] was the Second World War, in which the German Empire finally perished.[101]

In the end, the refutation of the war guilt question did not lead the German people on 'the path to liberty' by shaking off the constraints imposed by the Allies at Versailles, but aided the development of the National Socialist dictatorship. After January 1933 the war guilt question soon lost its sense of urgency, as the new regime began with a radical redrawing of German policy and a bid to restore Germany's great power status. Under the new regime, the revision of the Treaty of Versailles was no longer an end in itself, or the final goal of foreign policy, but became the starting point for the achievement of further, more wide-ranging foreign policy aims. Of course, the ground for these aims of the National Socialist government had already been prepared during the Weimar years, not least by the revisionist propaganda of the *Auswärtiges Amt* in the immediate postwar years. As Holger Herwig points out:

> Nazi expansionism clearly fed upon the fertile intellectual basis laid down for it by the patriotic self-censors in the 1920s. In other words, Adolf Hitler's radical 'revisionism' was already well rooted in public and elite opinion under the Weimar Republic.[102]

After 1933 the nature of the German critique of the peace treaty changed, as it concentrated on revealing the legal shortcomings of the settlement by focusing on international law. The fight against the Versailles Treaty in the media had lost its urgency, and the debate on war guilt in Germany officially came to a conclusion in 1937.[103] In a speech in the Reichstag on 30 January 1937, Adolf Hitler summed up the process of leading the German nation from the life of a 'leper' among the other nations, following the Treaty of Versailles, back to great power status. 'Above all', he declared, 'I solemnly revoke the German signature on the declaration, blackmailed from the former, weak government against its better judgement, that Germany was guilty of the war.' This, in Hitler's words, amounted to a 'restoration of the honour of the German people'.[104] In the same year the *Zentralstelle* and the Working Committee were dissolved. Their task was seen as done, and the expense was no longer considered necessary. Although the journal *Berliner Monatshefte* (formerly *Die Kriegsschuldfrage*) continued to be published until 1944, Alfred von Wegerer was no longer its editor, and there was a marked decrease in popular interest in the war guilt question.[105]

Germany's former enemies were willing to accept these developments in Germany for their own reasons, as Evans and Pogge von Strandmann explain: 'Under the Allied response of appeasement, a willingness to modify the peace terms grew steadily and it appeared politically unwise to insist on sole German responsibility for 1914.'[106] Moreover, outside of Germany, enquiries into the outbreak of the First World War came to be regarded as less important in the face of the threat of a renewed European or World War by the late 1930s, while in Germany, with the effective abandonment of the Treaty of Versailles, there was no longer any perceived need to revise its hated war guilt ruling. It was finally official that Germany had not started the World War, and that the ruling of Versailles had been an unfair victors' *Diktat*. Germany's European neighbours on the whole no longer argued against this new orthodoxy.

One of the most influential, and 'classic' German revisionist accounts of the origins of the war published during this time was a two-volume study by Alfred von Wegerer, entitled *Der Ausbruch des Weltkrieges 1914*. It summed up the official German opinion which Wegerer and his colleagues of the *Zentralstelle* had helped to shape. Wegerer claimed that he based his 1939 account on the available documents, including Russian and French, and on a large number of published memoirs, as well as on personal conversations he had with many of the men in charge of politics in 1914. His publication was intended as a 'solid, scientific end' to his fight against the Versailles war guilt thesis to which he had devoted himself for fifteen years until Hitler's declaration of January 1937. Wegerer's comfortable interpretation was considered a standard account in Germany until the early 1960s, and was even recommended to history teachers and students in textbooks, despite the fact that, in John Langdon's words, 'it has not aged gracefully'. Contrary to Wegerer's claims, he mainly based his 'tendentious and prejudiced' account on *Die Grosse Politik*, and only selected documents from other collections if they were favourable to Germany.[107]

In his study, Wegerer blamed the Entente powers for the escalation of the July Crisis, arguing for example that one of the main reasons why the war between Austria-Hungary and Serbia could not be localized was Russia's decision to support Serbia. France was guilty, too, for standing by Russia and supporting its ally, while Britain had feared that Germany might assume too powerful a position on the continent, if it defeated France in a European war, and became involved for that reason. From studying the diplomatic documents available, Wegerer concluded that in the last days of the crisis the desire to avoid a general war had been the strongest in Berlin, although he conceded that it had also been present everywhere else. He offered a very comforting interpretation in which the German government, if anything, had tried to avoid an escalation of the crisis, rather than being responsible for the outbreak of war. The first decisions had been taken in

Vienna, Wegerer's account alleged, and Germany had tried in vain to influence the Austro-Hungarian leaders to mediate on 29 July. Russia had threatened Germany with its general mobilization, and French desire for revenge had played its part. In all of this, Germany emerges as a passive party, unable to change or shape events as they were unfolding. In the end, Wegerer summed up, 'the outbreak of the world war was probably more fate than desire!'[108]

Twenty years after the end of the war, its origins seemed finally settled. In 1939 a new, more terrible war embroiled Europe and ultimately the world, a war for which Germany could not deny her responsibility after her total defeat in 1945. In the years immediately after the Second World War, the origins of the war of 1914 were initially of no pressing concern. Greater horrors had overshadowed the suffering which the First World War had caused, and other concerns took over from those of studying the war's origins. The question of responsibility seemed resolved by the compromise of the interwar orthodox view of a breakdown of alliances. For Germany, this was a comfortable consensus indeed, but one that would all too soon come under renewed scrutiny.

Notes

1 Adler, 'The War-Guilt Question', p. 17.
2 See Holger Herwig (ed.), *The Outbreak of World War I: Causes and Responsibilies,* 5th revised edn, Lexington and Toronto 1991, pp. 10–11.
3 Walter Rathenau, *Nach der Flut,* Berlin 1919, cited in Fritz Klein, 'Between Compiègne and Versailles: The Germans on the Way from a Misunderstood Defeat to an Unwanted Peace' in M.F. Boemke, G.D. Feldmann and E. Glaser (eds), *The Treaty of Versailles: A Reassessment after 75 Years,* Cambridge 1998, p. 203.
4 Wilhelm Marx, 'The Responsibility for the War', *Foreign Affairs,* 4, 1926, p. 178.
5 Adler, 'The War-Guilt Question', p. 4.
6 Marx, 'The Responsibility for the War', citations on pp. 177–8, 194.
7 Ibid., p. 179.
8 Some of this evidence is discussed below, Part 3.
9 Bernhard Schwertfeger (ed.), *Dokumentarium zur Vorgeschichte des*

Weltkrieges, 1871–1914, Berlin 1928, quote in Preface. See also Herwig, 'Clio Deceived', p. 102. Schwertfeger was also commissioned by the *Zentralstelle* to compile an eight-part guide to *Die Grosse Politik* for a general readership.

10 Herwig, 'Clio Deceived', p. 102f., quote on p. 103; Langdon, *The Long Debate*, p. 26.

11 Alfred von Wegerer, *Der Ausbruch des Weltkrieges 1914*, 2 vols, Hamburg 1939, 2nd edn, 1943, vol. I, preface, p. v. Wegerer's book is discussed in more detail below, pp. 112–13.

12 Alfred von Wegerer, *Die Widerlegung der Versailler Kriegsschuldthese*, Berlin 1928 (English translation: *A Refutation of the Versailles War-Guilt Thesis*, New York 1930). Other publications include *Wie es zum Grossen Krieg kam: Vorgeschichte des Weltkrieges*, Leipzig 1930, *Im Kampf gegen die Kriegsschuldlüge: Ausgewählte Aufsätze*, Berlin 1936, where a selection of his writings can be found. On Wegerer, see also Langdon, *The Long Debate*, pp. 21ff.

13 Langdon, *The Long Debate*, p. 26, note 21, who cites a letter Montgelas wrote in the summer of 1918, in which he referred to the war as preventive and thought that Germany 'consciously brought about the war as a preventive war'. While editing the Kautsky documents, and following the Treaty of Versailles, he changed his mind and denied German war guilt.

14 Cited in Berber, *Das Diktat von Versailles*, p. 1229.

15 Cited ibid.

16 Hindenburg's speech of 18 September 1927, ibid., pp. 1229f. See also Adler, 'The War-Guilt Question', p. 21.

17 Hindenburg's speech of 28 June 1929, in Peter Longerich (ed.), *Die Erste Republik: Dokumente zur Geschichte des Weimarer Staates*, Munich and Zurich 1992, p. 143.

18 Adler, 'The War-Guilt Question', p. 1.

19 Ibid., p. 10.

20 Warren I. Cohen, *The American Revisionists: The Lessons of Intervention in World War I*, Chicago and London 1967, pp. 28–9.

21 Adler, 'The War Guilt Question', p. 2.

22 Ibid., pp. 4-5.

23 S.B. Fay, *The Origins of the World War*, 2 vols, New York 1929, vol. I: *Before Sarajevo: Underlying Causes of the War*, vol. II: *After Sarajevo: Immediate Causes of the War*; vol. I, p. vii.

24 John E. Moser, *Twisting the Lion's Tail: Anglophobia in the United States, 1921–1948*, London 1999, p. 39.

25 Fay, *The Origins of the World War*, citations vol. I, p. v; vol. II, pp. 547–8.

26 Ibid., vol. II, pp. 550ff., citation p. 558.

27 Ibid., vol. I, p. vi.

28 H.E. Barnes, *The Genesis of the War: An Introduction to the Problem of*

War-Guilt, New York 1926. The differences between the interpretations of Barnes and Fay are highlighted by Langdon, *The Long Debate*, pp. 26ff.

29 Adler, 'The War-Guilt Question', pp. 16–17.

30 Cohen, *American Revisionists*, p. 75.

31 Ibid., p. 98.

32 See Adler, 'The War-Guilt Question', p. 18.

33 Cited in Cohen, *American Revisionists*, p. 79.

34 Barnes, *Genesis*, p. xi.

35 Ibid., p. xiii.

36 Ibid., pp. 661–2.

37 Cited in Adler, 'War-Guilt', p. 14.

38 Cited in Herrman Wittgens, 'Senator Owen, the Schuldreferat and the Debate over War Guilt in the 1920s', in Wilson (ed.), *Forging the Collective Memory*, p. 131. See also Moser, *Twisting the Lion's Tail*, p. 39.

39 Wittgens, 'Senator Owen, the Schuldreferat and the Debate over War Guilt in the 1920s', p. 132. Owen's 'overly long speech' (it amounted to over 40 pages) is summarized here.

40 Cited ibid., p. 133.

41 See John F.V. Keiger, 'Raymond Poincaré and the Ruhr Crisis', in Robert Boyce (ed.), *French Foreign and Defence Policy, 1918–1940: The Decline and Fall of a Great Power*, London and New York 1998, pp. 49–70, for background to the Ruhr occupation.

42 Ibid., p. 134.

43 Ibid., pp. 135–8.

44 Cohen, *American Revisionists*, pp. 97, 120.

45 Adler, 'The War-Guilt Question', p. 27.

46 Ibid., p. 28.

47 Jäger, *Historische Forschung*, p. 59.

48 Adler, 'The War-Guilt Question', pp. 7–8.

49 Catherine A. Cline, *E.D. Morel, 1873–1924: The Strategies of Protest*, Belfast 1980, p. 98.

50 E.D. Morel, *Morocco in Diplomacy*, London 1912, republished during the war as *Ten Years of Secret Diplomacy: An Unheeded Warning*, London 1915, citation on p. xvi. On Morel and the UDC, see also Marvin Swartz, *The Union of Democratic Control in British Politics During the First World War*, Oxford 1971, pp. 11ff.; Keith Robbins, *The Abolition of War: The 'Peace Movement' in Britain, 1914–1919*, Cardiff 1976, pp. 37ff.; Cline, *E. D. Morel*, pp. 98ff.

51 E.D.Morel, *Truth and the War*, London 1916, pp. 103/xi.

52 See Adler, 'The War-Guilt Question', p. 8. Morel's books proved extremely popular. 16,000 copies of *Truth and the War* were sold in 1916 alone, while *Ten Years of Secret Diplomacy* went through five editions during the war. Cline, *E.D. Morel*, p. 103.

53 Swartz, *Union of Democratic Control*, p. 178. Another British pacifist imprisoned for four and a half months in 1918 was the philosopher Bertrand Russell who, similarly to Morel, felt that Britain could have come to an arrangement with Germany before July 1914. He recalls that before the war he 'foresaw that a great war would mark the end of an epoch and drastically lower the general level of civilization. On these grounds I should have wished England to be neutral. Subsequent history has confirmed me in this opinion'. Russell's autobiographical account also describes fighting between pacifists and patriots during pacifist meetings. Bertrand Russell, 'Experiences of a Pacifist in the First World War', in *Portraits from Memory and other Essays*, London 1956, pp. 30–4. Apart from Russell, the UDC also received support from Norman Angel and Ramsay MacDonald.

54 Quoted in Jäger, *Historische Forschung*, p. 59.

55 Cline, *E.D. Morel*, p. 104.

56 Morel, *Truth and the War*, pp. xvi, xxii–xxiii.

57 See Heinemann, *Verdrängte Niederlage*, p. 231.

58 Jäger, *Historische Forschung*, pp. 59-60; Keiger, *Poincaré*, pp. 199–200. See, for example, Georges Demartial, 'La Guerre de 1914: Comment on mobilisa les consciences', *Current History*, 1922; Mathias Morhardt, *Les Vrais Coupables*, German transl. *Die wahren Schuldigen*, Leipzig 1925; Alfred Fabre-Luce, *La Victoire*, Paris 1924. On French revisionists, see also Jean-Baptiste Duroselle, *La Grande Guerre des Français, 1914–1918: L'incompréhensible*, Paris 1994, pp. 31–3.

59 Keiger, *Poincaré*, pp. 195, 197; Krumeich, 'Vergleichende Aspekte', p. 922; Adler, 'War-Guilt', p. 22. Demartial, 'La Guerre de 1914'.

60 Krumeich, 'Vergleichende Aspekte', pp. 922–4.

61 Keiger, 'Raymond Poincaré and the Ruhr Crisis', p. 51.

62 Adler, 'The War-Guilt Question', p. 23.

63 David Lloyd George, *War Memoirs*, vol. I, London 1924, p. 32. On Lloyd George's change of opinion regarding the Treaty of Versailles and the war guilt decision, see also Michael Graham Fry, 'British Revisionism', in M.F. Boemke, G.D. Feldmann and E. Glaser (eds), *The Treaty of Versailles*, pp. 565–601.

64 Cited in Alan Sharp, 'Lloyd George and Foreign Policy, 1918-1922', in Judith Loades (ed.), *The Life and Times of David Lloyd George*, Bangor 1991, p. 129.

65 Lloyd George, *War Memoirs*, vol. I, p. 32.

66 Hartmut Pogge von Strandmann, 'Britische Historiker und der Ausbruch des Ersten Weltkrieges', in Wolfgang Michalka (ed.), *Der Erste Weltkrieg*, pp. 929–52, p. 934, citation on p. 935.

67 Nevinson, cited in Adler, 'The War Guilt Question', p. 23.

68 Gooch, *Before the War*, vol. 2, p. v.

69 Herwig, 'Clio Deceived', p. 106.

70 Heinrich Kanner, *Kaiserliche Katastrophenpolitik*, Vienna 1922; idem,

Der Schlüssel zur Kriegsschuldfrage, Munich 1926; Richard Grelling, *J'accuse...*, Lausanne 1915; idem, *Le Campagne 'innocentiste'*, Paris 1925. See Adler, 'The War-Guilt Question', p. 7, note 46.

71 Information on Hermann Kantorowicz in Imanuel Geiss's Introduction to Hermann Kantorowicz, *Gutachten zur Kriegsschuldfrage*, edited by I. Geiss, Frankfurt 1967, pp. 11ff. (cited as Geiss, 'Introduction').

72 Herwig (ed.), *The Outbreak of World War I*, p. 2.

73 Cited in Geiss, 'Introduction', p. 35.

74 Letter to Hermann Lutz, cited ibid., p. 36, note 68.

75 Quoted in Herwig, 'Clio Deceived', p. 113; see also Geiss, 'Introduction', pp. 22–3. A year later, that decision was revoked, and Kantorowicz received his promotion. In *Der Geist der englischen Politik und das Gespenst der Einkreisung Deutschlands*, Berlin 1929, Kantorowicz gives a contemporary account of the German innocence propaganda.

76 Geiss, 'Die manipulierte Kriegsschuldfrage', p. 33. For a summary of Kantorowicz's arguments in English, see Robert A. Kann's review of the *Gutachten* in *Central European History*, 1, 1968; and Langdon, *The Long Debate*, pp. 36ff.

77 Articles in *Kölnische Zeitung*, 11 Dec. 1927 and *Archiv für Politik und Geschichte*, Heft i, 1928, cited in Lichnowsky, *Heading for the Abyss*, London 1928, translator's note, p. v.

78 See above, p. 30, for Lichnowsky's 1916 memorandum.

79 Introductory letter from Prince Lichnowsky in *Heading for the Abyss*.

80 Prince Lichnowsky, *Heading for the Abyss*, p. xxvi.

81 Ibid., translator's note, p. vii. Lichnowsky's memorandum and the omissions are discussed in Röhl, *1914: Delusion or Design?*, pp. 48ff.

82 B.E. Schmitt, *The Coming of the War, 1914*, 2 vols, New York 1930; idem, *The Origins of the First World War*, London 1958.

83 Langdon, *The Long Debate*, p. 44.

84 Ibid., pp. 44–5.

85 B.E. Schmitt, 'July 1914', in *Foreign Affairs*, No. 1, Oct. 1926, p. 147.

86 Ibid., p. 133; R. Poincaré, *Au Service de la France*, Paris 1926. In Britain, Sir Edward Grey also felt compelled to publish a justification. Viscount Grey of Fallodon, *Twenty-Five Years*, 2 vols, New York 1925.

87 Langdon, *The Long Debate*, p. 39.

88 John Keiger, 'France', in Wilson (ed.), *Decisions for War*, p. 145.

89 Krumeich, 'Vergleichende Aspekte', p. 920.

90 Ibid., p. 921.

91 Pierre Renouvin, 'How the War Came', in *Foreign Affairs*, Apr. 1929, p. 384.

92 Cited in Langdon, *The Long Debate*, p. 44. P. Renouvin, *Les Origines immédiates de la guerre*, Paris 1925. An English translation, *The Immediate Origins of the War*, was published in New York in 1927.

93 Jäger, *Historische Forschung*, p. 68.
94 Cited in Herwig (ed.), *The Outbreak of World War I*, p. 7.
95 Langdon, *The Long Debate*, p. 4.
96 K. Zilliacus, *The Mirror of the Past: Lest it Reflect the Future*, London 1944, p. 129.
97 Ibid., p. 121.
98 V.I. Lenin, *Imperialism – The Last State of Capitalism*, in *Selected Works*, English translation, Moscow 1968, pp. 169–257, citations on pp. 240, 171. See also Joll, *Origins*, pp. 146–7.
99 Schaer's report cited in Geiss, 'Die manipulierte Kriegsschuldfrage', p. 46.
100 For the argument of the indirect admission of guilt, see ibid., p. 48. On 30 August 1932, Hermann Goering, acting as president of the Reichstag, dissolved the Commission and ordered the destruction of all available volumes of its report. Herwig, 'Clio Deceived', p. 108.
101 Geiss, 'Die manipulierte Kriegsschuldfrage', p. 50.
102 Herwig, 'Clio Deceived', p. 89.
103 Jäger, *Historische Forschung*, pp. 45–6, 66–7.
104 Text of the speech in Berber, *Das Diktat von Versailles*, vol. 2, p. 1231.
105 Jäger, *Historische Forschung*, p. 64.
106 Evans and Pogge von Strandmann (eds), *The Coming of the First World War*, p. vi.
107 Langdon, *The Long Debate*, p. 23.
108 Wegerer, *Ausbruch*, vol. 1, pp. 118ff.; vol. 2, pp. 88ff., 124ff., 414, 423.

Part 3

The Origins of the War and the Question of Continuity in German History

Introduction

After 1945 the terms of the Peace Treaty of Versailles were widely regarded on the Allied side as having been a serious mistake. It followed that the German share of responsibility for the First World War was gradually reduced. R.J.W. Evans and H. Pogge von Strandmann[1]

In the 1950s it was common among German historians to refer to the 'unleashing' of the Second World War in contrast to the 'outbreak' of the First. Walter Hofer's definition of this distinction became generally accepted, and made obvious the perceived difference between the origins of the two wars. 'A volcano "breaks out" [erupts], an epidemic "breaks out" – the war of 1939 did not "break out" in this sense', Hofer explained.[2] Rather, the Second World War had been prepared, planned and consciously *unleashed*. For the First World War, by contrast, the term 'outbreak' was used. The implication was that a distinct difference existed between the origins of the two wars, in accordance with the interwar orthodoxy that the war of 1914 had come about not as a result of intention or design, but as an inevitable event, almost an act of nature, like the eruption of a volcano. As the continuing debate on the origins of the First World War was to demonstrate, however, such assumptions did not go unchallenged, and a wide range of new interpretations was advanced. According to some historians, the war had been deliberately *unleashed*, while others asserted that it had *broken out*, without anyone's conscious intent. There are also, of course, a variety of modifications of the argument in between these two extreme positions.

The following section begins by examining the debate during the immediate postwar years, in which revisionist views were still widely held among American and British academics and the common perception of European nations 'stumbling into war' in 1914 was still the accepted interpretation among the West German public and the historical fraternity. It will then explore how Fritz Fischer's arguments about the origins of the war, advanced in the early 1960s, exploded this comfortable orthodoxy, and will investigate the impact of Fischer's theses and the sometimes hostile responses to them in the context of Germany in the 1960s. Despite the distance in time, the war guilt controversy was central to the question of identity in the Federal Republic. Fischer's work refuted the view that Germany had been innocent in the events that had led to war in 1914, and suggested that at Versailles the Allies had in fact arrived at the correct conclusion about German war guilt. Fischer's arguments provoked not only a re-evaluation of current views, but also a shift in emphasis from diplomatic and political history to a concern with social and economic history. This was reflected in the way historians sought to explain the origins of the war – the focus on foreign policy was replaced in many quarters by an increased interest in domestic policy as the underlying cause for an expansionist and aggressive foreign policy. Increasingly, historians began to concentrate on the underlying structures of Wilhelmine Germany, rather than on individual decision-makers. As will be seen, the study of new primary source material also became an important aspect of the debate, in which two opposing sides argued over the role of individual decision-makers, the importance of certain key events, and the authenticity of the available primary evidence. Although the initial reaction to Fischer's views by Germany's eminent historians was outrage, in the long term Fischer's work sparked a renewed interest in the old topic of the origins of the First World War, and encouraged new ways of examining the problem.

The debate after the Second World War: towards a comfortable consensus

German policy in 1914 did not aim for the unleashing of a European war; it was primarily determined by the alliance obligations vis-à-vis Austria-Hungary. [. . .] Certain circles in the German General Staff believed Germany's chances of victory were greater in 1914 than in the following years; such considerations did not, however, determine the policy of the German government. Franco–German Historians' Commission, 1951[3]

In 1945 Germany was a very different place than it had been following the defeat in 1918. This time there could be no denying that the country had lost the war, nor could there be any doubting that Germany had started it. Germany suffered a total defeat, and was left occupied and divided by its enemies. The founding of two separate German states in 1949 as a result of the lost war was an outward sign of defeat, and of a decisive break in German history. In West Germany, the nature of that defeat, total surrender and capitulation, as well as the painful realization of the crimes committed under the National Socialist regime, led to a serious crisis of identity. As a result, it seemed to be all the more important to insist that Germany had not caused the First World War, that there could be no 'pattern' of provoking war, no inherently aggressive policy that was essentially 'German'. Given the horrors of the Second World War, delving into the origins of the First World War was in any case not high on anyone's agenda in the immediate postwar years. A central theme of West German historians in those difficult first years of the new Federal Republic was the *discontinuity* of German history in the twentieth century and the attempt to explain National Socialism as an aberration in modern German history.

In East Germany, on the other hand, historians emphasized the *continuity* of German history between the Kaiser's Empire, Hitler's Reich and the West German Federal Republic. The new Communist system aimed to set itself apart by identifying 'bourgeois' West German history and the capitalist West German state with the German Reich that had gone to war in

1914 and again in 1939. West Germany was thus placed in a tradition of aggressive imperialist history in an attempt to discredit and devalue the new Federal Republic.[4] In East Germany, the question of the origins of the First World War was not particularly controversial, partly because here the belligerent history of the last decades was considered to have come to an end with the decisive break that had led to establishment of two separate states: the East German Republic considered itself divorced from that uncomfortable history, while West Germany was regarded as the continuation of it. As Andreas Dorpalen shows, Marxist historians

> see no fundamental difference between Germany's conduct and that of other states, merely one of degree. Germany's imperialism is found especially virulent because as a latecomer to the imperialist race it had acquired only a small share of the world's riches and thus was especially anxious to see the world divided.

East Germany's historians did not feel the need to whitewash Imperial Germany's prewar policy, they were not concerned with attributing shares of blame to different countries, even less so to individual decision-makers.[5] Rather, as Dorpalen explains, East German accounts started from the premise

> that all powers considered war as a proper and adequate way of settling conflicting claims – not a last desperate resort to be avoided if at all possible. Thus Britain, too, is included among the deliberate warmongers: London's reluctance to side unequivocally with France and Russia among the post-Sarajevo crisis is interpreted as a precautionary measure designed so as not to deter Germany from going to war – a war that Britain is alleged to have wanted in order to rid itself of its German competitor.[6]

While there was no controversy in the GDR in the 1950s over Germany's implication in the origins of the First World War, there was heated debate among Marxist historians over the policy of the Social Democratic leaders in 1914, who had assured the government of their cooperation and who had willingly supported the war. The Marxist labour historian Jürgen Kuczynski had challenged the view that only the party leadership had been at fault, but blamed instead the workers for their own actions.[7] However, this debate was nothing like the renewed controversy on the origins of the First World War which would erupt only a few years later in the Federal Republic.

In the West, most historians (and the German public) continued to reject the assumptions made by the Allies at Versailles that Germany had been to blame for the outbreak of war in 1914. The interwar orthodoxy of the European nations having 'slithered' into the First World War was still a popular point of view, while it was commonly argued that Hitler had been a mere aberration, a 'sudden interloper'.[8] In the 1950s, the orthodoxy of collective responsibility was still confidently advanced in the Federal Republic. Moreover, in the aftermath of the horrors of the Second World War, there was initially no great concern to investigate the causes of war in 1914, particularly in Germany, which now had more than enough uncomfortable history to come to terms with. Extensive document-based research was in any case largely impossible until 1956, when the Allies began to return German documents that they had seized in 1945.

At the first West German Historians' National Meeting (*Deutscher Historikertag*) since the war in 1950, the eminent historian Gerhard Ritter emphasized the 'victory of Germany's main theses' in the international historians' debate of the 1920s as a great achievement of German historiography.[9] As far as Germany's historians were concerned, the debate on the origins of the First World War was over. A Franco-German Historians' Commission of 1951, which included both Ritter and the French historian Pierre Renouvin, recommended the treatment of the subject in French and German school-books along the lines of the interwar orthodoxy. Political importance was attached to such an international agreement, because in the 1950s, West Germany was needed as an ally by Britain, France and the United States against the Cold War threat posed by the Soviet Union, and for this aim the country's rehabilitation was required. Much like in the inter-war years, arguments about Germany's involvement in the origins of the First World War could only have served to hinder that process of reintegration.

Fritz Fischer commented later that the agreement of the Historians' Commission and the general consensus of the early 1950s had been arrived at against the threat of a third world war, following the shock of the Korean War, and that it also needed to be considered against the background of the contentious issue of West Germany's rearmament.[10] Given the tensions of the early 1950s, it seemed politic to end the dispute on the origins in favour of a general compromise reminiscent of Lloyd George's interwar views, which had equally aimed at resolving tensions in the light of a worsening international climate. By 1955 West Germany had been accepted as a partner into NATO, a certain sign that the country was distancing itself from its past and moving towards greater international integration and recognition.

As a result of such political considerations, the revisionist views of German historians had been publicly endorsed and confirmed on an international political level. The Historians' Commission came to the following conclusion:

> The documents do not permit attributing a conscious desire for a European war to any one government or people. Mutual distrust had reached a peak, and in leading circles it was believed that war was inevitable. Each one accused the other of aggressive intentions, and only saw a guarantee for security in an alliance system and continual armament increases.[11]

The debate on the origins of the war looked set to be relegated to history. In 1955 the historian Walther Hubatsch confidently asserted that 'the history of the years 1914 to 1918 is more thoroughly researched than almost any other epoch. The historian moves everywhere on safe ground'.[12] Both the First World War's origins and its course seemed adequately researched as a topic, and historians relied on the official military histories and document collections which had been published since the early 1920s and completed after the Second World War.[13]

However, the comfortable consensus of the interwar years had already been challenged outside of Germany by the Italian senator and journalist Luigi Albertini, who had studied the available documents for ten years, and whose impressive three-volume study entitled *The Origins of the First World War* had been published in Italy during the Second World War. His findings only became known to a wider audience in the 1950s, when his work was published in English translation.[14] Albertini pointed the finger at Germany as being the country most responsible for the outbreak of war, although he conceded that it had been encouraged by Austria-Hungary, and that its decision-makers had aimed for a localized Austro-Serbian conflict, rather than a European war. Austria-Hungary's decision-makers had not been passive or reluctant in the events of July 1914, but responsibility also attached to Bethmann Hollweg, for example, for not supporting Britain's mediation proposals. Albertini also considered the Entente guilty to some extent, arguing that Sasonov escalated the crisis with Russia's general mobilization, while Poincaré failed to hold Russia back. Serbia, too, could have acted differently by cooperating fully with Austria's demands. Crucially, given the development of the interwar debate, Albertini attempted to provide a more dispassionate account by separating the question of the origins of the conflict from that of the rights and wrongs of the war. His volumes thus present less of a judgement and, perhaps because they were written from a greater distance, they were not motivated by the same moral outrage that influenced so many commentators writing in the immediate postwar period.[15]

Although Albertini's seminal work was based on much new primary evidence and was available in English from 1952 onwards, the impact of his work in Germany was initially very limited, especially given the lack of a German translation (to this day). However, Albertini's thorough study has led the way for most subsequent investigations; indeed, as Samuel Williamson points out, 'many later historians, seeking novelty, often find that Albertini has in fact already made their point or certainly suggested or implied it'.[16]

In Britain, the anti-revisionist position was most effectively supported by A.J.P. Taylor, who saw German policy in 1914 as part of a consistent German tradition from Bismarck to Hitler and who argued, like Albertini, that Hitler had not been an aberration in German history. Moreover, he maintained that German policy since 1871 had upset the fragile European balance of power. Germany's refusal to accept its position in Europe led almost automatically to increasing international tensions, culminating in the outbreak of war. Taylor summarized and advanced his anti-revisionist views in several publications.[17] In *War by Time-Table,* he interpreted the escalation of the July Crisis ultimately as a result of the military preparations of the major powers, and in particular of the Schlieffen Plan, Germany's infamous deployment plan. 'When cut down to essentials, the sole cause for the outbreak of war in 1914 was the Schlieffen plan – product of the belief in speed and the offensive', he claimed.[18] This was certainly too simplistic an interpretation of such a multi-faceted problem, as John Langdon criticizes: 'He simplifies a very complex situation to the point of monocausation, in some ways doing to the anti-revisionist position what Harry Barnes did to the revisionist. Taylor was the most prominent writer on the July crisis during the 1950s, but the serious student should look elsewhere for a balanced, detailed overview.'[19]

In Germany, Ludwig Dehio was the only scholar who broke out of the 1950s orthodoxy, for example by pointing to the similarities between Prussian militarism and Hitler, but his writings were largely dismissed by his colleagues and failed to have an effect on the established view. When his arguments became too critical, he was even censored by the publishers of the journal *Historische Zeitschrift,* whose editor he had been since 1945. Dehio's theses (accepting German war guilt and explaining German decisions in 1914 in terms of foreign policy concerns) provided an important stimulus for a new approach to the history of the First World War, and encouraged the Hamburg historian Fritz Fischer to re-examine German policy during the First World War.[20]

Despite these few discordant voices outside Germany, and even fewer within, the consensus that absolved Germany from her former war guilt accusation still held sway – 'the scholarly stagnation was perfect', in Imanuel Geiss's words.[21] The impact of Albertini, Taylor and Dehio, while not negligible, had been far from dramatic. However, this was to change with the arrival on the scene of a radically different interpretation of the origins of the First World War: the theses of the historian Fritz Fischer.

Fritz Fischer's new challenges to an old consensus

Under the disguise of a historical controversy, discussion about the book became also, by implication, a political debate about Germany's immediate past and about the foundation of two German states in 1949.

R.J.W. Evans and H. Pogge von Strandmann[22]

The debate on the origins of the war quickly changed when the most controversial contribution yet was made by the German historian Fritz Fischer. For the West German historical establishment, his extremely anti-revisionist claims were unacceptable, particularly when expressed by an insider like Fischer. His new and challenging interpretations exploded into the comfortable postwar orthodoxy regarding the origins of the First World War. The 'safe ground' that Hubatsch had described not only began to move, but to open up.[23] The debate began in Germany's most prestigious historical journal, the *Historische Zeitschrift,* in 1959, when Fischer published an article outlining his preliminary findings on the origins and nature of the war, on which his first major book on the subject, *Griff nach der Weltmacht,* would be based.[24] Fischer argued in his controversial publications that Germany's decision-makers in 1914 had deliberately risked a European war, in full realization that an Austro-Serbian conflict might escalate and that a localized war was unlikely to remain contained. German policy should not be interpreted as mere reaction to the threats and actions emanating from countries around it. Rather, he claimed that the German leadership had pursued an aggressive foreign policy in the years before 1914, and they had regarded the July Crisis as a golden opportunity to achieve some of their expansionist aims. Moreover, even more controversially, he maintained that Germany's leaders went to war in order to achieve annexationist war aims, that he had found evidence of the nature of these war aims (the so-called September-Programme), and that these aims had been similar to those pursued by Hitler in the Second World War. Worse still, he argued that the German war aims programme was supported by all political parties, including the majority SPD, by moderate industrialists, like Rathenau, by virtually all German academics, and across the board in all the German states. Thus, rather than blaming a small number of decision-makers, such an argument attributed responsibility for the outbreak of the war to a much wider range of Germans. According to Fischer's views, the policy that led to the outbreak of war was not one of blunders, but of design.

The impact of Fischer's thesis, and the vitriolic reaction to it, are perhaps difficult to comprehend today, but their importance cannot be stressed too strongly. The Australian historian John A. Moses summed up its significance in 1975:

> Once in a decade or generation the world of historians may be startled by the publication of some truly striking piece of research which not only shatters accepted images by revealing new material but also raises new questions about the total validity of earlier methodologies. Such a piece of research is Professor Fritz Fischer's *Griff nach der Weltmacht*.[25]

Moses's use of vocabulary is particularly apt regarding the Fischer controversy. Fischer's opponents were indeed 'startled' by the publication of his work, and by its implications for German history. He had undertaken detailed research in West and East German archives and based his arguments to a large extent on primary sources, making his work indeed a 'striking piece of research'. He 'shatter[ed] accepted images' with the help of this new evidence, and by asking new questions about the work that had preceded his own. To the German historical establishment, but also to Germany's conservative government, this was a provocation that they could not ignore. Many younger Germans, however, welcomed Fischer's courage in addressing such a taboo subject and attempting to destroy some of the old legends surrounding German history. In 1969 Karl-Heinz Janssen characterized the initial debate as a precursor to the students' revolts of 1968, arguing somewhat sarcastically that Fischer's attacks on the bourgeois-conservative classes and on industry and finance capital had 'tasted of revolution', and had therefore been attractive to some younger Germans.[26] Looking back on the controversy after forty years, Gerd Krumeich explains the appeal of Fischer's views to students like himself in the 1960s:

> No one in the anonymous mass of students [listening to Fischer's lectures], be it in Hamburg or elsewhere, had ever really thought about German war-aims in the First World War or the July Crisis of 1914. But all understood that someone there had the courage to turn against the establishment and to ask the 'continuity'-question in a way that the students wanted to pose it. We followed Fischer particularly because he provoked the staid older men to a fury, who continually pontificated in seminars on the 'demonic nature of power', on German spirit and German fate, on Bismarck's historic grandeur and such like. In reality the argument about the outbreak of war in 1914 served merely as a substitute war (*Stellvertreterkrieg*), because actually we had a completely different question, which only few dared to pose, of course. This was the question of Auschwitz, and how it could have happened![27]

Clearly, more was at stake than 'merely' the origins of the First World War, and this is important to remember in trying to understand the hostility which Fischer faced following the publications of his theses. Fischer's views addressed at once both world wars and Germany's role in them, and any investigation into the country's recent past was bound to touch raw nerves. Questions about the outbreak of war in 1914 were always thinly disguised questions into the origins of war in 1939, and the horrors that followed it, as Krumeich's recollections show.

Although Fischer's 1961 publication began by examining the July Crisis in detail, the bulk of the text was not concerned with German policy before the war, but with wartime decision-making. However, it was the prewar analysis in particular that provoked the most criticism. A close look at the available evidence led Fischer to conclude that the German government had to accept the 'decisive part of the historical responsibility' for the general war that resulted from the July Crisis (much in line with Albertini's earlier findings). Germany had wanted the Austro-Serbian war, and had made the conflict possible by giving Austria-Hungary the so-called 'blank cheque' on 5 July and by encouraging it to proceed forcefully against Serbia. Hoping for British neutrality, Germany had consciously taken and accepted the risk that a localized war between Austria-Hungary and Serbia might escalate into a European war in which Germany, France, Russia and possibly Britain would become embroiled.[28] The following excerpt gives a flavour of the argument that Fischer advanced:

> Given the tenseness of the world situation in 1914 – a condition for which Germany's world policy, which had already led to three dangerous crises (those of 1905, 1908 and 1911), was in no small measure responsible – any limited or local war in Europe directly involving one great power must inevitably carry with it the imminent danger of a general war. As Germany willed and coveted the Austro-Serbian war and, in her confidence in her military superiority, deliberately faced the risk of a conflict with Russia and France, her leaders must bear a substantial share of the historical responsibility for the outbreak of the general war in 1914.[29]

For the German historical fraternity and those educated

readers who had 'grown up' with the revisionist stance of Wegerer and others, Fischer's arguments were difficult to accept, and they constituted a radical departure (by a German scholar, at least) from the accepted and more comfortable opinion that all European states were equally to blame for the outbreak of war.[30] Although Fischer had clearly intended to stir up the historical consensus, he could not have predicted that his book would provoke such a passionate and long-lasting debate. Rather, he thought that, in contrast with the interwar years, when political constraints influenced the way historians examined the origins of the war, some distance had been created which would make a more matter-of-fact discussion possible. 'Today, in the perspective created by the Second World War and in the completely different political conditions prevailing in Europe, [the topic] has become history, and can be made the object of dispassionate consideration', he argued in *Griff nach der Weltmacht*.[31] Fischer's opponents, however, did not consider the topic history, nor did they agree with his radical revision of the accepted orthodoxy. They set about defending the established view, and their arguments with Fischer and his followers resulted in one of the most important historical controversies of the twentieth century.

Fritz Fischer and his critics

The key professional positions were still held by many men who had been trained in Imperial Germany and begun their careers in the Weimar period – Gerhard Ritter, Hans Herzfeld, Hans Rothfels. [. . .] Totally lacking were those critical peers [. . .] who had left Germany after January 1933 never to return. Georg Iggers[32]

Fischer's publication *Griff nach der Weltmacht* in 1961 (literally 'Grasping for World Power', the English edition being entitled less provocatively *Germany's Aims in the First World War*) marked the beginning of the so-called Fischer controversy. It also marked the end of the self-censorship that eminent

German historians had so far practised primarily for patriotic reasons. The collective war guilt interpretation of the interwar years was finally being questioned openly and, as a result, the apologists found themselves on the defensive.

In their case for the established orthodoxy, Fischer's critics concentrated particularly on three main points of his argument: the connections that he demonstrated between Germany's policy in the age of *Weltpolitik* and the war aims of Imperial Germany during the war; his new interpretation of the July Crisis and the increased amount of responsibility that Fischer attributed to German policy in the events that led to the outbreak of war; and in particular to Chancellor Bethmann Hollweg's role in prewar decision-making.

Central to Fischer's *Griff nach der Weltmacht* was a document he discovered in the files of the Reich-Chancellery in Potsdam which seemed to reveal that Germany's war aims during the war matched the intention of the prewar years to achieve a position of hegemony for Germany, first in Europe and ultimately world-wide. What is more, some of these war aims reminded his readers of those pursued by Hitler during the Second World War. The document, dated 9 September 1914 and subsequently dubbed 'September-Programme', was a memorandum written by Chancellor Bethmann Hollweg's private secretary Kurt Riezler, detailing the Chancellor's views about the aims of Germany's policy for the time when peace agreements were to be made. Five weeks into the war, Germany's Schlieffen Plan seemed to be delivering its promise of a quick victory, and the Chancellor expected peace negotiations in the near future. The 'September-Programme' was one of the key documents to come to light as a result of Fischer's work. The German Chancellor's future vision of Europe following a Germany victory included plans of annexations of territory belonging to Germany's European neighbours, a customs union that would guarantee German economic hegemony and a German colonial empire in Africa. The memorandum set out how to establish and guarantee

> security for the German Reich in west and east for all imaginable time. For this purpose France must be so weakened as to make her revival as a great power impossible for all time. Russia must be thrust back as far as possible from Germany's eastern frontier and her domination over the non-Russian vassal peoples broken.

In Fischer's words, 'the realisation of this programme would have brought about a complete revolution in the political and economic power-relationship in Europe'.[33] To Fischer, the 'September-Programme' was a 'blueprint' for world power. 'It was an expression of German striving for European hegemony, the first step toward "world domination" ', as he summed up in a later publication.[34]

To Fischer's opponents, this claim was unconvincing. They argued that a memorandum written in early September 1914, a time when Germany was fighting a successful campaign on all fronts, could not serve as evidence for *prewar* aims. Until that date, German troops had been fighting the war on two fronts with great success, and it is likely that the political decision-makers considered an early victory against at least one of Germany's enemies to be imminent. Egmont Zechlin emphasized that the memorandum was a 'preliminary programme' which was replaced in October. It was not about territorial war aims, Zechlin contended, but was rather an interim suggestion of how to organize Germany's economic influence abroad so as to defeat Britain.[35] According to Fischer, however, the extensive territorial demands detailed in the memorandum were not just motivated by Germany's recent military successes, nor were they merely wishful thinking on the part of Germany's political rulers. Rather, in his opinion, these demands were a continuation of the policy pursued before the outbreak of war by leading industrialists, military and political decision-makers and, crucially, these policies had been supported outside of that narrow group of the country's leaders by all political parties and many interest groups. Worse still, proponents of the discontinuity thesis struggled to explain away the similarities of German war aims in both world wars.

To a large extent the hostile reception and the widespread debate that followed the publication of *Griff nach der Weltmacht* among historians and in the press, on radio and television, was due to the continuity that Fischer's research seemed to indicate between the old German Reich and Hitler's 'Third Reich'. By implying such a continuity from Bismarck to Hitler, Fischer's work threatened to overthrow the current orthodoxy of the 'Third Reich' having been an anomaly, a brief and somewhat inexplicable aberration in Germany's history, thus burdening Germany with even more guilt, and with an even more uncomfortable history. Given Germany's already damaged reputation, it seemed highly desirable to refute such further charges. The official reaction to Fischer's publications reflected this attitude. The president of the West German Bundestag, Eugen Gerstenmaier, for example, claimed in a Bundestag speech in 1964 that it went 'too far' to attribute to the Germans the same amount of guilt and responsibility for the First as for the Second World War, and he publicly denounced Fischer's thesis.[36] Government bodies and the conservative governing parties at the time, the CDU/CSU (*Christlich-Demokratische Union* and its Bavarian sister party *Christlich-Soziale Union*), were outspoken opponents of Fischer. Conservative politicians pointed out that Fischer's views would damage Germany's reputation abroad and would burden German foreign policy in times which were already precarious enough. It had taken the Federal Republic ten years after the war had ended to manage to regain a quasi-sovereign status by having been allowed to join NATO in 1955, and the country was still in a relatively vulnerable position (both internally and externally) in the early 1960s. Fischer's theses were not considered helpful as regards the desire of West Germany's government to achieve more wide-ranging integration in the West. One critic, Michael Freund, summed up the implications of Fischer's arguments for German history as a whole, alleging that if both the war of 1914 and that of 1939 had come about through the 'planned unleashing of a world war' by a

German dictator, 'then Hitler had always governed us and would always govern us'.[37] While such a statement might almost seem hysterical today, it is worth remembering that German historians were writing in a very specific situation after the Second World War and, given the explosive nature of the topic, Fischer's theses were bound to provoke a heated debate. It is easier to understand the defensiveness of the West German government and historians in the light of the crudeness of such 'from Bismarck to Hitler' arguments which were sometimes advanced among Germany's former enemies, according to which a particular type of German national character was responsible for the atrocities of the Second World War. This, of course, was not something that Fischer had ever maintained.

Franz Josef Strauss of the Bavarian CSU demanded in 1965 that the government should employ all available means to combat such a 'distortion of German history and of the image of Germany today'. Accounts such as Fischer's were regarded as counterproductive to the development of the Western community by conjuring up 'images of a militaristic, warmongering and revenge-seeking Germany'.[38] To some critics, the main danger resulting from Fischer's arguments was that the low national self-esteem of Germans would be further damaged by his allegations, as though it was not bad enough, in Gerstenmaier's words, 'that we have to answer for Hitler's atrocities'.[39] Given the high-profile Eichmann trials in Jerusalem and those of Auschwitz SS guards in Düsseldorf, as well as the increasingly radical student protests which threatened the conservative government by demanding political change and a proper reckoning with Germany's recent past, there seemed indeed enough occasion to answer for atrocities committed in German history. Unsurprisingly, the government was not keen to have further wrongs added to the already disastrous list. Even the oppositional SPD (*Sozialdemokratische Partei Deutschlands* – German Social Democratic Party) kept fairly quiet in the early years of the debate, perhaps in an attempt not to alienate the conservative sections of society and to appear to conform with the system in the CDU-governed Federal Republic.[40]

Fischer's critics were quick to counter his 'heretical' claims, concentrating initially on the question of German war guilt, and the character and role of Chancellor Theobald von Bethmann Hollweg. They were convinced of Bethmann's innocence, and at most were willing to concede that he had been influenced and manipulated by the military, and that his decisions had at times amounted to blunders. They were unable to accept Fischer's view of Bethmann Hollweg pursuing aggressive foreign policy aims. To Fischer's critics, Bethmann had played a positive role in and before 1914, and his attacks on this 'good German' caused indignation. To portray Bethmann as a politician who pursued expansionist policies meant turning him into a scapegoat. Golo Mann's reaction was particularly indignant:

> I do not think that we know him much better or differently following Fischer's publication. He [Bethmann Hollweg] was conciliatory and weak, [. . .] he wanted to stay at the top and please everyone [. . .], and of course Bethmann thought in a strictly monarchical and traditional Prussian way. [. . .] But the man was no 'conquering beast'.

Mann went as far as to say that, whatever Bethmann's shortcomings, his supposed desire for *Weltpolitik* was incredible: 'we would refuse to believe it, even if a letter emerged in which Bethmann Hollweg had demanded the Germanization of the planet.'[41] Mann accused Fischer of using the mass of documents that he had assembled to force

> the construction of a continuity between 1900, 1914, 1918, 1925, 1939. Bülow and Bethmann, Stresemann the Foreign Minister, Adolf Hitler: they all had essentially made the same politics and the First World War had been started like the Second, that is to say by a power that wanted war in order to found a world-Empire.

Mann's main concern was the implication this thesis had for

the new German Republic, and for the country's quest to be accepted as a civilized nation in the Western world. If both Hitler's and Stresemann's foreign policy had essentially been bent on 'conquering and ruling on the continent', would not by implication the same still be true for Germany? 'English enemies of the Federal Republic are inclined to believe it. [. . .] Bethmann Hollweg, Stresemann and Hitler: one step further in this game of continuities, and Adenauer would be the fourth in this group.'[42] Mann's criticisms demonstrate clearly the fear aroused in Germany in the wake of Fischer's publications – what would the Western world think of Germany, and what were the implications of Fischer's work for German standing abroad, as well as for Germany's self-esteem? Ironically, what Fischer's critics failed to see was that, arguably, the suppression of the truth about Germany's role prior to 1914 and the unwillingness of successive Weimar governments to come to terms with Germany's past had made the coming to power of National Socialism possible in the first place.

An additional grave concern was the fear that Fischer's theses would lend legitimacy to the East German interpretation of history. Although the building of the Berlin wall in 1961 meant that 'from now on the GDR could no longer be ignored',[43] until the late 1960s the West German government refused to recognize the existence of the GDR (under the so-called Hallstein doctrine of 1955, which was only modified under Willy Brandt in 1968). Fischer's views were considered threatening because they were seen to lend credence to the East German view that a division of Germany was justified.

Gerhard Ritter, one of Germany's eminent historians, was Fischer's most critical and outspoken opponent, but he was joined by the majority of the German historical profession at the time. Ritter reacted swiftly to Fischer's perceived provocation. In his 1962 review of Fischer's book, he condemned *Griff nach der Weltmacht* as a first climax in the current trend of darkening the German historical consciousness (*Selbstverdunkelung*), a development that he considered to have originated in the defeat of 1945 and one which had replaced the earlier opposite extreme of self-idolization (*Selbstvergötterung*). To Ritter, the book amounted to a 'renewal of the guilt accusation of Versailles' and it reminded him of the 'anti-German war propaganda of 1914'.[44] Ritter's own indignant response to Fischer is reminiscent of the outrage with which Germans greeted the Treaty of Versailles and attempted to fight it. Ritter summed up his reaction to the publication of *Griff nach der Weltmacht*: 'I could not put the book down without feeling deep melancholy: melancholy, and anxiety with regard to the coming generation.'[45] He seems to have envisaged a future in which young Germans would have to carry the burden of responsibility for the outbreak of both world wars, in which they would be regarded as justifiably punished with defeat and partition, and in which the possibility of a reunification no longer existed. Ritter's concern was also with Fischer's portrayal of Bethmann Hollweg who, in Ritter's words, emerged as a 'cunning power-politician (*Machtpolitiker*) who played with unscrupulous carelessness with Germany's fate'.[46] In a government-sponsored publication, a pamphlet in a series edited by the *Bundeszentrale für politische Bildung* written specifically for teachers and pupils, Ritter explained the particular importance of the question of the origins of the First World War for Germans. The war was, in his words, 'one of the most important historical conditions of our current life', and the question of responsibility was

> particularly stirring for us Germans, because if it was caused solely or primarily by the excessive political ambition of our nation and our government, as our war-opponents claimed in 1914, and has recently been affirmed by some German historians, then our national historical consciousness darkens even further than has already been the case through the experiences of the Hitler times![47]

Given Germany's precarious position in the 1960s, Ritter warned that such a development 'could become dangerous' and, echoing the interwar notion that historians had to write history in order to further their nation's historical consciousness and awareness, he outlined that a historian's task was to help bolster the political self-image of the nation by way of the representation of history that he creates.[48]

Fischer's critics identified a number of areas in his work which they considered dubious. They questioned his methodology, for example by accusing him and those historians who supported his findings (labelled the 'Fischer or Hamburg school') of adopting a contradictory approach by using diplomatic and political documents to prove their argument that German foreign policy before the war had been influenced by domestic concerns. Fischer was also charged with approaching history with hindsight, particularly in relating Hitler's foreign policy aims to those of Bethmann Hollweg and the Imperial government. Wolfgang Mommsen criticized Fischer for drawing conclusions from verbal statements, rather than from actual political events, and in particular objected to the 'moralistic tone' in Fischer's work.[49] In addition, it was alleged that Fischer focused too narrowly on Germany, and that he interpreted the actions of the other European governments as mere reactions to German moves, while his approach ignored the culpability of other nations. Comparisons with the policy of the other major powers would have made the differences as obvious as the similarities, Golo Mann and other critics argued. Fischer had already anticipated this criticism and attempted to address it in his foreword by arguing that an investigation of the war aims of the other nations would require a separate book to be written.[50] Nonetheless, his critics were right to point out that an investigation of the origins of the war from only the German perspective painted a narrow picture. Subsequent research into the diplomatic, economic and social history of the other major combatant countries would fill this gap.

The emotional nature of the debate was reflected in the personal criticisms advanced against Fischer. In an atmosphere that is almost unfathomable today, he was charged with being a disloyal traitor who was 'soiling his own nest'. He was subjected to professional and personal criticism, and accused of secretly being supported by East Germany. This suspicion arose because Fischer had been the first Western scholar to be allowed access to East German archives, and because some of his critics – wrongly – accused Fischer of being a Marxist, because of his emphasis on domestic policies and investigation of the role of industrialists and big business in the origins of the war, and because he explicitly excluded Karl Liebknecht and Rosa Luxemburg from the otherwise almost all-encompassing list of Germans who had favoured the aggressive war aims which he highlighted. Hostility towards Fischer was such that some of his conservative colleagues even refused to shake his hand in public at the International Historians' Convention in Vienna in 1965.[51] In the previous year at the German Historians' Convention in West Berlin, Ritter and Fischer clashed over Ritter's allegation that Fischer had fabricated and deliberately misinterpreted documentary evidence. Fischer in turn accused Ritter of continuing 'the tradition of apologetic journalism and historiography which began in 1914 or 1918 and which regarded it as a national duty not to clarify and analyse but to justify, or at least "understand" the evolution and the actions of the Prusso-German national state'.[52] In the same year, Foreign Minister Gerhard Schröder withdrew funds which had already been committed by the *Goethe Institut* in an attempt to stop Fischer from embarking on a lecture tour of the United States. The withdrawal of funds had been prompted by the intervention of three prominent historians (Gerhard Ritter and Arnold Bergstässer of Freiburg University, and Hans Rothfels of Tübingen). Government officials tried to get Fischer to postpone, if not cancel, his trip, and suggested as a compromise that two other German historians should accompany him to advance a different point of view and 'correct' Fischer's theses. In response, twelve prominent American historians complained publicly in the weekly newspaper *Die Zeit* against this treatment, and in West Germany criticism against such censorship was not only raised by Fischer's supporters but also, for example, by his critic and colleague Egmont Zechlin, who insisted on the safeguarding of liberty of scholarship.[53]

The Fischer controversy reveals as much about Germany in the 1960s as it does about Imperial Germany. In the light of what we have identified earlier as historians' 'patriotic concerns' when writing history, Germany's established historians of the 1960s were to a large extent motivated by a desire to clear Germany of Fischer's 'charges'. To many of them, born, like Ritter, in the Wilhelmine period, the First World War was part of their own personal history. Moreover, it is important to remember in this context that in the early 1960s the new West German Republic was trying to establish itself as a country that was part of a Western alliance at a time when the Cold War posed a real and tangible threat, particularly to the divided Germany. The new West German state was in a precarious position between East and West, and any inkling of a tradition of aggressiveness might make it appear in an unfavourable light, and might suggest that the current state of partition and occupation should perhaps continue indefinitely, and that West Germany was no suitable alliance partner for the Western powers. Postwar Germany, after the First as well as after the Second World War, was a place in which historians were expected to put 'national interests' first – and those definitely did not include throwing new and uncomfortable light on the origins of the First World War. Hermann Kantorowicz had already commented on this state of affairs in the 1920s, when his findings about the origins of the war, which did not support the current revisionist orthodoxy, were suppressed by the establishment. He noted:

> For in Germany – and indeed all over the Continent – it is by no means considered sufficient that an historical work should tell the truth in accordance with the convictions of the author. In a work dealing with higher policy it is held without saying that the author should enter upon his investigation in the interests of his own nation and against its antagonists, and that his work shall be 'patriotic', and the outcome of 'national feeling'.[54]

Nothing much had changed by the 1960s, and both the German government and many conservative historians were as keen as ever to keep the revisionist orthodoxy alive, for fear of the damage that Fischer's provocative theses might inflict on the new Republic. Holger Herwig explains the concerns at the time:

> The damage [from Fischer's theses] to the Bonn regime's self-image would be devastating: hence, the rebarbative attempts by prominent West German historians such as Gerhard Ritter and Karl Dietrich Erdmann as well as Foreign Minister Gerhard Schröder to prevent the spread of Fritz Fischer's views beyond the Federal Republic.[55]

The CDU-led government (under Konrad Adenauer until 1963, and then under Ludwig Erhard) saw its arguments in favour of a future German reunification undermined by Fischer's allegations (although Adenauer was willing to forgo a reunification in favour of an integration of the FRG in the Western economic and military structures – an aim for which Fischer's theses were, however, equally unhelpful). With hindsight, John Langdon questions the validity of these concerns. 'Given the Cold War and the balance-of-power requirements of NATO and the Warsaw Pact, what chance did German reunification have anyway? Fischer may have betrayed this cherished ideal, but it would never have been achieved in 1961 in any case.'[56] And yet, we should take seriously the concerns of contemporaries who did not have the benefit of hindsight, and who felt that Fischer's publications seriously undermined Germany's standing in the Western world.

The debate that was started by Fischer's publications was of a scale quite unlike any other historical controversy. Ironically, the very public nature of the debate turned the book into something of a best-seller, unusual for a work of over nine hundred pages and advancing complicated and detailed arguments. Within a few years, *Griff nach der Weltmacht* had been published in several editions, and had been translated into English, French, Italian and Japanese. In

1977 Fischer already spoke of more than 300 reviews and articles on the subject.[57] Today, books and articles which address the controversy are beyond reading for a single historian. The debate was initially very public, as both sides used the media (newspapers, radio and television) to argue their corner, particularly in 1964, the year which commemorated the outbreak of both world wars (fifty and twenty-five years ago respectively). Such anniversaries heightened the public interest in the debate, and led to emotive discussions on television and in the print-media.[58] Eugen Gerstenmaier's Bundestag speech condemning Fischer's writing was delivered in 1964 against this background.[59]

Until 1964, the debate was largely shaped by Fischer's critics, and their desire to prove Fischer wrong ensured that this new round of war guilt discussion was similar in intensity to that of the interwar years. The critics were motivated by a conservative and nationalistic approach to history, and the pro- and anti-Fischer lobbies were divided by their political concerns for the new Federal Republic which can be summed up as either supporting or rejecting a new foreign policy direction for Germany at the time.[60] In Michael Freund's view, for example, Fischer's book was 'stuck in the year 1919', and amounted to something 'equally as bad as the innocence-lie of the years after 1918, to a mere reversal of the innocence-lie, that is to say a warmed-up war guilt lie of the Allies in its crassest form'. Freund complained that 'nobody is served if one smears the entire German history with Hitler's dirt'. He was convinced that German policy in 1914 had not been a grasp for world power, but rather 'the grasp of a dying man for life'. In his angry reply to Fischer's work, he left no doubt where the real dangers of this new interpretation lay:

> Fischer wanted to overcome the innocence lie, but the negative of a lie is never the truth. The war guilt accusation of the Allies against Germany, a silly and evil allegation, and the equally evil and silly counter-claim that the war guilt article expressed a devilish desire to destroy, has already once ruined a German republic. Once is enough.[61]

In addition to negative reviews of Fischer's work, Gerhard Ritter mounted further detailed criticism in the third volume of his major four-volume study *Staatskunst und Kriegshandwerk*. The volume was dedicated entirely to an enquiry into Bethmann Hollweg's role in the war years, and was entitled 'The Tragedy of Statesmanship: Bethmann Hollweg as War Chancellor 1914–1917'. Ritter attempted to 'rescue' the Chancellor from Fischer's criticisms, and summed up his approach in countering Fischer's views in the Preface.

> [Fischer's] basic thesis is that Bethmann Hollweg, hitherto always shown as [a] pusillanimous compromiser and appeaser, was actually a practitioner of power politics with ambitious ideas of conquest, and hence a kind of precursor to Adolf Hitler; but this argument has convinced me no more than it has the great majority of professional historians in Germany and elsewhere. This misinterpretation may survive in the popular prints, but it is unlikely to carry much weight in the world of scholarship. For that reason alone it did not seem worth my while to freight this book with protracted polemics [. . .]. At the same time it seemed essential, indeed unavoidable, to show in my Notes, from the original documents, the numerous instances in which Fischer's account is based on arbitrary misinterpretation of his sources. Only in this way can the danger be stemmed of allowing an incorrect historical picture to become fixed. [. . .] Free of the national-liberal tinge that marks the accounts of most of my predecessors, as well as of the radical reversal of that bias that has become discernible since 1945 (as in the case of Fischer), I have tried to analyse the source material with the greatest care and cautiously to feel my way into whatever situation prevailed at the time, to the end of coming as close as possible to historical reality.[62]

The implication, thus, was both that Fischer had not attempted to portray 'historical reality' as closely as possible and, crucially, that such a depiction of 'historical reality' was actually possible to achieve, and that it could be arrived at with a cautious and judicious use of the available primary sources. Such views only helped to increase the emphasis the opponents put on documents, and they explain why it was possible for both sides to interpret documents in different ways to help them prove their particular 'historical reality'. At the time of writing his response to Fischer, Ritter did not expect that much further evidence would emerge that would lead to a rewriting of his own interpretation of events. Anticipating the opening of the archives in London and Paris fifty years after the outbreak of the war, Ritter suspected that 'many details in the picture I project may have to be corrected or supplemented. I must say, however, that I do not expect any great surprises'.[63]

Support for Fischer's conclusions

Startling as some of [Fischer's] conclusions must at first appear, it seems unlikely that they can be seriously challenged in view of the weight of the evidence that the author adduces. **Times Literary Supplement, 1962**[64]

While Fischer had received relatively little support from West German historians in the 1960s, his theses were rather better received outside the Federal Republic. In East Germany, Fischer's thesis of a continuity of aggression in German history, which seemed to confirm the Marxist interpretation of the origins of the war as a necessary result of capitalism and imperialism, was welcomed, although ironically, given the accusations raised against Fischer in the West that his approach was 'Marxist', if anything, in the East it was criticized for not being Marxist enough.[65] In a review article, Fritz Klein, one of East Germany's leading historians on the First World War, summarized what he saw as the importance of Fischer's contribution in helping to bring about 'a real German historical consciousness', which he regarded as 'a precondition for the life of the coming generation'. This consciousness would develop and solidify when Germans began to realize that they must free themselves of imperialism. 'Fischer's book is of great value for this process of realization', Klein maintained.[66] In 1968–9 a historians' collective headed by Fritz Klein published a three-volume account entitled *Germany in the First World War,* which argued along Marxist–Leninist lines that the war had been the result of 'monopolistic capitalism'. Germany's leadership and the desire for imperialist expansion were seen as one of the causes of the war, and much of this work was based on the documentary evidence provided by Fischer's research.[67]

The West German debate was of relatively little consequence to East German historians, and Fischer's work caused no comparable sensation in the GDR, as Klein recalls in his memoirs:

> That Germany bore the main responsibility for the outbreak of the world war of 1914, that the demand for extensive war aims was determined primarily by the leading economic circles, and that the expansive war policy of the German Reich was merely a continuation of policies pursued by German policies and German élites long before 1914, which also did not come to an end with the first defeat of 1918: arguments of this kind were to us neither new from a scholarly point of view, nor politically irritating.[68]

Klein's statement contains the key to the different understandings of the importance of Fischer's theses in East and West Germany: in the East, Fischer's views were not politically controversial because Marxist historians had taken German war guilt, as well as that of the other imperialist powers, for granted. According to this point of view, Germany's imperialism had been particularly virulent, and the country bore the largest share of guilt. The East German state did not place itself in a German tradition, and the inglorious German past was portrayed as not belonging to the new East Germany. The divide between the two Germanies had just been made visible and had become more clearly demarcated with the building of the wall to 'protect' East Germans from the 'fascist' West German state. East German historians were keen to stress the continuity in German history from Bismarck to Hitler and post-1945, because it was the idea of a *discontinuity* in German history that could potentially undermine the existence of the separate East German state. If the discontinuity thesis could be proven, and if it could be argued that National Socialism had been an aberration, then demands to reunify Germany could be voiced. For East Germans, the continuity thesis in (West) German history not only served the fight against imperialism, but was also part of the class struggle in which it was thought that the progressive class in Germany had achieved victory in 1949 over the forces of reaction and militarism which had dominated German history, bringing to a head a process that had begun in 1848. The idea of continuity in German aggressive foreign policy served the East German establishment, who favoured a complete break in German history, as represented by the partition of Germany in 1949.[69] In West Germany, by contrast, the topic was of particular political importance, because the Federal Republic did not see itself divorced from Germany's past history, and because conservative elements within the new state did not want to see German history sullied with the charge of a history of aggressive war aims and the unleashing of two world wars.

Fischer's views were also well received by a number of foreign historians, such as the Austrian Rudolf Neck, who considered Fischer's *Griff nach der Weltmacht* 'one of those products of the German spirit which encourage the friends of the Germans again and again not to despair of the German kind (*am deutschen Wesen*) despite everything'. In a positive review of Fischer's book, he merely quibbled that Austria-Hungary's role had been underestimated, arguing that 'one had also played with fire at the Ballhausplatz'.[70] Positive reactions also came from the Swiss historian Adolf Gasser and the American Klaus Epstein, who considered Fischer's work to amount to more than the usual revision of a historical interpretation. Rather, this was 'a break-through which resembled in many ways a revolutionizing of the current views of the politics of Imperial Germany in the First World War'. From this point on, it could no longer be maintained that German policy had been without direction or aimless, Epstein argued.[71] In France, Jacques Droz contended that Fischer had not only written history, but had also made it by rewriting the apologetic history of Germany's past and forcing a revision of the orthodox views.[72] In Britain, Fischer's views generally had a positive reception. There was support for his arguments, for example from James Joll and John C.G. Röhl. A review in the *Times Literary Supplement*, while pointing out the need for 'equally comprehensive studies of the war aims of the other belligerents in the First World War', was full of praise for Fischer's achievement.

> Professor Fischer's book 'Bid for World Power [. . .]' is a brilliant example of history written from the original records to throw light not only on the period immediately covered but on earlier and later periods too. It is by far the most comprehensive study of its subject yet produced and, startling as some of its conclusions must at first appear, it seems unlikely that they can be seriously challenged in view of the weight of the evidence that the author adduces.[73]

Within West Germany, Fischer initially had support from only a small number of historians, some of whom had been his students at Hamburg, such as Imanuel Geiss and Helmut Böhme. Geiss's interest in the origins of both World Wars was motivated by desire to avoid further conflagrations in the future. In the age of nuclear warfare, this reflected an important political concern, and Geiss arrived at the conclusion that peace in Europe could only last if Germany did not pursue any political goals other than that of preserving the status quo. Certainly it should not be part of Germany's foreign policy aims to attempt a reunification of the two Germanies. Geiss was convinced that any further attempt at *Weltpolitik* on Germany's part would lead to a third major war.[74] Aside from a number of publications on the subject, Geiss edited an important collection of documents on July 1914 which was intended to provide a broader audience with primary evidence to back up Fischer's claims and was published in time to mark the 1964 commemoration of the beginning of the war.[75]

Following the discussion of the issue at the 1964 German Historians' Convention, the debate began to change in tone and style, as more German historians came to accept Fischer's arguments, or were at least partially convinced by them. There was an increasing willingness to check and re-evaluate the dominant apologetic interpretations of German history. In between the two hard-line positions of Fischer and his critics, a variety of interpretations began to develop, as German historians were willing to concede that Imperial Germany may have played a more decisive role in the July Crisis than they had previously thought, and that its leaders may have embarked on a preventive war in 1914, intending to break out of its encirclement of hostile powers. Nonetheless, Fischer's claims about aggressive war aims remained difficult to accept for many German historians.[76]

New consensus and new debate: Fischer's *War of Illusions*

Few documents on the history of imperial Germany have caused as much of a stir – but also as much racking of brains – amongst historians as the entry for 8 December 1912 in the diary of [. . .] Admiral Georg Alexander von Müller. **John Röhl**[77]

Fischer followed up his 1961 claims about German war aims with a second major study, in which he focused his attention on Germany's policies during the immediate prewar years. *Krieg der Illusionen (War of Illusions)*,[78] first published in 1969, argued even more forcefully that Germany's leading decision-makers had been willing to seize the opportunity offered by a crisis in the Balkans, such as the one provoked by Franz Ferdinand's assassination, to bring about war. Fischer argued that leading decision-makers in Berlin decided as early as December 1912 that they should embark on a war in the not-too-distant future, and his overview of German history from

1911 to 1914 was aimed at proving that Germany had indeed wanted war in 1914.

While the 'September-Programme' and German war aims had been central to *Griff nach der Weltmacht*, this second major publication on the subject placed another key event at the centre of its investigation. In December 1912 the Kaiser had held a now infamous meeting with some of his military and naval advisers. Against the background of war in the Balkans, and having been advised that Britain would not remain neutral in a future war between Germany and France, Wilhelm II had used this new certainty to argue for unleashing a war. While his advisers had agreed, and the Chief of Staff Helmuth von Moltke had even demanded a war 'the sooner the better', Admiral von Tirpitz had requested a postponement of 'the great fight' for one-and-a-half years because his navy was not yet ready. Evidence for this secret meeting emerged from the diary of the Kaiser's Chief of the Imperial Naval Cabinet, Admiral von Müller. According to Müller's account, the Kaiser 'envisaged the following' at the meeting:

> Austria must deal energetically with the foreign Slavs (the Serbs), otherwise she will lose control of the Slavs in the Austro-Hungarian monarchy. If Russia supports the Serbs, which she evidently does [. . .] then war would be unavoidable for us too. We could hope, however, to have Bulgaria and Rumania and also Albania, and perhaps also Turkey on our side. [. . .] If these powers join Austria then we shall be free to fight the war with full fury against France. The fleet must naturally prepare itself for the war against England. [. . .]
>
> General von Moltke: 'I believe a war is unavoidable and the sooner the better. But we ought to do more through the press to prepare the popularity of a war against Russia [. . .].'
>
> H[is] M[ajesty] supported this and told the State Secretary [Admiral von Tirpitz] to use his press contacts, too, to work in this direction. T[irpitz] made the observation that the navy would prefer to postpone the great fight for one and a half years. Moltke says the navy would not be ready even then and

> the army would get into an increasingly unfavourable position, for the enemies were arming more strongly than we, as we were very short of money. [. . .][79]

On the basis of such evidence, Fischer argued that war had been decided upon in Berlin as early as December 1912, and that the meeting was proof of the warlike spirit among Germany's leading decision-makers. He claimed that the massive army bill of 1913, the preparation of public opinion for war in the press, and efforts to win new allies resulted directly from the meeting. While most German historians refused to believe Fischer's interpretation that the war of 1914 had been decided on 18 months before its outbreak, his views received support from Adolf Gasser in Switzerland and John Röhl in Britain. In an important and detailed document collection on the war council, published in 1977, Röhl was able to refute some of the criticisms raised against the Fischerite interpretation of the importance of the war council.[80] In response to critics who held that 'there is not the slightest evidence to support the argument that William II's excited order to prepare the country for war by means of an official press campaign was followed up by deeds',[81] Röhl amassed much evidence to the contrary. Although it has ultimately not been possible to prove a direct link between the discussions of 1912 and the decision to go to war in 1914, the meeting can serve as impressive evidence of how decision-making was conducted in Imperial Germany at the highest level: without consulting the civilian government, such as the Chancellor and Foreign Secretary, the Kaiser and his military and naval advisers made decisions behind the scenes. Moreover, as John Röhl observes,

> the 'war council' itself must be regarded as one of the most obvious signs that the Army had regained its traditional position of pre-eminence in Prussia-Germany after the collapse of Tirpitz's originally grandiose naval plans and the fiasco of the Agadir Crisis of 1911.[82]

The controversy around the war council highlighted in

particular the difficulties that can result from using documents to prove a particular point of view. Fischer's critics claimed that he had overestimated the importance of the meeting, given that Müller's diary recorded: 'This was the end of the conference. The result amounted to almost 0.' In other words the meeting had hardly been the important event that Fischer claimed it had been. However, John Röhl was able to demonstrate with the help of the original diary that the published version contained an incomplete citation. The complete original diary entry read: 'This was the end of the conference. The result amounted to almost 0. The Chief of the General Staff says: War the sooner the better, but he does not draw the logical conclusion from this, which is to present Russia or France or both with an ultimatum which would unleash the war with right on our side. In the afternoon I wrote to the Reich Chancellor about the influencing of the press.' Müller's summary of the meeting's results as 'zero' was due to his disappointment that the bellicose mood of the participants had not led to more decisive action. Only a look at the original diary had made it possible to refute the allegations of Fischer's critics and demonstrated that to Müller the meeting had been evidence of a desire for war, and that he, at least, regretted that nothing further had come of it immediately. Röhl's detailed investigation also revealed that the Chancellor, Bethmann Hollweg, had been informed of the meeting the same day, contrary to claims that he had been left in the dark about the event, an argument used by critics to deny that any real importance attached to the meeting in December 1912.[83]

In *War of Illusions*, Fischer argued that Germany bore the main share of responsibility for the outbreak of the war, due to her expansionist foreign policy aims. According to Fischer, Germany had embarked on a 'preventive war'. This did not mean, however, that Germany's decision-makers had attempted to prevent an attack by their neighbours, but rather that they had wanted to prevent a situation from developing in which Germany would no longer be strong enough to challenge her neighbours – a fine, but important distinction.

Fischer disagreed with the view that war in 1914 had been a preventive war in the sense of preventing an imminent attack by Russia with offensive action, as was commonly held among historians in the Federal Republic at the time. In Fischer's words, the preventive war of 1914 'was an attempt to defeat the enemy powers before they became too strong, and to realise Germany's political ambitions, which may be summed up as German hegemony over Europe'.[84]

In addition, Fischer maintained that an aggressive foreign policy had been employed by Imperial Germany's ruling élite in order to placate public opinion and divert attention from domestic problems, an argument that had first been advanced by Eckhart Kehr in the early 1930s. The emphasis on the 'primacy of domestic policy' (*Primat der Innenpolitik*), rather than foreign policy motivations, opened up further aspects of the controversy, in which historians have debated to what extent domestic politics determined foreign policy decisions in Wilhelmine Germany. It also made the study of the social history of Wilhelmine Germany a popular subject among historians in the 1970s. Volker Berghahn was one of the main proponents of the view that German policy had been motivated by a desire to divert and to some extent avoid domestic problems. In his opinion, 'the country's ruling élites were increasingly haunted by the nightmare of impending internal chaos and external defeat so that an offensive war appeared to be the only way out of the general deadlock'.[85] In the late 1960s and early 1970s, the study of the underlying structures of Wilhelmine Germany, rather than a concentration on the role of individual decision-makers, became the focus of a group of historians at the University of Bielefeld (most prominently Hans-Ulrich Wehler and Jürgen Kocka). They, too, emphasized the primacy of domestic policy, rather than focusing primarily on foreign policy in attempting to understand the history of Wilhelmine Germany and the origins of the First World War. The Bielefeld school's views echoed those of Eckhart Kehr and Hans Rosenberg, and were epitomized in Wehler's *Das deutsche Kaiserreich* in 1973. According to

Wehler, the problems of the German Empire stemmed from the discrepancy between a modern economy and an unmodern or outmoded political system which had not introduced democratization and parliamentarization. The ruling authoritarian Prussian élite attempted to preserve the status quo and to manipulate the German people, while feeling increasingly threatened by internal and external foes. Where Fischer had identified a conscious and deliberate grasp at world power, based on over-confidence on the part of Germany's rulers, Wehler considered the First World War to have been a desperate 'flight forward' which had become almost unavoidable.[86]

By the 1970s, the controversy about the origins of the war had lost some of its momentum. Historians continued to argue over different ways to interpret the history of Imperial Germany, but no longer felt quite so strongly about the 'charge' that Germany had caused the war. Now they debated whether the war had been willed to achieve foreign policy aims, or in order to divert or placate domestic tensions, rather than refusing to accept that Germany had played a key part in the events that had led to the outbreak of war. The debate became increasingly confined to the writings and discussions of academics, so that by 1973 Arnold Sywotteck concluded from the lack of a public controversy that the 'historiographical investigations about the national history [of Germany] hardly touch upon the historical-political consciousness of the Federal Republic'.[87] In contrast with the years of the Weimar Republic, when the topic had been of almost continuous significance, the subject of war guilt was no longer discussed widely or used in the political discourse of the Federal Republic after the initial outrage following Fischer's first publications. Unlike the Weimar governments, the governments of the Bonn Republic had no need to conjure up the image of an unfairly blamed Germany. If anything, it was in their interests not to raise the contentious topic. Historians, however, continued to debate the finer points and nuances of the differing arguments.

The search for new evidence

Riezler's diary was thus turned into a weapon against Fischer. **Bernd-Felix Schulte**[88]

Fischer's wide use of primary sources in both of his contentious books led to a renewed interest in documentary evidence about the origins of the First World War. As Francis L. Carsten pointed out in a review of *Griff nach der Weltmacht* in 1963, 'historians who might feel inclined to contradict [Fischer's] conclusions will find this difficult without repeating his researches carried on during many years'.[89] Fischer's emphasis on document-based arguments resulted in a quest from both sides to find further primary evidence and make it available to others in scholarly editions. Following Fischer's publication of *Griff nach der Weltmacht*, a large number of edited document collections have made primary source material available to historians. Among them are Imanuel Geiss's two-volume document collection *Julikrise und Kriegsausbruch 1914* (of which abridged German and English editions were published in 1965 and 1967 respectively), John Röhl's publication of memoranda by Prince Karl Max von Lichnowsky and Prince Philipp zu Eulenburg, the diaries of Kurt Riezler, edited by Karl Dietrich Erdmann, and the diaries of the journalist Theodor Wolff by Bernd Sösemann, to name only a few.[90] As a result of the attempts on both sides to support their theses with documentary evidence and to present their arguments as based on primary source material, students and scholars were able to benefit from the resulting flood of publications, and the available evidence is constantly being added to with new publications. However, because of the importance historians involved in the debate began to attach to documents as a means of 'proving' their point of view and 'disproving' the opponents arguments even ensued over the authenticity of certain evidence, and the reliability of published editions of documents (as we have seen above, for example, regarding Görlitz's edition of the Müller diaries).

Other problems of document interpretation resulted from

the fact that the particular emphasis given to Bethmann Hollweg's role in July 1914 had turned the debate to a large extent into one that was based on personalities. James Joll points out the problems that can arise from such a focus:

> Once this is so, then the interpretation of documents necessarily depends on the interpretation of character; for the way in which one reads the documents is determined by one's general view of the nature and motives of the writer of the documents, and divergent views of a man's character will result in differing interpretations of what he writes.[91]

Indeed, it has been a characteristic of the debate that historians were unable to agree on the interpretation of certain key documents, such as Müller's diary entry detailing the events of the war council. Similarly, Bethmann Hollweg's attitude in the weeks before the outbreak of war, as it was revealed in the diary of his personal assistant Kurt Riezler, could be interpreted either as evidence of the Chancellor's pessimism and fear in 1914, or of his policy of 'bluff' during the July Crisis.

Given the importance attached to the role of Bethmann Hollweg who, as we have seen, has been portrayed as essentially peace-loving but misguided by the anti-Fischer 'camp', and as warmongering and in pursuit of aggressive foreign policy aims by Fischer and his supporters, it is not surprising that the diaries of Bethmann Hollweg's close political adviser and secretary, Kurt Riezler, were a documentary source eagerly awaited by both sides. More criticism and debate about documents followed the publication of Riezler's diaries – in fact, one could speak of a 'Riezler-diary controversy' which ensued in the early 1980s, some years after the diaries were first published by Karl Dietrich Erdmann in 1972. Bethmann Hollweg's own personal papers were destroyed at some time during or after the Second World War, a fact which gave particular significance to the diaries of his close adviser Riezler. Even before Erdmann's edition of the diaries was published, they had already been surrounded by controversy. On the basis of what he had already seen of the diaries prior to their publication, Erdmann, one of Fischer's critics, alleged that Fischer's thesis regarding German policy in July 1914, and particularly regarding Bethmann Hollweg's role, could be proven wrong with the help of Riezler's writings. Erdmann's own views of the origins of the war echoed Lloyd George's sentiment that no government actually wanted war, but that none had wanted to prevent it either. As ever, this was a comfortable half-way house as far as many Germans were concerned.

That any of Riezler's diary entries for the crucial prewar years could be published at all must be regarded as a stroke of luck, given that Kurt Riezler had instructed his brother Walter to destroy them after his death in 1955. The latter, realizing the potential importance of the documents, and following the advice of Riezler's long-term friend Theodor Heuss after consultation with historians, decided against destroying the diaries. Nonetheless, it took several more years before Walter Riezler handed the volumes to Erdmann, acting as editor on behalf of the Historical Commission of the Bavarian Academy of Science, and even longer before Riezler's daughter gave her consent for a publication.[92] However, in the intervening years Erdmann, who had had the benefit of reading the documents prior to their publication, claimed that the diaries made it 'impossible to remove Germany from the active role that she had played in the July Crisis of 1914'. While they confirmed some of Fischer's claims regarding Bethmann Hollweg's conscious risking of war in July 1914, importantly they did not support his later claims that the German government had aimed for war at least since December 1912 and that the Wilhelmstrasse had unleashed a war to realize European hegemonial plans.[93] Both sides therefore awaited the publication of the diaries with great anticipation. Fischer and Ritter had only been allowed to see excerpts before the publication, but when the entire text was finally available for scrutiny, it seemed to confirm Erdmann's view of Bethmann Hollweg. Erdmann placed great importance on Riezler's evidence, and came to the following conclusion about German policy in 1914:

> The conception of Bethmann Hollweg's policy in the July crisis, such as it emerges from the Riezler diaries, fits neither into the pattern of a Germany pushed into a war against her will, nor of a Germany wilfully pushing into war. Egmont Zechlin found a very adequate term for this attitude. He called it '*präventive Abwehr*' (preventive defence). This seems to me to be more to the point than 'preventive war', although Bethmann Hollweg himself, some time later, called the First World War 'in a certain sense' a preventive war. Fischer shares the opinion that preventive war is not the right term, because on the side of the Entente there was objectively no intention of attacking Germany. In my view, the term *präventive Abwehr* fits better than preventive war, because Germany, though taking the risk of war, had hope of disrupting the Entente without a war.[94]

Clearly, Riezler's diary was a crucial piece of evidence in the ongoing debate, particularly as it was used by the anti-Fischer side, who claimed that the publication refuted 'conclusively Fritz Fischer's theses about Germany's part in the beginning of war in 1914 and her alleged "grasp for world power" ', as an entry in a standard biographical dictionary of German History claimed.[95] However, doubts were soon raised about the authenticity of the documents that Erdmann had made available in his edition. In a review of the edition, the Austrian historian Fritz Fellner considered the publication of the diaries 'a disappointment of all concrete expectations'. Fellner's detailed review raised early doubts about the authenticity of the diary entries for July 1914, and he concluded: 'The Riezler diaries do not reveal anything and do not prove anything.'[96]

However, a real controversy did not begin until the early 1980s, when the principal attack against Erdmann's edition was launched by the historian Bernd Sösemann (Sösemann was at this time preparing his own document edition of the journalist Theodor Wolff's diaries), who criticized Erdmann's edition primarily on technical grounds, because Erdmann had not mentioned that the diaries he edited contained substantial gaps, and that, according to Sösemann, some 30 volumes of the original material, covering the crucial years 1907–14, were missing, while some pages were cut out of volumes which survived, such as those for August 1914. This, crucially, made Germany's policy in July 1914 appear less belligerent than the 'Fischer school' had claimed. Erdmann also had not alerted his readers to the fact that for the most important times, July and August 1914, the diary was not kept in its usual format in small exercise books, but was available only on loose pages, which differed in style from the rest of the diaries, and suggest that Riezler perhaps rewrote (and possibly edited) crucial sections of his writings, or that, at worst, they had been tampered with at a later date, perhaps even in the light of the Fischer controversy.[97] Fritz Fischer launched his own critique of Erdmann's edition and referred to the 'state secret of the Riezler diaries'. His investigation showed that Riezler had read extracts from his diaries to an American diplomat during the Second World War, and that those extracts had contained clear evidence that Bethmann Hollweg had desired a war in 1914. And yet, evidence to that effect did not emerge from Erdmann's edition of the diaries.[98] The suspicion was raised that some more incriminating material had been removed, either by Riezler himself, or by someone else after his death. As far as critics of Erdmann's edition are concerned, while he has provided an invaluable service in editing the documents and providing a thorough introduction on Kurt Riezler himself, he failed to indicate potential problems with the source, and the reliability of the diary has to be seriously questioned.

At the same time as the Riezler diaries caused controversy, Bernd Sösemann's own scholarly edition of Theodor Wolff's diaries was published. It contains the testimony of several key witnesses who, in private conversation with Wolff, had spoken of Germany's role in the events that led to war, including Bethmann Hollweg and the Foreign Secretary Gottlieb von Jagow. The evidence published by Sösemann suggested that among Germany's leading politicians and industrialists, it was believed that the Wilhelmstrasse had caused the war, albeit by accident rather than design.[99] Given that Wolff's diary contains records of conversations with many influential politicians in the years 1914–19, and that its authenticity is not in doubt, it is a more rewarding source for historians than Riezler's diaries, whose importance had been rather exaggerated prior to their publication.

Indicative of the importance of the debate in Germany is the fact that the controversy over Riezler's diaries soon spread from historical journals to national newspapers, which were willing to devote considerable space to discussions about the authenticity of the text, and to the connected question of the origins of the First World War. The opponents were even able to discuss their views on television.[100] Although the debate was conducted in the main by professional historians and a few journalists, it was of concern to a large number of educated Germans, and had still not lost its political relevance.

The vehemence of the debate about the diaries and the extent of the allegations made against Erdmann (which amounted to conspiracy theories in which historians of the 'Fischer school' accused their opponents of deliberately falsifying or omitting evidence in order to undermine Fischer's views) has been symptomatic of the Fischer controversy and its aftermath. For both sides, much was at stake in their attempts to prove their opponents wrong, not least professional reputations, as accusations of unprofessional scholarship were frequently levelled at the opposite side.

The importance attached to contemporary evidence made the Riezler diary controversy particularly heated. In the end, the diary failed to confirm once and for all the views of one or the other side in the debate, and the controversy surrounding its authenticity only added to the mistrust between the different factions. As neither side could convince the other of its point of view, the debate moved into another round, characterized by some consensus, as well as continuing controversy over certain contentious issues.

The end of the Fischer decade

In 1970 Fischer himself summed up some of the criticisms that had been voiced against him, when he speculated about what prompted this violent reaction among his colleagues:

> I had apparently violated a national taboo. Ever since the collapse of the Third Reich, historians have tended to neglect the First World War, focusing attention instead on Adolf Hitler and the Second World War. [...] German history before and after Hitler seemed to be 'unproblematic'. [...] In July 1914, Germany had been drawn into war; and for the next four years, she fought desperately for her very existence. In September 1939, on the other hand, Hitler deliberately precipitated war, a fact that no one in Germany will dispute; and for the next six years, he continued to pursue his grandiose plans for conquest.
>
> For historians schooled in this tradition, my book was nothing short of treason. I had demonstrated beyond any doubt that Germany had similar aims in both world wars, and since this similarity could not be denied, my critics resorted to a variety of methods to obscure the unpleasant truth.[101]

Ten years after the controversy first began in earnest, Imanuel Geiss, one of Fischer's younger colleagues at Hamburg University and a prominent contributor to the debate, also attempted to explain the reason why Fischer's views caused such upset and outrage among German historians and the public.

> For an explanation of the largely irrational, in any case vehement reaction against Fischer of most older historians in the Federal Republic and a part of the public, one has to understand the central position that the First World War occupied until recently in the German national consciousness. This war was the German heroic time of our century, upon which many of the older generation – those who are today 50–90 years old – look back with a mixture of wistful pride and national grief (particularly over the political and territorial losses through Versailles). Back then the Germans, allegedly victims of a seemingly conspiratorial encirclement, fought against the proverbial 'world of

> enemies' under the banner of Kaiser and Reich, to which still today the secret or even open sympathy of a significant part of the older [. . .] generation extends. Numerous older German historians fought in the First World War as German or Austrian officers [. . .]. An elemental part of the 'war-experience' myth was the consciousness of Germany's relative or total innocence in the outbreak of the First World War.[102]

Despite the fact that nearly fifty years had passed since the beginning of the war, to many Germans, and to Germany's established historians in particular, the war was not 'history', but continued to play a part in their consciousness. It required a new generation of historians, further removed from the events of 1914 –18, to approach the subject more objectively.

In 1971 Joachim Remak began an article on the origins of the war with a confident statement: 'Fritz Fischer's decade has ended. It began, neatly enough, in 1961 with *Der Griff nach der Weltmacht*, and drew to a close, in 1969, with *Krieg der Illusionen*. In between, there has been more discussion, scholarly or otherwise, than has been caused by any other single historian in our lifetime.'[103] Remak could not have foreseen that even more debate would result from the attempts of Fischer's critics and his defenders to assert their positions, such as the controversy of the Riezler diaries, which only began a decade after Remak's article was published, or that his own advocacy of examining the policies of other European powers in 1914 ('Were not there some Frenchmen, too, in 1914, or some Serbians?' he asked) would become part of further floods of publications on the vexed question of the origins of the war.

And yet, it is true that after the initially hostile reaction of many of Fischer's German colleagues, some compromise positions have been advanced since the 1970s. His work had destroyed once and for all the illusion of a German Reich surprised by war and innocent in its outbreak, and when the first indignation of the controversy died down, most historians agreed that Germany played a much more active role in the events that had led to war than many had liked to admit prior to Fischer. In 1972, when the debate had seemingly come to an end, Imanuel Geiss summarized the results of the controversy and the current consensus thus:

> The old innocence thesis from 1914 to 1960 is dead. The retreat to the position of 'we-all-slithered-into-war' is finally blocked. The predominant part of the German Reich in the outbreak of the First World War and the offensive character of German war aims is no longer debated and no longer deniable.[104]

Geiss was optimistic about the positive consequences of the Fischer controversy for the German population as a whole, as he explained in the same publication:

> A German who today believes his historians (albeit still the younger ones) that there was no 'encirclement' before 1914, that the First World War was no defensive German war, but in the main a German war of aggression and conquest, will no longer today misuse Versailles and the reparations or the world economic crisis as a great national excuse for the rise of National Socialism. [...] A German who has come to such a realization will further concede that the Germans also have to pay a price for the Second World War, begun and morally rightly lost by Germany, not only against the West, but also against the East.[105]

In other words, Germans had to accept their defeat in the Second World War and the redrawing of the map of Europe that followed, including in particular the acceptance of the contentious Oder–Neisse border between Germany and Poland in the East as a justified and legitimate postwar border settlement.[106] In the strained relations between West and East Germany, a détente was only just developing following Adenauer's resignation in October 1963, and Willy Brandt's new *Ostpolitik* remained in its infancy during the rest of the 1960s. Only following Brandt's succession of Kiesinger as Chancellor, and with the *de facto* recognition of the GDR and the acceptance of the Oder–Neisse border in August 1970 did it begin to look as if West Germans were finally coming to terms with their new borders and that they no longer had plans to redraw the map of Europe. Seen in this broader context, the importance of the debate in post-Second World War Germany becomes transparent. For the Federal Republic, there was always more at stake than simply an understanding of events in 1914. The debate over the origins of the war was of direct political relevance in the 1960s and 1970s, much as it had been in the 1920s and 1930s, because at both times post-war border changes and a reduction of Germany's power and status were at stake, and a defeated Germany had to try to come to terms with the results of a lost war. Moreover, after 1945 the idea that Germany, due to peculiarities in the country's historical development, had followed a special path which differed from the countries around it, was discussed among historians in Germany and abroad. This debate of a German *Sonderweg* gave the question of the origins of the First World War further significance, although it is a concept that did not go unchallenged. Implicit in the assumption of a *Sonderweg* is the view that there might have been a right and a wrong way for states to develop, a notion that historians no longer advocate with the same certainty they once did.[107]

Despite Geiss's optimistic assessments of the current state of debate, however, arguments continued between those who favoured a defensive war thesis, those who thought Germany acted offensively in 1914, and those who considered the war to have been preventive.[108] These different approaches and continuing debates are the subject of the final part of this book.

Notes

1 Evans and Pogge von Strandmann (eds), *The Coming of the First World War*, p.vi.

2 See Gottfried Niedhart (ed.), *Kriegsbeginn 1939: Entfesselung oder Ausbruch des Zweiten Weltkrieges*, Darmstadt 1976, p. 5, citing Walter Hofer, *Die Entfesselung des Zweiten Weltkrieges*, 2nd edn, Stuttgart 1955, p. 11.

3 Agreement of the Franco-German Historians' Commission of 1951. 'Deutsch-französische Vereinbarung über strittige Fragen europäischer Geschichte' (May and October 1951), *Geschichte in Wissenschaft und Unterricht*, 3, 1952, pp. 288–99.

4 Jäger, *Historische Forschung*, pp. 106/120.

5 Andreas Dorpalen, *German History in Marxist Perspective: The East German Approach*, London 1985, p. 286. On the perception of Fischer's views in East Germany, see also Willibald Gutsche, 'The Foreign Policy of Imperial Germany and the Outbreak of the War in the Historiography of the GDR', in Gregor Schöllgen (ed.), *Escape into War? The Foreign Policy of Imperial Germany*, Oxford 1990, pp. 41–62.

6 Dorpalen, *German History in Marxist Perspective*, p. 285. Non-Marxist historians like Keith Wilson and Niall Ferguson have recently repeated similar arguments. See below, Part 4, for details.

7 The debate, which was fought out in the newspaper *Neues Deutschland* and in a number of articles in the East German journal *Zeitschrift für Geschichtswissenschaft*, is described in Dorpalen, *German History in Marxist Perspective*, pp. 287ff.

8 James Retallack, *Germany in the Age of Kaiser Wilhelm II*, Basingstoke and London 1996, p. 9.

9 Cited in Arnold Sywotteck, 'Die Fischer-Kontroverse: Ein Beitrag zur Entwicklung des politisch-historischen Bewußtseins in der Bundesrepublik', in Imanuel Geiss and Bernd Jürgen Wendt (eds), *Deutschland in der Weltpolitik des 19. und 20. Jahrhunderts*, Düsseldorf 1973, p. 27. Given the callous way in which those theses had been constructed and advanced in the interwar period, this was hardly an achievement of which to be proud (see above, Parts 1 and 2).

10 Fritz Fischer, *Juli 1914: Wir sind nicht hineingeschlittert. Das Staatsgeheimnis um die Riezler-Tagebücher. Eine Streitschrift*, Hamburg 1983, p. 49. The importance of the Korean War for Germany is analysed, for example, by Lothar Kettenacker, who also charts the history of West Germany's integration from Cold War to détente and eventual reintegration. *Germany since 1945*, Oxford 1997, pp. 53–99.

11 'Deutsch-französische Vereinbarung über strittige Fragen europäischer Geschichte', p. 293. See also Frank McDonough, *The Origins of the First and Second World Wars*, Cambridge 1997, p. 25.

12 Walther Hubatsch, *Der Weltkrieg 1914/1918*, in Leo Just (ed.), *Handbuch der deutschen Geschichte*, vol. IV, 2nd Section, Konstanz 1955, p. 2. A second revised edition of this text was published by the West German Ministry of Defence in 1966, in which Hubatsch had changed his confident statement only slightly: 'Researchers in all countries are more or less agreed on the main features of the events – as long as ideological constraints do not impede the objective treatment.' *Der Erste Weltkrieg*, Bundesministerium der Verteidigung (ed.), Bonn 1966, p. 10.

13 Bruno Thoss, 'Der Erste Weltkrieg als Ereignis und Erlebnis: Paradigmenwechsel in der westdeutschen Weltkriegsforschung seit

der Fischer-Kontroverse', in Wolfgang Michalka (ed.), *Der Erste Weltkrieg*, pp. 1012–43, p. 1012. The official histories included: Reichsarchiv (ed.), *Der Weltkrieg 1914–1918*, 14 vols, Berlin and Frankfurt/M. 1920–56; Marine-Archiv (ed.), *Der Krieg zur See*, 23 vols, Berlin 1920–65.

14 Luigi Albertini, *Le origini della guerra del 1914*, 3 vols, Milan 1942–43; English translation *The Origins of the War of 1914*, 3 vols, London 1952–57. For a discussion and summary of Albertini's arguments, see Langdon, *The Long Debate*, pp. 50ff.; Samuel R. Williamson (ed.), *The Origins of a Tragedy: July 1914*, Chapel Hill, 1981, pp. 1ff.

15 Langdon, *The Long Debate*, pp. 60/61.

16 Williamson (ed.), *Origins of a Tragedy*, p. 20.

17 A.J.P. Taylor, *The Course of German History*, London 1945; *The Struggle for Mastery in Europe, 1848–1918*, New York 1954; *War by Time-Table: How the First World War Began*, London and New York 1969. A summary of Taylor's arguments can be found in Langdon, *The Long Debate*, pp. 62ff.

18 Taylor, *War by Time-Table*, p. 121.

19 Langdon, *The Long Debate*, p. 64.

20 Ludwig Dehio, *Gleichgewicht oder Hegemonie?* Krefeld 1948; idem, *Deutschland und die Weltpolitik im 20. Jahrhundert*, Munich 1955. Despite his early work on the German prewar policy, Dehio became an outspoken critic of Fischer's views, perhaps particularly so because his work had inspired Fischer who had taken it to an extreme position. See Geiss, *Studien*, p. 130. On Dehio, see also Stefan Berger, *The Search for Normality: National Identity and Historical Consciousness in Germany since 1800*, Providence and Oxford 1997, pp. 58–9.

21 Ibid., p. 123. On other German scholars writing after 1945, see Berger, *The Search for Normality*, pp. 56ff.

22 Evans and Pogge von Strandmann (eds), *The Coming of the First World War*, p. vii.

23 Geiss, *Studien*, p. 123. On the impact of Fischer's views on the political scene in Germany, see, for example, Edgar Wolfrum, *Geschichtspolitik in der Bundesrepublik Deutschland: Der Weg zur bundesrepublikanischen Erinnerung, 1948–1990*, Darmstadt 1999, pp. 231ff.

24 Fritz Fischer, 'Deutsche Kriegsziele, Revolutionierung und Separatfrieden im Osten 1914–1918', *Historische Zeitschrift*, 188, 1959; idem, *Griff nach der Weltmacht: Die Kriegszielpolitik des kaiserlichen Deutschland 1914/18*, 1st edn Düsseldorf 1961 (English translation: *Germany's Aims in the First World War*, London 1967).

25 John A. Moses, *The War Aims of Imperial Germany: Professor Fritz Fischer and his Critics*, University of Queensland Papers, vol. I, No. 4, St Lucia 1968, p. 213.

26 Karl-Heinz Janssen, 'Aus Furcht und Verzweiflung: Das deutsche Angriffsmotiv im August 1914', *Die Zeit*, No. 12, 21 March 1969, p. 62.
27 Gerd Krumeich, 'Das Erbe der Wilhelminer', *Frankfurter Allgemeine Zeitung*, 4 Nov. 1999, p. 56. It should be noted, however, that Fischer did not consider himself a leader of the student movement, nor had particular sympathies for its aims. See Bernd Jürgen Wendt, 'Fritz Fischer: Leben, Werk und Wirkung', in Kersten Krüger (ed.), *Fritz Fischer (1908–1999): Schenkung der Gelehrtenbibliothek Fritz Fischer an die Fachbibliothek Geschichte*, Veröffentlichungen der Universitätsbibliothek Rostock 2000, S. 26.
28 The events of July 1914 are discussed in the Introduction.
29 Fischer, *Germany's Aims*, p. 88.
30 Among the first critics from the historical fraternity were Erwin Hölzle and Ludwig Dehio and, as we have seen, outside of Germany Albertini had advanced similar views of German culpability.
31 Fischer, *Germany's Aims*, p. ix.
32 Georg Iggers, Introduction, in Iggers (ed.), *The Social History of Politics: Critical Perspectives in West German Historical Writing Since 1945*, Leamington Spa 1985, p. 22.
33 For the September-Programme, see Fischer, *Germany's Aims*, pp. 103ff.
34 Fischer, *World Power or Decline: The Controversy over Germany's Aims in the First World War*, Norton 1974 (transl. of *Weltmacht oder Niedergang? Deutschland im Ersten Weltkrieg*, Frankfurt 1965), pp. 44–5.
35 Egmont Zechlin, 'Probleme des Kriegskalküls und der Kriegsbeendigung', in idem, *Krieg und Kriegsrisiko: Zur deutschen Politik im Ersten Weltkrieg*, Düsseldorf 1979, pp. 41ff. (The paper was first presented at the German Historians' Convention in 1964.)
36 Cited in Sywotteck, 'Fischer-Kontroverse', p. 28. When the speech was reprinted in an official government bulletin in 1966, even some of Fischer's critics thought that this went a step too far. See Langdon, *The Long Debate*, p. 77.
37 Michael Freund, 'Bethmann-Hollweg, der Hitler des Jahres 1914?' in Lynar (ed.), *Deutsche Kriegsziele*, p. 175.
38 Cited in Jäger, *Historische Forschung*, p. 143. On the involvement of prominent politicians such as Strauss, Gerstenmaier and Erhard see also Wolfrum, *Geschichtspolitik in der Bundesrepublik Deutschland*, p. 233.
39 See ibid., p. 144.
40 This interpretation in Sywotteck, 'Fischer-Kontroverse', p. 45. See also Stefan Berger, 'The German Tradition of Historiography, 1800–1995', in Mary Fulbrook (ed.), *German History since 1800*, pp. 477–92, p. 479.

41 Golo Mann, 'Der Griff nach der Weltmacht', in Lynar (ed.), *Deutsche Kriegsziele,* pp. 189–90.
42 Ibid., p. 192.
43 Kettenacker, *Germany since 1945*, p. 63.
44 Gerhard Ritter, 'Eine neue Kriegsschuldthese? Zu Fritz Fischers Buch "Griff nach der Weltmacht"', *Historische Zeitschrift,* 194, 1962, pp. 667–8, reprinted in Lynar (ed.), *Deutsche Kriegsziele,* pp. 121–44, citation p. 144. A look at Ritter's personal biography goes some way towards explaining his reaction to Fischer's theses. Ritter, born in 1888, had spent his formative years in Wilhelmine Germany, and had been deeply affected by the collapse of 1918. He had resented the republic that had replaced the monarchy, and had initially favoured some of Hitler's foreign policy. However, he eventually found himself on the side of resistance to Hitler, having joined Carl Friedrich Goerdeler's conservative and military resistance group. He had been introduced to Goerdeler by Dietrich Bonhoeffer. Following the assassination attempt of 20 July 1944, Ritter spent several months in prison. After 1945, he continued to believe in Prussia as an ideal, and regarded the years under National Socialism very much as an aberration in German history. See Andreas Dorpalen, 'Gerhard Ritter', in H.-U. Wehler (ed.), *Deutsche Historiker,* Göttingen 1973, pp. 86–99.
45 Cited in James Joll, 'The 1914 Debate Continues: Fritz Fischer and his Critics', in H.W. Koch (ed.), *The Origins of the First World War: Great Power Rivalry and German War Aims,* 2nd edn, London 1984, pp. 30–45, p. 31. See also Gregor Schöllgen, 'Griff nach der Weltmacht? 25 Jahre Fischer-Kontroverse', *Historisches Jahrbuch,* 106, 1986, pp. 386–406, p. 392.
46 Ritter, 'Eine neue Kriegsschuldthese?', p. 144.
47 Gerhard Ritter, *Der Erste Weltkrieg: Studien zum deutschen Geschichtsbild,* Bundeszentrale für politische Bildung, Heft 64, Bonn 1964, p. 11.
48 For further information on Ritter's critique of Fischer, see Langdon, *The Long Debate,* pp. 101–9.
49 W.J. Mommsen, 'Domestic Factors in German Foreign Policy before 1914', *Central European History,* vol. 6, No. 1, 1973, p. 8.
50 Mann, 'Der Griff nach der Weltmacht', p. 187; Fischer, *Germany's Aims,* p. x. John Langdon identifies a number of areas of contention, ranging from 'errors and exaggerations' to the 'political implications' of Fischer's work. *The Long Debate,* pp. 74ff.
51 Richard J. Evans, *In Hitler's Shadow: West German Historians and the Attempt to Escape from the Nazi Past,* London 1989, p. 113; Jäger, *Historische Forschung,* p. 143; Wendt, 'Fritz Fischer: Leben, Werk und Wirkung', pp. 13–29. Fischer's critics also focused on his past in order to discredit him, pointing in particular to his membership of

the NSDAP and the fact that he was able to advance his academic career during the 1930s. Fischer in fact never claimed to have withstood the onslaught of National Socialism without some concessions to the regime, although, as Wendt argues, his Nazi party membership number (5,846,569) demonstrates that Fischer did not join until he had to for professional reasons (ibid., p. 18). Nonetheless, compared to Ritter's resistance credentials, Fischer's past was certainly less commendable, at least in the eyes of his critics.

52 Cited in Langdon, *The Long Debate*, p. 74. The proceedings at the convention can be followed in *Versammlung deutscher Historiker in Berlin, 7–11. Oktober 1964. Beiheft zur Zeitschrift Geschichte in Wissenschaft und Unterricht*, Stuttgart 1965.

53 Fischer, *Juli 1914*, pp. 70–1; Langdon, *The Long Debate*, p. 77. The trip was finally funded by the American Council of Learned Societies.

54 Cited in John A. Moses, *Politics of Illusion: The Fischer Controversy in German Historiography*, London 1975, p. 5.

55 Herwig (ed.), *The Outbreak of World War I*, p. 3.

56 Langdon, *The Long Debate*, p. 84.

57 Cited in Schöllgen, *Jahrbuch*, p. 393.

58 Geiss, *Studien*, p. 144.

59 For Gerstenmaier's speech see above, p. 134.

60 Jäger, *Historische Forschung*, pp. 141f.

61 Freund, 'Bethmann-Hollweg: Der Hitler des Jahres 1914?', pp. 178ff.

62 Gerhard Ritter, *Staatskunst und Kriegshandwerk: Das Problem des Militarismus in Deutschland*, 4 vols, Munich 1959–68, vol. 3: *Die Tragödie der Staatskunst*, 1964. English translation *The Sword and the Scepter: The Problem of Militarism in Germany*, translated by Heinz Norden; vol. 3, *The Tragedy of Statesmanship – Bethmann Hollweg as War Chancellor 1914–1917*, 3rd edn Miami 1972, pp. 2–3.

63 By the late 1960s, vociferous critics among Fischer's German colleagues included, among others, Andreas Hillgruber, Egmont Zechlin, Karl-Dietrich Erdmann and Wolfgang J. Mommsen, although increasingly, as will be seen below, their disagreements with the Fischer school were a matter of emphasis, rather than an outright denial of the important role that Germany had played in the events that had led to war in 1914. For a detailed discussion of their arguments, see Langdon, *The Long Debate*, pp. 100–29.

64 *TLS* (no author) 3140, 4 May 1962, p. 323.

65 See e.g. Fritz Klein, 'Die westdeutsche Geschichtsschreibung über die Ziele des deutschen Imperialismus im Ersten Weltkrieg', *Zeitschrift für Geschichtswissenschaft*, vol.10/8, 1962, pp. 1808–1836.

66 Ibid., p.1836.

67 Fritz Klein et al. (eds), *Deutschland im Ersten Weltkrieg*, 3 vols, Berlin 1968-69. See also Willibald Gutsche, *Der gewollte Krieg: Der deutsche*

Imperialismus und der Erste Weltkrieg, Berlin 1984; Fritz Klein, 'Der Erste Weltkrieg in der Geschichtswissenschaft der DDR', *Zeitschrift für Geschichtswissenschaft*, 42, 1994, pp. 293–301.

68 Fritz Klein, *Drinnen und Draussen. Ein Historiker in der DDR. Erinnerungen*, Frankfurt/Main 2000, p. 239. On the reception of Fischer's theses in the GDR see Matthew Stibbe's forthcoming article 'The Primacy of Ideology? The Fischer Controversy over German War Aims in the First World War and its Reception by East German Historians, 1961–1989'.

69 Cf. Sywotteck, 'Fischer-Kontroverse', p. 46. For East German interpretations of the origins of the First World War, see e.g. Klein et al. (eds), *Deutschland im Ersten Weltkrieg*; Wolfgang Schumann and Ludwig Nestler (eds), *Weltherrschaft im Visier*, Berlin 1975; Willibald Gutsche, *Sarajevo 1914: Vom Attentat zum Weltkrieg*, Berlin 1984. For an assessment of Fischer's alleged use of Marxist analysis, one of the criticisms levelled at Fischer, see Langdon, *The Long Debate*, pp. 76–81.

70 R. Neck, 'Kriegszielpolitik im Ersten Weltkrieg', in Lynar (ed.), *Deutsche Kriegsziele*, citations pp. 157/148.

71 K. Epstein, 'Die deutsche Ostpolitik im Ersten Weltkrieg', ibid., p. 160. For an American interpretation of the Fischer debate see also Konrad H. Jarausch, 'World Power of Tragic Fate? The Kriegsschuldfrage as Historical Neurosis', *Central European History*, 5, 1972, pp. 72–92.

72 See Jäger, *Historische Forschung*, p. 151. For positive reviews of Fischer's *Griff nach der Weltmacht*, see e.g. Jaques Droz, *Les Causes de la Première Guerre mondiale: Essai d'historiographie*, Paris 1973; F.L. Carsten's review in the *English Historical Review*, 78, 1963, pp. 751–3; H.W. Gatzke's review in the *American Historical Review*, 68, 1962, pp. 443–5; P. Renouvin, 'Les Buts de guerre de l'Allemagne (1914–1918) d'après les travaux de Fritz Fischer', *Revue Historique*, 80, 1962, pp. 381–90; Epstein, 'Die deutsche Ostpolitik im Ersten Weltkrieg', *Jahrbücher für die Geschichte Osteuropas*, 10, 1962, pp. 381ff.

73 *TLS* (no author) 3140, 4 May 1962, p. 323.

74 See Jäger, *Historische Forschung*, pp. 139/40 for a summary of these political motivations.

75 Geiss (ed.), *Julikrise und Kriegsausbruch*.

76 See also Jäger, *Historische Forschung*, pp. 151–2.

77 John Röhl, *The Kaiser and his Court: Wilhelm II and the Government of Germany*, Cambridge 1996, p. 162.

78 Again, Fischer had previously published some of his findings in the *Historische Zeitschrift* before the publication of the book in 1969. 'Weltpolitik, Weltmachtstreben und deutsche Kriegsziele', *Historische Zeitschrift*, 199, 1964, pp. 265-346; idem, *Krieg der*

Illusionen (Engl. transl.: *War of Illusions: German Policies from 1911–1914*, London 1975).

79 Fischer, *War of Illusions*, pp. 160 ff. For an analysis of the diplomatic background to the meeting see Stevenson, *Armaments*, pp. 251ff. The Müller diaries had already been analysed by John Röhl in the same year, and the published diary, edited by Walter Görlitz, found to be incomplete. Fischer based his analysis on Röhl's findings in 'Admiral von Müller and the Approach of War, 1911–1914'. The complete diary entry can be found here.

80 Most of the relevant documents and a detailed analysis of the events can be found in Röhl's document collection, 'An der Schwelle zum Weltkrieg: Eine Dokumentation über den "Kriegsrat" vom 8. Dezember 1912', *Militärgeschichtliche Mitteilungen*, 21, 1/1977. For an account in English, see Röhl, 'Admiral von Müller and the Approach of War', and idem, *The Kaiser and his Court*, ch. 7. See also Fischer, *War of Illusions*, pp. 160ff.; Adolf Gasser, *Preußischer Militärgeist und Kriegsentfesselung 1914: Drei Studien zum Ausbruch des Ersten Weltkrieges*, Basel and Frankfurt/M. 1985. Historians who have denied the importance of the famous meeting include Wolfgang J. Mommsen, 'Der Topos vom unvermeidlichen Krieg: Außenpolitik und öffentliche Meinung im Deutschen Reich im letzten Jahrzehnt vor 1914', in idem, *Der autoritäre Nationalstaat*, Frankfurt/M. 1990, pp. 380ff.; in English idem, 'Domestic Factors in German Foreign Policy before 1914'; E. Zechlin, 'Die Adriakrise und der "Kriegsrat" vom 8. Dezember 1912', in *Krieg und Kriegsrisiko: Zur Deutschen Politik im Ersten Weltkrieg*. Düsseldorf 1979; L.C.F. Turner, *The Origins of the First World War*, London 1970. For a detailed bibliography on the war council, see Röhl, *The Kaiser and his Court*, pp. 255–6. A discussion of the war council and further references can also be found in Mombauer, *Helmuth von Moltke*, pp. 135–43.

81 Mommsen, 'Domestic Factors in German Foreign Policy before 1914'.

82 Röhl, *1914: Delusion or Design?*, p. 31.

83 Röhl, 'An der Schwelle zum Weltkrieg'. Müller's diary was published by W. Görlitz (ed.), *Der Kaiser … Aufzeichnungen des Chefs des Marinekabinetts Admiral Georg Alexander von Müller über die Ära Wilhelm II.*, Göttingen 1965. For a critique of the edition, see Röhl, 'Admiral von Müller', pp. 651–73 and idem, *The Kaiser and his Court*, p. 163, where Röhl argues that there were 'profound and complicated reasons for the confusion surrounding this document [the war council diary entry]. A major cause of the trouble was that the Müller diaries were originally published in a deliberately distorted and mutilated form.'

84 Fischer, *War of Illusions*, p. 470.

85 Volker Berghahn, *Germany and the Approach of War in 1914*, 1st edn 1973, p. 213.

86 Hans-Ulrich Wehler, *Das deutsche Kaiserreich, 1871–1918*, Göttingen, 1973, Engl. transl. *The German Empire, 1871–1918,* Leamington Spa 1985. On Wehler's recent interpretations of the link between German foreign and domestic policy see *Deutsche Gesellschaftsgeschichte*, vol. 3: *Von der 'Deutschen Doppelrevolution' bis zum Beginn des Ersten Weltkrieges*, 1849–1914, Munich 1995. On the historiography of the German Empire, see also Chris Lorenz, 'Beyond Good and Evil? The German Empire of 1871 and Modern German Historiography', *Journal of Contemporary History*, 30, 1995, pp. 729–65.

87 Sywotteck, 'Fischer-Kontroverse', p. 33.

88 Bernd F. Schulte, reader's letter to *Die Zeit*, No. 33, 12 Aug. 1983.

89 Carsten, Review of *Griff nach der Weltmacht*, p. 752.

90 Geiss (ed.), *Julikrise und Kriegsausbruch*; Geiss (ed.), *Juli 1914* (English transl. *July 1914*); Röhl (ed.), *Zwei deutsche Fürsten zur Kriegsschuldfrage*, English transl.: *1914: Delusion or Design?*; Karl Dietrich Erdmann (ed.), *Kurt Riezler: Tagebücher, Aufsätze, Dokumente*, Göttingen 1972; Sösemann (ed.), *Theodor Wolff: Tagebücher 1914–1918*.

91 Joll, 'The 1914 Debate Continues: Fritz Fischer and his Critics', p. 35.

92 The history of the publication, and of the controversy over the diaries, is detailed in Agnes Blänsdorf, 'Der Weg der Riezler-Tagebücher: Zur Kontroverse über die Echtheit der Tagebücher Kurt Riezlers', *Geschichte in Wissenschaft und Unterricht*, 35, 1984, pp. 651–84. For an account in English, see Langdon, *The Long Debate*, pp. 109ff. The diaries were published by Karl Dietrich Erdmann, *Kurt Riezler: Tagebücher, Briefe, Dokumente*, Göttingen 1972. For a bibliography of the relevant newspaper articles and publications around the Riezler controversy, and a strong attack of Erdmann, see Bernd Felix Schulte, *Die Verfälschung der Riezler Tagebücher: Ein Beitrag zur Wissenschaftsgeschichte der 50er und 60er Jahre*, Frankfurt/M., Bern and New York 1985. For the debate in the German press, see e.g. Karl-Heinz Janssen, 'August '14: Wahrheit auf Raten. Zwei Historiker streiten um Tagebücher: Wurde die deutsche Kriegsschuld am Ersten Weltkrieg im nationalen Interesse verschleiert?, *Die Zeit*, No. 24, 10 June 1983; Karl Dietrich Erdmann, 'Die Tagebücher sind echt. Streit um ein historisches Dokument, das ins Zwielicht geraten ist. Eine Antwort', *Die Zeit*, No. 28, 8 July 1983; and letters to the editor, *Die Zeit*, No. 33, 12 Aug. 1983. The 'duel' between Erdmann and Bernd Sösemann, the historian who first doubted the authenticity of the text that Ermann edited, was largely conducted in the pages of the *Historische Zeitschrift*.

93 Erdmann's response to allegations from Bernd-Felix Schulte, cited in Schulte, *Die Verfälschung der Riezler Tagebücher*, p. 16, note 4.

94 Erdmann's views on Bethmann Hollweg in 'Zur Beurteilung Bethmann Hollwegs', *Geschichte in Wissenschaft und Unterricht*, 15, 1964, pp. 525–40. In English, his views can be found in 'War Guilt 1914 Reconsidered: A Balance of New Research', in Koch (ed.), *The Origins of the First World War*, pp. 342–70, citation on p. 366.

95 Rössler-Franz, *Biographisches Wörterbuch zur deutschen Geschichte*, cited in Schulte, *Die Verfälschung*, p. 17.

96 Fritz Fellner, Review of *Kurt Riezler: Tagebücher, Aufsätze, Dokumente*, in *Mitteilungen des Österreichischen Instituts für Geschichte*, 1973, pp. 490–5.

97 The latter claim was made by Bernd-Felix Schulte, *Die Verfälschung der Riezler Tagebücher*, who suspected foul play on behalf of the anti-Fischerites. Without advancing a similar conspiracy theory, other commentators also questioned the authenticity, or at least the completeness, of the diaries Erdmann edited.

98 Fischer, *Juli 1914*.

99 Sösemann (ed.), *Theodor Wolff*, see e.g. vol. I, No. 88, 357, 340. See also Röhl, 'Germany', pp. 27ff.

100 The debate began in the *Historische Zeitschrift*, and was then taken up by *Die Zeit*. *Der Spiegel*, *Die Welt* and *Frankfurter Allgemeine Zeitung* also featured articles on the debate, as did numerous regional newspapers, such as *Hamburger Abendblatt*, *Main Echo* and *Münstersche Zeitung* as well as the *Norddeutscher Rundfunk* and *Bayerisches Fernsehen*. It made a reappearance very recently, when, in response to an article on the Fischer controversy by Gerd Krumeich in the *Frankfurter Allgemeine Zeitung*, Bernd Sösemann reminded readers in a letter to the editor that Riezler's diaries had been tampered with. In response, Agnes Blänsdorff reiterated her earlier defence of Erdmann's edition. See *FAZ*, 4 Nov. 1999; letters on 12 and 19 Nov. 1999. In March 2001, Sösemann published another critique of the Riezler diary edition in *FAZ*, 14 Mar. 2001, alleging that Erdmann had obviously needed 'a well sharpened sword against his opponent Fischer' and had therefore conveniently overlooked the problematic nature of the source that he edited.

101 Fischer, *World Power or Decline*, Foreword, p. vii.

102 Geiss, *Studien*, p. 112. Geiss's role in the developing controversy is examined in detail in Langdon, *The Long Debate*, pp. 86ff.

103 Joachim Remak, '1914 – The Third Balkan War: Origins Reconsidered', *Journal of Modern History*, 43, 1971, reprinted in Koch (ed.), *The Origins of the First World War*, p. 86.

104 Geiss, *Studien*, p. 188.

105 Ibid., pp. 195–6.

106 As part of the controversy, the doctoral thesis by one of Fischer's students, Imanuel Geiss, on German war aims in Poland during the First World War was greeted with outrage by conservative Germans,

a fact that testifies to the particularly emotive nature of the debate regarding Polish territory in post-1945 Germany. Imanuel Geiss, *Der Polnische Grenzstreifen 1914–1918: Ein Beitrag zur deutschen Kriegszielpolitik im Ersten Weltkrieg,* Lübeck and Hamburg 1960. Reactions to this publication are analysed in Geiss, *Studien,* pp. 124–5.

107 On the reinterpretation of the idea of a German *Sonderweg,* see Berger, *The Search for Normality*, pp. 64–5.

108 See Jäger, *Historische Forschung,* p. 156.

Part 4

Post-Fischer Consensus and Continuing Debates

Introduction

It is beyond doubt that Fritz Fischer's research, based on intensive study of the sources, has had a profound effect on German historical writing. Whether one accepts his main theses or not, the results of his work now form an integral part of any analysis of the foreign policy of Imperial Germany. Gregor Schöllgen[1]

In response to Fischer's challenge to the established orthodoxy, and following years of hostile debate, different schools of thought developed in Germany (the 'Hamburg school' and the 'Bielefeld school', for example), and the lines between the various factions became blurred. Certainly, the majority of scholars remained unconvinced by Fischer's interpretation of German foreign policy as a straight line, with Germany's decision-makers aiming for war for several months before it was finally unleashed in 1914, as his interpretation of the 'war council' suggested. Nonetheless, his research provided the much needed impetus for German historians to re-examine the available evidence in order to understand why war broke out in 1914.

Increasingly, the 'opponents' began to focus on smaller details of the controversy. As younger historians entered the debate, they were able to examine German history more dispassionately than historians like Ritter and Fischer, for whom the First and Second World Wars had been part of their personal histories. To this generation of younger historians, the question of the origins of the war was indeed history, worthy of exploration, but not linked to their own histories. Increasingly, too, historians began to emphasize the role of the other belligerent powers in 1914, thus shifting the emphasis of Fischer's focus from Germany and extending the debate. Some of the nuances in the debate, as well as recent investigations into the role of other countries in the events that led to war, will be examined in the final part of this book. The emerging consensus and continuing debates demonstrate to what extent Fischer's controversial claims have become accepted by historians, and how much of them still remains contested ground.

Nuances in the debate in the wake of the Fischer controversy

The 'Fischer controversy' overturned the orthodoxy of the 1950s without any one view replacing it, and Fischer has rightly claimed that it helped democratise not only the historical profession but German society generally. **David Stevenson[2]**

The end of the Fischer controversy did not lead to total agreement over the origins of the First World War, although few would underline today the old, apologetic interpretation of nations slithering accidentally into war. Three main interpretations emerged among German historians in the wake of the Fischer controversy: that of Fischer and his followers, who argued that Germany went to war in 1914 due to ambitious foreign policy aims, that of Wolfgang Mommsen, Hans-Ulrich Wehler and Volker Berghahn, among others, stressing the domestic situation of the Kaiserreich as determining foreign policy and concentrating on the structures within Wilhelmine Germany, and that of Egmont Zechlin, Karl Dietrich Erdmann and Andreas Hillgruber, who emphasized foreign policy and strategic considerations as determining German policy and argued that Germany wanted to preserve its freedom of action and embarked on a 'calculated risk' in 1914.

Fischer's and Wehler's arguments have already been analysed above. In response to both schools of thought, West German conservative historians began to reinterpret Germany's role in the years prior to the outbreak of war, and many continued to portray German policy in 1914 as essentially defensive, while not denying, however, that the Fischer school was right to emphasize Germany's large share of responsibility for the outbreak of the war. The debate continued in academic publications, but also made a reappearance in public media. In a 1982 article in the *Frankfurter Allgemeine Zeitung*, Egmont Zechlin characterized the defensive nature of German policy in 1914 as aiming for a 'defensive preventive war', while emphasizing the desire of German statesmen to support Austria-Hungary. He underlined the decisive role that 'fate' had played in bringing about the war and, echoing Erdmann, argued that while no one had actually wanted the war, equally no one had been prepared to avoid it.[3] The debate was still considered of sufficient public interest in the early 1980s for this national daily paper to print lengthy articles on the subject and provide a forum for further debate on the origins of the war.[4]

A compromise position between the Fischer view and that of his critics was, for example, advanced by Klaus Hildebrand, whose position reflected the extent to which most conservative historians were willing to accept the Fischer thesis. While attributing 'initiating responsibility' to the German leadership for events during the July Crisis, he claims that Germany 'did not "unleash" the First World War according to a plan, in order to realize offensive aims'. Nor were German actions entirely defensive. It can also not be maintained, according to Hildebrand, that Germany 'attempted an external "escape forward" into the war because of her utter desperation regarding the lack of an internal escape (*Ausweglosigkeit*) out of her situation'.

> Rather, [German policy in 1914] was about overcoming by means of an offensive action a defensive [situation] which was

> no longer considered bearable, and asserting herself as a great power among the great powers, as a state in the state system of Europe.[5]

While this constitutes a radical departure from the innocence thesis of the interwar and immediate postwar years, it is nonetheless more apologetic than the views of Fischer and his followers.

In the 1980s critics of the Hamburg and Bielefeld schools went further in their attempts to explain and excuse German decision-making in and before 1914 by concentrating on geopolitics as the reason why the German Reich had been different from its western neighbours. In this interpretation, Wehler's assertion that the political culture in Imperial Germany had been ill at ease with the economic developments of the Reich was countered by the argument that Germany's problems stemmed from its peculiar position at the centre of Europe. Klaus Hildebrand describes Germany's history as marked by a special consciousness (*Sonderbewusstsein*) – a term first used by Karl Dietrich Bracher – resulting from the country's 'existence between the worlds of the West and the East'. In Hildebrand's words, Germany was a country that was allowed to 'exist, but not grow', a fact that caused Germans 'continuous difficulties and led them to fear, justifiably, for the future of the Reich'.[6] In the early 1980s Gregor Schöllgen argued in favour of an interpretation of German policy in and before 1914 as essentially defensive, rather than offensive. Schöllgen advocated that one should 'accentuate [. . .] the *defensive* element in German policy' more than Fischer had done. According to Schöllgen, the continuity in German history is also a 'continuity of fear', resulting from the country's vulnerable position surrounded by great powers.[7] These views, which stress Germany's 'precarious' geopolitical situation, have more recently been emphasized by Schöllgen in an essay collection entitled *Escape into War?* According to Schöllgen, the Fischer school is mistaken in still insisting on the theory of a war of aggression. Instead he concurs with Hillgruber's interpretation, as advanced in his 1977 study on the July Crisis, of a 'conception of a calculated risk for the achievement of limited power political changes by exploiting situations of international crisis'.[8] Schöllgen argues that the German Reich was trapped in a 'vicious circle' in the decades before the outbreak of the First World War. As a result, Germany was confronted by a 'serious dilemma', as Schöllgen explains:

> It was a European great power; as such, it desired – and was indeed compelled – to pursue great-power politics in order to maintain its position. But in the Age of Imperialism, great-power policy was synonymous with world-power policy, or, as it was called in Germany, with *Weltpolitik*. By pursuing world-power politics, the German Reich actually contributed substantially to the destruction of the balance of power which was in many respects essential for the existence of a German great power in Europe.[9]

According to such lines of argument (which are very reminiscent of those advanced in Germany during and immediately after the war), Germany's leaders could not really have acted differently than they did in 1914, and they were acting defensively, rather than offensively, in the light of hostile alliances around Germany that hemmed its development and threatened its status and future security. Moreover, compared to Britain and France, Schöllgen evaluates Germany's *Weltpolitik* as 'fairly modest', rather than 'grasping for world power', as Fischer had contended. In this interpretation, the overall impression of Germany's position in 1914 is viewed fatalistically: 'it appears that *because* German policy advanced, it was also *bound* to decline'.[10] Geopolitical arguments were advocated by other, largely politically conservative historians, for example by Michael Stürmer and Klaus Hildebrand. According to Stürmer, German history before the war had been shaped by what he calls the 'German dilemma'. The German people, 'situated in the strategic heartland of Europe', needed a strong nation state as a guarantee against future invasions.

Germany's geostrategic position presented Germany 'with the impossible task of squaring the circle'. Moreover, in Stürmer's opinion, Germany's geostrategic dilemma 'is still with us. Germany, unlike Britain, does not enjoy the advantages of being an island'.[11]

Such arguments did not go unchallenged. In the 1980s geopolitics became a part of the academic and public discussions in the Federal Republic, with little awareness, as Hans-Ulrich Wehler criticizes, of the parallels to such discussions in National Socialist Germany. In such analyses, there is talk of Germany's *Mittellage* (position at the centre of Europe), of geostrategic constraints, or plainly of geopolitics. The implication of these theories is that geography was Germany's fate, that the country was endangered due to its central position in Europe, and that the new German Reich after 1871 had been constantly threatened on account of its geostrategic position. In other words, it was not the actions and desires of the men in charge of Imperial Germany, or the shortcomings of the political system and structures, but simply the constraints that fate had put on the German Reich, which were responsible for the politics that led to war in 1914. Wehler has questioned this apologetic interpretation, wondering whether Germany was indeed as encircled as its decision-makers made out, and whether its situation 'at the heart of Europe' was really as precarious as the apologists claim. What about Switzerland or Poland, he asks – there is no history of aggression in these countries, and yet their geopolitical situation is similar to Germany's.[12] A proponent of the geopolitical argument would probably reply that neither of those countries was a 'great power', and would point to Germany's industrial and financial strength and the size of its population as reasons why being located 'in the middle' had been intolerable for Imperial Germany. According to this point of view, Imperial Germany had had no choice but to become a great power and to embark on power politics – it was either that or be swallowed up by the powerful states around it.

Conservative geopolitical interpretations emerging since the 1980s clearly echoed the apologist stance of the 1950s, although this time they were not without their fair share of critics. James Retallack dismisses views which rely on alliance 'mechanisms' and Germany's 'exposed geostrategic position' to explain the origins of the war, and highlights what he regards as their main aim: 'Such analyses seek to shift the blame elsewhere: either toward the other Great Powers or toward the abstracted international system.'[13] Helmut Böhme's critique of geopolitics highlights its apologetic intentions:

> In this argumentation, the right to world power amounts practically to a duty for war, to normal European politics, or it is understood in the context of a war of cultures. Germany did not have a choice in 1914 if she wanted to keep up in the contest of European grand nations.[14]

Why were such apologetic and reactionary geopolitical arguments raised again in Germany in the 1980s? The answer, as ever, lies with the political background against which historical debates develop. In this case, it was the new political direction which Germany embarked upon following the change of government in 1981, when the conservative Christian Democrat Helmut Kohl took over the chancellorship from the Social Democrat Helmut Schmidt. Further impetus was provided by the 1990 reunification of Germany, as a result of which '"power politics" as history and fate of the "country in the middle" is once again demanded' in certain quarters.[15] James Retallack points out the significance of the contemporary conservative political climate which 'has led some conservative historians to propose a more positive, nationalist view of German history'.[16] This was a radical departure from the critical days of the 1960s. By the 1980s, both world wars were sufficiently far removed in time for some younger historians to question again the orthodox views on German history, which since the heady days of the Fischer controversy had been that Germany had to bear a large, if not the largest, share of responsibility for the outbreak of war in 1914. For many Germans, the period of apologies and guilt was coming to an end. Patriotism, so long a dirty word in postwar Germany, and a nationalist view of German history, were encouraged once again in the conservative Federal Republic. Mary Fulbrook comes to similar conclusions about German history in the 1980s:

> it cannot be argued that history was in some way 'objective' and apolitical in West Germany. Strenuous attempts were made in the 1980s by West German Chancellor Helmut Kohl, assisted by historians such as Michael Stürmer and Andreas Hillgruber and the philosopher-historian Ernst Nolte, to shape popular historical consciousness in the interests of 'normalising' the German past and constructing a new national identity, through the selective presentation and reinterpretation of the past in museums and exhibitions as well as articles and books.[17]

Of course, this reinterpretation of German history in an attempt to create a more positive national identity for West Germans did not apply just to the First World War. The history of National Socialism, of the Second World War and the Holocaust was also the subject of revision and reinterpretation, culminating in another high-profile historical debate, the famous *Historikerstreit* (historians' debate) which began in 1986.[18] Following German reunification four years later, a positive interpretation of German history became even more desirable, and was readily advanced by Germany's conservative historians.

The rise of a renewed interest in geopolitics was not an exclusively German phenomenon, and has been attributed to a concurrent rise of nationalism and a decline of internationalism, in particular of international working-class movements, a trend that was heightened in the wake of the failure and ultimate collapse of the Soviet Union and its European satellites. Miles Kahler describes the appeal of geopolitics in certain quarters, not only in terms of explaining the past, but also in terms of justifying current political decisions:

> Used and misused by spokesmen for starkly different points of view, geopolitics fits most neatly with the nationalist and conservative side of the political spectrum, where it was born. Geopolitics is useful as a restraint on the diversion of resources to domestic welfare ends, since it posits requirements for any great power that wishes to retain its status. Through the liberal use of terms such as 'rimlands', it urges an endlessly expanding strategic role for the great power and justifies renewed competition in the Third World. The geopolitical frame of mind also fits well (as it did before 1914) with a vision of international competition and struggle that denies the possibility of sustained cooperation.[19]

The geopolitical explanations of the origins of the First World War that we have already encountered fit this last point well. Coupled with a denial of the possibility of international cooperation or a peaceful resolution to international crises, this point of view fatalistically presupposes that a conflict was inevitable in 1914. Consequently, no one was really to blame for the outbreak of war: a neat return to the comfortable interwar consensus.

There was another reason why the old topic of the origins had once again become the focus of historians by the early 1980s. After all, a new consensus existed by that time which was based to large extent on the Fischer school's findings. This meant there was again an established orthodoxy to be refuted by a new generation of historians. Much of Fischer's interpretation had begun to trickle down into general histories and school textbooks, and his views were becoming generally more accepted by the academic community. A detailed investigation into how the subject of the outbreak of war was discussed in West German school-books in the late 1970s revealed that – with the notable exception of Bavarian school-books, which tended to omit the Fischer debate altogether – Fischer's views had filtered into West German school-books and were being taught at schools by a new generation of historians. Klaus Bruckmann, a critic of Fischer's views, undertook to study the extent to which the origins of the First World War were then taught along Fischer's line. He came to the conclusion that the evidence he found of Fischer's views in German school-books amounted to 'history as indoctrination'.[20] If Fischer's once seemingly heretical claims now constituted the new official line, albeit watered down and stripped of some of their most contentious allegations, such as the question of war aims and the long-term planning of the conflict, then his critics felt the need to prevent further 'indoctrination' with his views by forcefully advancing a counter-argument.

Outside of Germany, other factors determined the nature of the debate and of the developing scholarship on the origins of the war. Some studies undertaken in the late 1970s and early 1980s have to be seen in the context of the conflict between the international superpowers during the 1970s. In 1979 the American Miles Kahler compared the conflicts of the pre-1914 era between Britain and Germany with those between the Soviet Union and the United States in the 1970s. Although he comes to the conclusion that the analogy is 'appealing but flawed', the reasons for examining the origins of the First World War so long after its outbreak can be seen in the international events and tensions of the time, which carried with them the frequent and seriously felt risk of escalation into a third world war.[21] Much like in the interwar period, it seemed as if an understanding of why previous world wars began might lead to an understanding of whether another such war might break out. Current crises, such as the Chinese–Vietnamese conflict of 1979, and rising tensions between the USSR and the United States, were the background to such investigations. The superpower arms race of the 1970s and 1980s, and in particular the nuclear arms race, which was becoming increasingly fierce, heightened the interest in the arms race of the great powers before 1914.[22] Writing in 1981, Samuel R. Williamson identified what he considered to be obvious parallels between the situation prior to the First World War and political developments at the time: 'the similarities between the world of alliances and arms races in the years before 1914 and the international situation of the early

1980s pose crucial questions about the future of modern civilization', he warned.[23]

An example of a study claiming to be motivated by current political concerns is Geoffrey Barraclough's investigation of the 1911 Agadir Crisis, which the author portrays as one of the 'long-term causes' of the First World War. The work was ultimately motivated by a wish to discover parallels between the events that had led to war in 1914, and the international tensions in the early 1980s, the background against which the book was written. Thus Barraclough concludes:

> It needed no unusual perspicuity in 1911 to foresee, as Bebel did, the great *Kladderadatsch*, the total collapse of the existing system. The trouble was that no one took any notice. If no one takes notice today we can expect our own *Kladderadatsch*, the only difference being that it will be far more complete. [. . .] To retell the story of 1911 would be pointless if it had no bearing on our present predicament. [. . .] If Agadir has any lesson to teach [. . .] the final lesson must be: no more Agadirs. But, looking around the world today, with all its multiple flash-points, who would dare to predict that?[24]

In times of international crises and tension, in the 1970s and 1980s as much as in the interwar years, collective responsibility for the outbreak of war was emphasized in many quarters. Both times, it was an attempt to try to prevent future conflicts by pinpointing the shortcomings of international rivalries and imperialism. The assumption was that if they had led to war before, they could easily do so again. Not surprisingly, the wars in the Balkans at the end of the twentieth century reminded many commentators of the fact that the First World War had begun with a Balkan quarrel, and many feared that tensions in the region would once again trigger a greater European or even world catastrophe. David Stevenson's study of the outbreak of the First World War was written against this background in 1997, and the author explains why he considers an understanding of the escalation of earlier Balkan tensions into a world war might be important:

> As this study was being written, images of Sarajevo flickered nightly across Western television screens, and commentators recalled that events there eighty years ago had started a world war. Although global politics in the 1990s have so far been less perilous than in the early twentieth century, with the break-up of the familiar framework provided by the Soviet–American Cold War they may not remain so. The most likely future is one of a return to a world of several competing Great Powers, manoeuvring in a hazardous environment of ethnic conflict, rivalry for markets and resources, and armaments races. If this happens, it will be more relevant than ever to examine why the pre-1914 Balkan tension so disastrously escalated.[25]

The parallels between international crises at the end of the twentieth century and those at the end of the nineteenth did not escape the attention of historians. In the uncertain Cold War world, the origins of the First World War seemed to contain valuable lessons on the escalation of crises, and the old topic continued to be of political relevance. In the light of criticisms of Fischer's one-sided approach, historians increasingly looked outside of Germany for clues as to why the international crisis of 1914 escalated into a world war. What they tended to find, as we will see, is that a good case can be made for allocating some of the blame for the outbreak of the war to governments outside of Germany.

Assessing the role of the other belligerent powers in 1914

Too much concentration on Berlin's role slights developments taking place in Austria-Hungary, Russia, Serbia and the Balkan states in the months before July 1914. Samuel R. Williamson, Jr.[26]

Not all historians agree that Germany was significantly more to blame for the outbreak of the First World War than other nations, and most would still maintain that a focus on Germany to the exclusion of other countries presents too one-sided a picture. Studies of individual countries demonstrate different levels of culpability – depending on the focal point of the historian, different countries appear more or less prominently involved or guilty. The Balkan tensions that 'plagued' Europe in the prewar years clearly are of crucial importance, as are the decisions taken by the various European governments in July 1914. Following Fischer's lead, historians began to concentrate on the long-term causes of the war, and on evaluating the roles played by the decision-makers in different European capitals. Their work has demonstrated that Germany's leaders are not the only ones whose motivations we need to understand and that the rest of Europe did not merely *react* to Germany's actions. Rather, research into the policies of Germany's European neighbours has revealed that the responsibility for the outbreak of war cannot be solely attributed to Germany. Historians have particularly focused on the role of the governments in Vienna, London, Paris, St Petersburg and Belgrade, and we will look at each case in turn here.

Austria-Hungary

Austria-Hungary has become a focal point of historical investigations, not surprisingly, given the fact that it was the Dual Monarchy's declaration of war on Serbia that set in motion the chain of mobilizations and declarations of war from which the main European powers could not extricate themselves. Albertini's investigation of the July Crisis had already led him to conclude in the 1940s that 'Berlin could encourage and spur on to attack, but the initiative was taken by Austria'.[27] As John Langdon points out, prior to Fischer's *Griff nach der Weltmacht*, Austria-Hungary's significant share of responsibility for the outbreak of war had been taken for granted. Fischer departed from this position, not by exonerating Austria-Hungary, but by focusing on Berlin to the extent of ignoring Vienna. 'His copious denunciations of German intentions bleached Austrian actions into a colorless record of unswerving submission to the wishes of Berlin.'[28] Much in contrast with the impression one might get from Fischer's accounts, Samuel R. Williamson's study of Austria-Hungary identifies the important role played by Vienna's decision-makers, among others. He objects to 'too much concentration on Berlin's role', which negates, in his opinion, the importance of decisions being taken in Austria-Hungary, Russia, Serbia and the Balkan states in the months before July 1914.[29] Williamson's own investigation of Austria-Hungary's role in the events of 1914 leads him to conclude that decisions taken in Vienna, far from being negligible or of secondary importance to those taken in Berlin, were consciously designed to lead to war.

> In Vienna in July 1914 a set of leaders experienced in statecraft, power and crisis management consciously risked a general war to fight a local war. Battered during the Balkan Wars by Serbian expansion, Russian activism and now by the loss of Franz Ferdinand, the Habsburg leaders desperately desired to shape their future, rather than let events destroy them. The fear of domestic disintegration made war an acceptable policy option. The Habsburg decision, backed by the Germans, gave the July crisis a momentum that rendered peace an early casualty.[30]

Similarly, Robert Evans has argued that the 'high policy-makers of the Monarchy actively provoked the war because they saw the circumstances of the assassination as themselves a fateful provocation to Austria-Hungary'. His study points to 'a remarkable unanimity' among the decision-makers in Vienna to use the crisis for a reckoning with Serbia. In the last days of July, 'Vienna was certainly not waiting for instructions; indeed, the Habsburg capital exhibited a rare harmony of its military and civil leadership', Evans asserts.[31]

The Austrian historian Fritz Fellner has concluded from a detailed study of the so-called Hoyos mission of 5 July 1914 (which resulted in the famous 'blank cheque' guarantee of German support for Austria) 'that the unleashing of the war could be attributed in no small part to the activities of younger diplomats in the Viennese foreign office'.[32] Leading statesmen in Vienna considered an expansionist foreign policy a way out of the stagnation and problems of internal politics. Moreover, with the death of Archduke Franz Ferdinand, one of the main Austrian proponents of peace, and of internal reconstruction and change, had been lost. As John Leslie pointed out in his investigation of Austria-Hungary's war aims, 'it is difficult to escape the conclusion that war was welcomed, even deliberately provoked, by those who grasped it as a substitute catalyst for the change they could no longer expect from the now empty Belvedere [Palace in Vienna]'.[33] In other words, just like in Berlin, internal and external problems were to be solved with the help of war. Internally, the Dual Monarchy faced the problem of how to accommodate and appease a multitude of different nationalities, some of whom, particularly the Serbs, sought to undermine the Monarchy and demanded independence, while externally, Austria-Hungary's great power status had been increasingly reduced and the country seemed in danger of becoming a 'second-rate' power. An aggressive foreign policy was supported by Austria-Hungary's Chief of the General Staff, Franz Conrad von Hötzendorf, who had long been keen for a 'reckoning' with Serbia, leading him to welcome the crisis of 1914. His belligerence was backed and encouraged by other Austrian military and political leaders. 'By removing the main restraint on his bellicosity, Sarajevo gave Conrad his unique opportunity to demand categorically the preventive war against Serbia he had been seeking since 1906 and deprived Berchtold [the Austro-Hungarian Foreign Minister] of his main argument against action – the archduke.'[34] Similarly, Williamson asserts that 'Conrad's desire for war set him apart from most of the other actors in the July crisis. Whereas many would accede to the developing situation with regret or caution, he welcomed the crisis.'[35]

However, Fellner is convinced that Germany and Austria-Hungary essentially wanted two different wars. The escalation of the conflict into a European war 'was exclusively the consequence and result of a determined German policy, which did not start to operate only in the last days of July', Fellner asserts, in line with the Fischerite view that Germany's leaders had specific aims in mind when they set about encouraging Vienna's statesmen to make demands of Serbia. Moreover, according to Fellner 'the war could have been localized if the German Empire had not deliberately organized its escalation'. German policy during the July Crisis amounted to 'a betrayal of the ally who had been promised support', as Germany was not willing to provide the help that she had promised in a localized war. According to Fellner, 'Austria-Hungary bears the responsibility for planning a local third Balkan War against Serbia – the responsibility for the escalation of the conflict into a European war does not lie with Austria-Hungary, it lies in Berlin'.[36] It is difficult to see, however, how the war could have been localized, as Fellner claims, given Russia's determination to come to Serbia's aid, and Austria-Hungary's intention not to settle for a diplomatic victory.

Holger Herwig's assessment of Vienna's role sums up the current consensus regarding Austria-Hungary's involvement in the events of 1914:

> For too long, Anglo-Saxons remained mesmerized with the *fin de siècle* Vienna of Gustav Mahler, Arthur Schnitzler, Gustav Klimt, Arnold Schönberg, and Sigmund Freud, and refused to accept that the home of Sacher Torte and Kaffee mit Schlag, or Karnival and Musikverein, could have initiated the great folly of 1914. But the initiative for war lay in Vienna. Habsburg and not Hohenzollern decided to settle accounts by military rather than diplomatic means. Both the direction and the pace of the July crisis were dictated by Vienna. [. . .] Vienna first resolved for war, sought German assurances, and then exploited them once received.[37]

According to Herwig, focusing on Berlin in July 1914 is not enough, for the Austro-Hungarian Chief of the General Staff's 'aggressive stance' dictated decisions, Emperor Franz Joseph shared the general's mind-set, and Berchtold played 'the pivotal role'.[38]

More recently, Günther Kronenbitter has examined the relationship between the alliance partners Germany and Austria-Hungary, focusing in particular on the relationship between the two Chiefs of the General Staff, Helmuth von Moltke and Franz Conrad von Hötzendorf. He notes that their attempts at coordinating their strategies were shaped from the beginning by their different political and strategic aims. Kronenbitter, too, comments on Conrad's desire to fight and defeat the Serbs, and on the acceptance in Vienna that a clash would be unavoidable. But he places more emphasis on Berlin in bringing about an escalation of the crisis into a world war: 'One can interpret the relationship of the alliance partners in such a way that during the last phase of the July Crisis at the latest, Germany attempted without scruples to rearrange the war against Serbia, which had been decided upon in Vienna, into a decisive world-political war (*Entscheidungskampf*).'[39] Such detailed studies of Austria-Hungary's policies and war aims proved that significant roles were played outside Berlin, too. Without the initial willingness of Vienna's statesmen for a 'reckoning' with Belgrade, Berlin's decision-makers would not have been able to use this particular crisis as the trigger for war. Ultimately, however, there is some consensus that Berlin at the very least encouraged Vienna (for example by issuing the 'blank cheque') or, at worst, that pressure was put on Austria-Hungary to act before it was too late.

Great Britain

Britain, too, has become the focus of historians who have attempted to establish the responsibility for the escalation of the crisis of 1914. After all, as we have seen, German politicians had maintained ever since July 1914 that British policy had to some extent been responsible for the outbreak of war, because Britain's leaders had not made their intentions of supporting France and Belgium clear from early in the crisis, and views such as Bethmann Hollweg's had shaped public perception of British policy in the interwar years.[40] However, it would be wrong to assume that such points of view only existed on the enemy's side. Some contemporary British statesmen, notably Lloyd George, blamed Grey's foreign policy for the outbreak of war, and even suggested that Belgium had not been the real reason for Britain's entry into the conflict. Already in the early months of the war, some members of the cabinet discussed in private whether Grey's foreign policy had been responsible for the escalation of the July Crisis, and they continued to do so after 1918.[41]

Lloyd George's *War Memoirs* ensured that Grey's alleged shortcomings were also discussed publicly after the war. They included, in Keith Wilson's words, 'a sustained and vitriolic attack on the persona of Sir Edward Grey and on his handling of British foreign policy throughout the [July] crisis'. In his memoirs, Lloyd George echoed the criticisms raised by Bethmann Hollweg, while acknowledging the difficulties Grey had faced due to the split in the cabinet. His conclusions were damning: 'Had he [Grey] warned Germany in time of the point at which Britain would declare war – and wage it with her whole strength – the issue would have been different.'[42] Lloyd George came to the conclusion that 'Edward Grey is one of the two men primarily responsible for the war'.[43]

In the light of such accusations against Grey's decision-making, the investigation of Britain's role in the origins of the First World War was to attract a number of scholars. Although many British historians were willing to believe Fritz Fischer's thesis of German war aims, there remained the perceived need to investigate Britain's part in the events that had led to war, as James Joll emphasized in an introduction to the English translation of *Griff nach der Weltmacht*:

> Even if Fischer's work reinforces the belief that the German leaders bear the greatest weight of responsibility for the outbreak and prolongation of the First World War, it therefore imposes all the more strongly on British historians the duty of looking again at the record of the British government.[44]

In Britain, historians did not have access to documents in the

Public Record Office until 1967, the same year that Joll's introduction and the English translation of Fischer's first book on the subject was published. The opening of the archives led to a flood of publications on the subject.

Zara Steiner's *Britain and the Origins of the First World War* was one of the first attempts at unravelling British policy in the events that led to war since Albertini's ground-breaking study. According to Steiner, Britain's policy and its 'diplomatic decisions tended to be a response to outward events and external situations', and were not motivated by domestic pressures (such as those resulting from the suffragette movement, from industrial unrest and from the Irish question), in contrast with the view advanced by Fischer and others that in Germany, aggressive and erratic foreign policy was to some extent a reaction to internal pressures and problems. Steiner concludes that Britain had played no active role in bringing about a crisis, and that Britain's policy in 1914 had been reactive and defensive. According to Steiner, Sir Edward Grey had been at pains not to provoke Berlin during July 1914. If his mediation proposals came to nothing this was 'because the Central Powers had other goals in mind'.[45]

The British historian Keith Wilson has defended Grey from his contemporary critics. He describes the 'great pressure' that Grey had been under from the Russians and the French to announce Britain's support for them in case of war and shows that the Russian Foreign Minister Sasonov even went as far as to blackmail Britain via thinly veiled threats directed at the British ambassador Buchanan. Wilson argues that 'a much-needed improvement in Anglo-Russian relations was the main item of business in the British Foreign Office at this time', citing the Anglo-Russian naval negotiations of the summer of 1914 as evidence. According to Wilson, Britain's foreign policy had 'an imperial scale of priorities' in 1914, and 'Grey's personal decision for war cannot be understood and appreciated fully if this background is not taken into account'.[46]

Evidently, outside of Germany, the Fischer debate did not lead to an end of the search for the reasons why war had broken out in 1914. Following the controversy, historians have continued to examine, and to some extent revise, the origins of the war. Since the 1980s, these 'neo-revisionists' focused on Britain's role, arguing that more flexibility on London's part might have avoided the escalation of the crisis into war. According to such interpretations, Germany had not posed any real threat to European security, and Britain's goals of ensuring its own security were clearer than any goals Germany might have had.[47] Thus David Calleo blames not just German aggression, but also the reaction of Germany's neighbours to that challenge:

> Geography and history conspired to make Germany's rise late, rapid, vulnerable and aggressive. The rest of the world reacted by crushing the upstart. If, in the process, the German state lost its bearings and was possessed by an evil demon, perhaps the proper conclusion is not so much that civilization was uniquely weak in Germany, but that it is so fragile everywhere. And perhaps the proper lesson is not so much the need for vigilance against aggressors, but the ruinous consequences of refusing reasonable accommodation to upstarts.[48]

Such arguments have had their share of critics. Donald Kagan is sceptical of these views, and wonders

> what 'accommodation' could the European states have made to the German 'upstart' that would have brought satisfaction to Germany and stability to Europe? [. . .] Wilhelmine Germany was not just another European nation seeking to maintain its national interests or even to advance it by means tolerable to its neighbors. From the early 1890s imperial Germany was a fundamentally dissatisfied power, eager to disrupt the status quo and to achieve its expansive goals, by bullying if possible, by war if necessary.[49]

Other historians, too, have emphasized the attitude of Britain *vis-à-vis* the perceived threat emanating from Germany. Recently, Niall Ferguson has addressed Britain's role and responsibility for the escalation of the July Crisis into war. Ferguson's account shows that Grey was almost in a no-win situation. The nature of the alliance system and what was known of German military strategy made it a foregone conclusion that if Austria, backed by Germany, were to make extreme demands of Serbia, and if Russia came to Serbia's defence, then France, too, would be drawn into the conflict. If Grey deterred Austria and Germany too forcefully, he might be sending signals to France and Russia that Britain would definitely be found on their side in a future war, and might thus encourage their aggression against Germany. Given the importance Britain attached to maintaining a balance of power in continental Europe, Grey was indeed in a tricky situation. According to Ferguson,

> part of Grey's strategy in trying to turn the ententes with France and Russia into quasi-alliances had been to deter Germany from risking war. However, now he feared that too strong a signal of support for France and Russia [...] might encourage the Russians to do just that. He found himself in a cleft stick: how to deter Austria and Germany without encouraging France and Russia.[50]

This is a good summary of Grey's predicament in July 1914. It is worth speculating that Bethmann Hollweg's late mediation proposal to Vienna (following weeks of insistence that no mediation should be entered into) would have been delivered sooner, and more forcefully, if the Chancellor had known earlier of Britain's definite resolve to come to France's aid in a European war. Certainly, this was the implication of Bethmann's statement to Goschen. Ferguson's views echo those of David Calleo, who reiterates early criticisms of Grey and argues that 'a decisive Britain, making clear either its support or non-support, might conceivably have prevented the conflict. To be sure, with the desperation prevailing in Vienna, St. Petersburg, and indeed Berlin, even a resolute Britain might not have smothered the crisis. In any event, Grey procrastinated until the chance was gone.'[51]

Ferguson's view of Grey amounts to a severe indictment of the Foreign Secretary's policy:

> Yet, in his determination to preserve the Entente with France, Grey was willing to make military commitments which made war with Germany more rather than less likely, sooner rather than later. By a completely circular process of reasoning, he wished to commit Britain to a possible war with Germany – because otherwise there might be war with Germany. Appeasement of France and Russia had once made sense; but Grey prolonged the life of the policy well after its rationale had faded.[52]

Grey remains an easy target, much as he was during and after the war, but the charges raised against him require some qualification. It is difficult to see, for example, how the ambivalence of Grey's policy can be seen as the cause of the war compared with the policies pursued by politicians in Berlin and Vienna at the same time. After all, it could be argued that Grey's hesitant attitude was motivated by the desire to *avoid* an escalation of the crisis, while German and Austro-Hungarian decisions were based on the explicit desire to *provoke* a conflict, albeit a localized one, rather than the world war that ensued. And while it is true to say that Bethmann Hollweg's policy in the prewar years and during July 1914 had been based on the hope of British neutrality (despite clear evidence to the contrary), the same cannot be said of Germany's military decision-makers, for whom Britain's entry into the war was of little consequence. The German General Staff was only too happy to have Britain included among Germany's enemies, while Bethmann Hollweg continued to hope for British neutrality.[53] Moreover, the British cabinet was divided in its attitude towards entry into the war, and Grey had been in no position to announce Britain's support of its allies in such a scenario.

An interesting aspect in the debate on British prewar decision-making is the question of why Britain became involved in the European war. Few historians would still maintain that the 'rape of Belgium' was the real motive for Britain's declaration of war on Germany (although ostensibly fighting for the neutrality of Belgium provided the popular motivation for that declaration), and some even argue that 'if Germany had not violated Belgian neutrality in 1914, Britain would have'.[54]

However, disagreement continues over who, in the eyes of Grey and the Foreign Office, ultimately constituted the more frightening future opponent: Germany or Russia. British policy-makers were concerned about the possibility of an overly powerful Russia, especially if Britain decided to stay neutral, and Russia won a war against Germany. The victorious Russian Empire would pose a direct threat to India, which is why the British Foreign Office considered it necessary to maintain good relations with France and Russia, even at the expense of similarly good relations with Germany. In the British Foreign Office, it was believed that 'it would be far more disadvantageous to have an unfriendly France and Russia than an unfriendly Germany'.[55] According to Ferguson, Britain's policy in the years before the First World War had become pro-Russian and anti-German, culminating in secret naval negotiations between Britain and Russia in 1914, of which Germany was well aware. 'All of this makes German fears of encirclement seem less like paranoia than realism', Ferguson contends. Moreover, he argues that the crucial moment at which the course for a conflict between Britain and Germany was set was not the Kaiser's war council of 1912, but a Committee of Imperial Defence meeting of August 1911, in which it was decided that Britain could not afford not to support France actively in a Franco-German conflict: 'It seems, therefore, that in a war between Germany and France in which England takes active part with the French, the result in the opening moves might be doubtful, but the longer the war lasted the greater the strain would be on Germany', recorded the minutes of the meeting. According to Ferguson, this evidence 'turn[s] Fritz Fischer on his head', because it demonstrates Britain's readiness to fight against Germany. However, there is a crucial difference which renders this argument unconvincing and limits the importance of the meeting. It did not lead to a decision to support France come what may, even if France were the aggressor and itself attacked Germany. Yet only if this had been the outcome of the meeting could it be considered comparable in importance to the war council. It is difficult to see how Fischer is turned on his head with this evidence, as critics of Ferguson's position have rightly queried: 'Just how that gathering "set the course for a military confrontation between Britain and Germany" we are left to deduce on our own', criticizes Holger Herwig.[56] The meeting, although doubtless important, seems to have been qualitatively different to that in Berlin in December 1912 in which the participants advocated unleashing a war in the near future.

At the same time, Ferguson judges Grey's fears that Germany might have wanted to break up the Entente and arrive at a separate agreement with France 'preposterous' and 'fantastic'.[57] However, given that this had indeed been the underlying objective behind many German international provocations, such as the First Moroccan Crisis, Ferguson's critics might argue that Grey's fears were actually well-founded.[58]

A further recent critic of Sir Edward Grey's prewar decision-making is John Charmley who, like Ferguson, questions the widely held assumption that Britain's involvement in the war of 1914 had been both inevitable and necessary. To Charmley, 'Grey was a cold warrior in a warm climate', and his policies contributed to some extent to the origins of the war. In contrast to the conclusions reached, for example, by Paul Kennedy, Charmley questions the validity of Grey's 'balance of power' concerns and his commitment to preserving it.[59]

It certainly seems fair to conclude that Grey appears to have misjudged the nature of the July Crisis and, according to Samuel Williamson, he 'failed to appreciate Vienna's desire for war'. Williamson maintains that 'Grey's failure to acknowledge the differences between this crisis and earlier ones constitutes a major failure of perception that severely reduced Britain's ability to manipulate the crisis toward a peaceful solution'. It is difficult to see how Britain might have been able to perceive that difference, given the secrecy that was in place in Vienna and Berlin. As has been demonstrated, historians have advanced forceful arguments indicting Grey's policy in July 1914. However, there still seems to remain a major difference which requires emphasis: while Vienna and Berlin were plotting behind the scenes in July, Britain's leaders were merely reacting to the situation with which they were confronted. Clearly, just as German decision-making should not be seen in isolation, neither should Britain's. Moreover, as Joachim Remak has argued, as far as

> Great Britain's responsibility for the final crisis and the outbreak of hostilities is concerned, it is indisputably less than Germany's. It was units of the German army, not of the British navy, who were sending shells into Belgium. Before the guns had been moved into position, however, it can scarcely be said that the British did much better in restraining the Eastern member of the Triple Entente than they would accuse the Germans of doing vis-à-vis Vienna.[60]

More recently, and in the light of Ferguson's provocative theses, the German historian Stig Förster has concluded that of all the great powers, Britain had the least interest in a general war, while its government could do little to prevent the catastrophe from developing on the continent. However, he concludes that Britain's leaders did not act terribly wisely in dealing with German aggression while trying to preserve a possible escape route for Britain, because this encouraged Berlin's hope for British neutrality.[61]

Förster certainly shares Ferguson's doubts that Britain's entry in the war had been in the country's best interest, given that there was no obligation to become involved. Britain's neighbour and Entente partner France, however, did not have the luxury of deciding for or against the war, as Germany's Schlieffen Plan would automatically embroil France in the fighting. And yet, France's role, too, has come under scrutiny from historians.

France

After Britain, France was the most obvious country to focus on in the post-Fischer debate. After all, there had always been voices (in France, as well as in Germany) which pointed at French *revanche* as a motive for French aggression and blamed France for the outbreak of war. 'Poincaré-la-guerre's' foreign policy had been the subject of particular scrutiny in the immediate postwar years. Had the French president plotted with his Russian allies in July 1914? Had Fischer been wrong in concentrating too much on Germany to the exclusion of other countries, such as France, whose prewar policy had been decidedly anti-German? John Keiger explains the nature of the allegations which have been made against French policies, and in particular against Poincaré's role in the July Crisis.

> France was an excellent scapegoat on to whom the blame could be shifted. Because in a war with Germany in 1870 she had lost the two provinces of Alsace-Lorraine, it was suggested that for virtually the next half-century she had prepared for a war of *revanche* against Germany to regain the lost territories. Because from 1912 France's new leader, Raymond Poincaré, who was a Lorrainer into the bargain, was determined to apply resolute policies and to strengthen the links with France's allies, particularly with Russia, it was suggested that he plotted a war of *revanche* against Germany. [. . .] Poincaré was charged with having encouraged Russia to begin the conflict. The idea of 'Poincaré-la-guerre' gained currency. It was picked up and used for all ends. In France it was put to political use when Poincaré's political opponents wished to stop him returning to power in 1926. In the end when the argument subsided, because facts had been manipulated and evidence distorted, inevitably confusion had resulted and some of the mud had stuck.[62]

Keiger's investigation of France's role in the origins of the First

World War suggests, however, that the allegations against Poincaré, raised among others by Albertini and Jules Isaac,[63] were largely unfair and unfounded. Poincaré had not urged the Russians to go to war during his visit to St Petersburg in July 1914, or once he had returned to Paris, Keiger concludes. Other historians have come to different conclusions about Poincaré's role. Gerd Krumeich's study of French armament policy before the First World War indicates that Poincaré had given strong support to the Russian ally because he feared that to give in to German pressure would lead to a split of the Entente. Although Krumeich sees Poincaré as a more active player than Keiger, he does not advocate the revisionist line of the interwar years. Rather, he contends that, ultimately, French decisions were motivated by 'years of fear of Germany's world-wide aspirations and aggression'.[64]

In a more recent study of the French Quai d'Orsay, M.B. Hayne concludes that Poincaré's actions in 1914 had essentially been defensive: 'Though Poincaré may have contributed to the coming of the First World War, the myth that he consciously conspired for or desired the war needs to be dismissed.' However, Hayne does not absolve all French decision-makers completely from blame. Rather, he attributes responsibility to the 'aggressive policies' of the French ambassador in St Petersburg, Maurice Paléologue. Hayne claims that his documentary evidence 'implicates the Ambassador substantially in the responsibility for the onset of war'. While the government in Paris was trying to avoid an escalation of the crisis, Paléologue, in St Petersburg, had established an 'ambassadorial dictatorship', and failed to inform Paris of events in the Russian capital. Moreover,

> without the consent of his government, Paléologue extended explicit support to Sazonov, the Russian foreign minister. His assurances actively encouraged the Russians to adopt a bellicose attitude, and thereby made an important contribution to the outbreak of a general war. It is difficult to envisage St Petersburg risking such a conflict without the support of Paléologue, who claimed to be acting in the name of France.[65]

Paléologue exaggerated German belligerence and Russia's desire for moderation during the last days of July, and had deliberately 'distorted, omitted, and delayed the transmission of essential information about Russian affairs'.[66] Despite such a strong indictment, however, Hayne is not convinced by the allegation, advanced for example by L.C.F. Turner, that Paléologue had conspired with the French military to bring about the war. Moreover, he claims that it would be wrong to see the ambassador 'as a mere warmonger. He was deeply suspicious of Germany and convinced that war was unavoidable. His patriotism was undeniable. Unfortunately, it encouraged him to follow an extreme course which, whatever Germany's motives, did much to prevent a peaceful resolution of the July crisis'.[67]

In contrast, Krumeich explains French foreign policy in the context of domestic political tensions which had forced Poincaré to accept René Viviani as premier, a man who differed in opinion to Poincaré, for example regarding the new law to increase military service to three years. Paléologue withheld information not because he was unsure of Poincaré, as Hayne's account might suggest, but because he feared Viviani's reaction might be more peaceable than his own, given that the premier supported Grey's mediation proposals. Where Keiger sees Viviani as Poincaré's puppet, Krumeich identifies him as an important personality who impeded Poincaré's decision-making. According to Krumeich Poincaré was a firm supporter of Russia's actions in July 1914 who was willing, like his allies in St Petersburg, to call Germany's bluff. Krumeich is not alone in arguing that French fear of Germany was due to German actions. Dominic Lieven, for example, maintains that 'if [. . .] in the three years prior to 1914 Paris did begin to view German action even outside its own sphere of interest as an overall threat to the balance of power and French security the chief blame for this must lie on Germany's own unnecessarily clumsy and aggressive diplomacy'.[68] Similarly, Joachim Remak asserts that 'the nation that can be held least responsible for the outbreak of the war is France. This is true even if we bear in mind all the revisions of historical judgements, and all the revisions of these revisions [. . .]. And it is so even if we use Fischer's approach, and ask ourselves just what the aims of France were, in the years that preceded the war and after'.[69] Although Remak concedes that French politics were motivated by the desire 'to undo the decision of Frankfurt' (the peace agreement following the Franco-Prussian war of 1870–71 in which France lost the provinces of Alsace and Lorraine), he emphasizes the restraints that France put upon itself, and how 'tentative and cautious the bid to recover the lost provinces was'. France did not go to war in 1914 to reclaim Alsace and Lorraine, but because Germany began a march on Paris.[70]

For all their differences, studies of French prewar policy reveal a strong anti-German attitude at the Quai d'Orsay, and a keen desire to stand by the Russian ally against German aggression. Certain parallels emerge between German and French decision-makers: while Paléologue was motivated by 'the deepest pessimism about relations between the powers and the conclusion that Germany was determined to unleash a major conflagration in the future',[71] the same fear of an uncertain future in which Germany would be at the mercy of its hostile neighbours motivated Bethmann Hollweg's decision-making during the July Crisis. Both were convinced that a war would be unavoidable in the near future. For both, Russia's attitude in the Balkan crisis which began with the assassination of Franz Ferdinand was crucial.

Russia

Of course, historians have also concentrated on Russia, the other great power to get embroiled in the war in 1914. Russia's role in the July Crisis is an obvious topic of investigation in the debate on the origins of the war, given that German propaganda during and after the war claimed that the Russian mobilization had made further diplomatic attempts at a peaceful solution to the July Crisis impossible. Dominic

Lieven has investigated just how important the general mobilization of the Russian army on 31 July had been.

> At first glance it would seem to have been crucial since Russia's move was answered immediately by Germany's mobilization and within two days by the outbreak of war. Even without the Russian mobilization there is, however, every reason to doubt whether by 30 July a European conflict could still have been avoided since, as Russian diplomats stressed, by then Austria and Germany had gone too far to retreat without serious damage to their prestige and to the stability of their alliance.[72]

What is more, evidence from the German archives confirms that Germany had decided on its own mobilization regardless of Russia's actions – it was only a stroke of luck that Russia's general mobilization was announced in time to make Germany's own military measures *appear* as a reaction to Russia's. This was another way in which Germany's decision-makers had attempted to give the impression of being attacked and to put the blame for the outbreak of the war on Russia.[73]

The role of the Franco-Russian alliance has also been investigated in this context. In many ways, Dominic Lieven has argued, the alliance was 'a logical consequence of the war of 1870–71', and insured France against further German aggression by ending its isolation. But what did it mean for Russia?

> Above all the alliance committed Russia to the defence of the European balance of power in the face of Germany's increasing might. Should Berlin seek to turn France into a German satellite by the use of force Russia would intervene. Russia thus denied Germany a free hand in Western Europe, just as the Dual Alliance of 1879 had signified Berlin's refusal to accept any Russian threat to the independence or existence of the Habsburg Monarchy. Though defensive, the alliance with France had its dangers for Petersburg.[74]

Lieven's investigation, *Russia and the Origins of the First World*

War, begins from the post-Fischer premise that 'in July 1914 Germany's rulers took most of the vital decisions which led to war and that in so doing they were in part guided by fears not only of the rapid growth of Russian military power but also of the effects that present and future political developments might have on its use'. While Lieven concludes that Germany's fears in this area were exaggerated, nonetheless he asserts that there was some justification for them. Russia was building a large navy similar to Tirpitz's German one, and the Russian army was increasingly rapidly in quantity and quality. 'Moreover, if German panic at the Russian menace was exaggerated it was scarcely more so than the perpetual British alarm about the Russian threat to India.'[75]

While adding an extra dimension to Fischer's German-centred point of view, such as pointing to the importance of the decision to support Serbia, even at the risk of war, taken by the Council of Ministers on 24/25 July, Lieven's findings nonetheless concur with Fischer's conclusions: 'Study of the July Crisis from the Russian standpoint indeed confirms the now generally accepted view that the major immediate responsibility for the outbreak of the war rested unequivocally on the German government.'[76] And yet, according to Keith Neilson, Russia played an important part in the events that led to war: 'While being far from willing war to occur, the Russian government was prepared, in light of the changes that had occurred in the five years since the Bosnian humiliation, to risk a conflict rather than abdicate its position as a Great Power.'[77]

Russia's role as protector of the Slavs has also been blamed for the escalation of the crisis. Certainly Russia made no secret of its intention to support Serbia in the July Crisis. Did Russia have any prior knowledge of the conspiracy behind the assassination of Franz Ferdinand, as has sometimes been presumed? Lieven has found no evidence for such a claim and denies any such involvement. Did Russia encourage Serbia to adopt a hard-line stance in response to the Austro-Hungarian ultimatum, as has sometimes been mooted? Samuel Williamson argues that on the basis of Serbian documents it can definitely be ruled out that Russia had encouraged Serbia to resist. The evidence reveals that 'Serbia had no intention of accepting any Habsburg ultimatum that infringed in the slightest on Serbian sovereignty', although Williamson concedes that 'in taking this stance, Pašić and his colleagues were obviously confident of Russian help'.[78]

Serbia

This leads us to the question of Serbia's role in the crisis. After all, it was the assassination of Franz Ferdinand by a Serbian-led terrorist that provided the trigger for war, and the First World War began with Austria-Hungary's declaration of war on Serbia. Austria-Hungary's decision-makers were convinced of the Serbian government's complicity in the assassination of the Archduke by a Bosnian Serb, although proof that some of them (although by no means the entire government) knew of the planned act of terrorism was not actually obtained until 1917 during the so-called Saloniki trial.[79]

In analysing Serbian decision-making during the July Crisis, Mark Cornwall argues that Belgrade's role was more decisive than historians have usually been willing to concede. When Austria-Hungary declared war on Serbia on 28 July, a period of uncertainty was finally coming to an end for the Belgrade government.

> The evidence suggests that during the previous month Serbia was far more independent and obstinate than historians have previously imagined. [. . .] Above all, Serbia throughout July 1914 was prepared to refuse Austrian demands incompatible with its status as a sovereign and 'civilized' state and, like the Great Powers, it would even risk war at this time to defend its status. This obstinacy stemmed partly from Serbia's new confidence after its expansion in the Balkan Wars [. . .]. As a result the government produced (from its own point of view) a very conciliatory reply, but one still hedged with reservations and still resistant over the vital points: despite Serbia's military

> weakness and near-isolation diplomatically, the kingdom was prepared on 25 July to run the risk of a localized war with Austria-Hungary. [. . .] By the end of July 1914, Pašić [Serbia's Prime Minister and Foreign Minister] knew that if Greater Serbia materialized, it would be out of the fires of a full European war. Serbia itself had helped to create this war because during the July crisis it was not prepared to return to the status of an Austro-Hungarian satellite.[80]

Joachim Remak focuses on the Austro-Serbian confrontation during the July Crisis and concludes from his findings that the war that broke out in 1914 was in many ways a 'third Balkan War'. Serbia played an important part in this crisis. 'Had Belgrade not been bidding for a Greater Serbia, there could have been a way out even after the Austrian ultimatum. Pašić, in that case, could have upset all of Austria's plans by accepting the ultimatum *in toto*.'[81] According to Remak, Serbia's leaders were willing to risk a conflagration because they hoped that, with Russia's help, a war against Austria could be won.

> The pursuit of Serbia's aims was worth a war with Austria. And if that should activate Europe's alliances, and bring about an Austro-German-Serbian-Russian-French war, so be it. No fears of international complications, after all, had been capable of forestalling two earlier Balkan Wars. Turkey was dying and now Austria was. 1914–1918 was the longest but by no means the only war of the Turkish succession. It was the Third Balkan War.[82]

As Manfried Rauchensteiner shows, the Serbian government was not in a conciliatory mood, and the carefully phrased answer to Vienna's ultimatum, while designed to gain the approval of the other European governments, did not amount to an unconditional acceptance of the demands made of Belgrade. That the Serbian government was clearly aware of the implications of its reply is evident from the fact that Serbia began its mobilization measures hours before delivering the answer to Austria's ultimatum.[83]

In summary, all these investigations into the role of Europe's governments in the prewar years share a common approach – to investigate the origins of the war not from the point of view of Germany's actions, but to focus instead on the other protagonists who were involved in the crisis. Examining the events which led to war from different perspectives has added new dimensions to the debate. Decisions were not just made in Germany; the men who controlled Europe's destiny were not just Bethmann Hollweg and Moltke, but they included Berchtold and Conrad, Grey, Poincaré, Paléologue, Sazonov and Pašić, to name but a few. Such interpretations have suggested that Fischer's narrow focus on Germany tells only a part of the story, albeit an important one or even, as some would argue, the most important one. The comparative perspective of these studies provides an insight into 'a world of international politics at once more complicated, more interactive and less unilateral than the Fischer view would permit or encourage'.[84] Most studies do, however, arrive at the conclusion that while some degree of blame attaches to other governments, it is not distributed equally, but that the main share of responsibility clearly lay with the decisions which were made in Germany.

The debate at the end of the twentieth century

The 'Fischer controversy' overturned the orthodoxy of the 1950s without any one view replacing it. David Stevenson[85]

At the end of this investigation, it might seem as if historians have analysed every possible angle and have advanced every plausible, and indeed some implausible, theories regarding the origins of the war. Can there be anything left to argue about? Surely, historians have arrived at a consensus which most can accept? As Stig Förster notes in a recent account of the origins of the war, it is now possible to approach an investigation of the events that led to war with less political baggage. But this does not mean that the general interest in the topic has abated. On the contrary, Förster detects an international trend of intensified discussion of the First World War as a whole, while key questions, particularly in view of the war's origins, remain unresolved despite all efforts.[86]

According to Förster, there is today hardly a serious historian who would dare to appear as an apologist for German policy prior to August 1914. Even such former critics of Fischer's views as, for example, Klaus Hildebrand have taken on board critical views of Imperial Germany's foreign policy, and their publications ensure that these views are no longer contentious or marginal.[87]

And yet, every new publication on the subject of the origins of the war is potentially full of surprises. In a recent book entitled *How the First World War Began: The Triple Entente and the Coming of the Great War of 1914–1918*, Edward McCullough asserts that 'Germany and Austria fought to maintain the status quo, while France and Russia fought to change it'. According to McCullough, German historians who conclude that Germany bore the main share of responsibility for the outbreak of war are motivated by some skewed desire to punish themselves:

> Germans of the Fritz Fischer school are impelled by the need to find a scapegoat for the disasters which overtook Germany, and the imperial government is readily available. As they no doubt realize that Germany had no way to escape being crushed by the Triple Entente once it came into being, they must make Germany responsible for its creation and for her own isolation.[88]

Not many historians today would support McCullough's conspiracy theory and argue that the Entente was to blame for the outbreak of war, while Germany and Austria-Hungary were innocent in the events that led from international crisis to European war. Indeed, this account is somewhat out of touch with the current state of scholarship about the causes and nature of the First World War (as its bibliography reveals). And yet, it demonstrates the way in which it is still possible, albeit with selective use of evidence, to advance such an extreme revisionist argument and that, for whatever reasons, some historians still feel compelled to do so.

However, while it is clear that there is still no general and final agreement on the reasons for the outbreak of war in 1914, we can nonetheless conclude that there is, indeed, some sort of consensus among most specialists at the end of decades of controversy. Many historians have moved to different areas of enquiry. The debate over the primacy of domestic or foreign policy is no longer of major concern to historians, and the interests in studying the war itself have shifted away from a quest for the attribution of national guilt towards structural argumentation. In the 1970s, pioneering studies on social and economic aspects of the war were undertaken (for example, by Gerald D. Feldman and Jürgen Kocka), while East German historians (such as Fritz Klein and Willibald Gutsche) highlighted the role of industry and the banks. By the 1980s, individual decision-makers began to return to the historical stage and their actions have once again become the subject of historians' scrutiny. At the other extreme, historians have reacted to criticisms that for too long, the history of the war has been written without due consideration of the people who fought in it, and died in it. As a result, historians have begun to investigate, for example, military history 'from below' (W. Wette), while the history of everyday life (*Alltagsgeschichte*) and cultural history became new focal points for historical investigation and have shaped the way the First World War is studied today. Historians have concentrated on studying the mentalities of groups or classes in society, and have managed to reveal a certain 'war mentality' among parts of the population of Europe. They have shown that without some readiness or even expectation of going to war among the people of Europe as well as among their leaders, war could not have broken out in 1914. In addition, historians have concentrated on examining the experience of 'ordinary soldiers' and of civilians in the years 1914–18, have focused on issues of remembrance and commemoration, and have revisited old common assumptions and myths around the war, such as the alleged enthusiasm for war among the European population in August 1914 (the so-called *Augusterlebnis*).[89] Today it is no longer possible to write the history of the First World War convincingly without taking on board these new approaches, which have thrown new light not just on the conduct of war, but also on its outbreak.[90]

However, historians have also continued to return to the origins of the First World War, and the topic has gained renewed significance since the late 1980s, when the re-emergence of troubles in the Balkans meant that European history seemed set to repeat itself. As Gregor Schöllgen explains, 'at a time which has experienced even the return of conventionally conducted war into the heart of Europe, the question whether the escalation of the summer of 1914 was unavoidable poses itself more urgently than before'.[91]

As to the war's origins, writing in 1999, Matthew Seligmann and Roderick McLean are confident that the debate is largely settled and that the attempts by recent apologists to shift the blame away from Germany have failed to make their mark:

> Although some of Fischer's views remain controversial, few historians would dispute the fact that Germany was more willing than virtually any other power to risk war in 1914. An attempt by neo-conservative German historians [such as Gregor Schöllgen] to revive the idea that German policy was essentially defensive has failed to undermine the new orthodoxy.[92]

Similarly, as we have seen, Stig Förster's most recent account stresses that no serious historian today could be an apologist for German policy prior to August 1914. He places great emphasis on Bethmann Hollweg and considers it 'a fact that Bethmann did not shy away from the risk of war during the July Crisis'. However, crucially, Förster argues that Bethmann had no concrete war aims other than the destruction of the Entente – a clear difference to Fischer's controversial theses about Bethmann's aggressive war aims. Förster argues that both Bethmann and the Chief of the General Staff Moltke dreaded the war they had previously wanted when the conflict finally became unavoidable. It is this very ambivalence, according to Förster, that gives the origins of the war aspects of absurdity. What makes the origins so difficult to fathom is precisely that 'the men who finally brought about the war moved in a realm of the absurd'. The question as to the real motives of these leaders can perhaps never be answered completely. Evidence of the absurdity of decision-making in the prewar capitals is also provided by recent studies of Europe's military leaders. Publications on the Prussian Minister of War Erich von Falkenhayn, the German Chief of the General Staff Helmuth von Moltke, and the Austro-Hungarian Chief of Staff Franz Conrad von Hötzendorf have demonstrated the degree to which these military leaders desired a war, but equally dreaded its outbreak. Falkenhayn's statement: 'Even if we perish over this, at least it was fun' of 4 August, Moltke's assertions that 'we are ready, the sooner the better for us', and Conrad's frequently expressed regret that the Dual Monarchy had missed previous opportunities for a reckoning with Serbia all have to be seen in this context.[93]

In the final analysis, Förster concludes that the leadership in Vienna and St Petersburg seem to have wanted the war, but they would have been unable to achieve their aims if Germany's policy had not escalated the July Crisis. Förster also makes an important point which is all too easily overlooked and is worth re-emphasizing at the end of this investigation into the origins of the First World War: whatever Germany's decision-makers aimed to achieve in 1914, it is not true to say that the majority of Germans wanted war. Not only were they not asked, but they were also systematically lied to, something that is also true of the other great powers, who all claimed to be fighting a defensive war in 1914.[94]

If this is the most recent consensus view, nonetheless apologetic views continue to be put forward, and there are still commentators who refuse to acknowledge Germany's large share of responsibility for the events that led to war. Thus, just when the German historical establishment has begun to accept the conclusions which result from Fischer's pioneering findings as much as from the victors' ruling at Versailles, other voices within Germany and elsewhere are still willing to dispute these conclusions. As recently as July 2001, the German conservative newspaper *Frankfurter Allgemeine Zeitung* took issue with a speech delivered by the German Chancellor Gerhard Schröder on the occasion of the opening of an exhibition on the history of the Federal Republic, when he talked of the 'unimaginable crimes of National Socialism' and the two world wars of the twentieth century which had been begun (*angezettelt*) by Germans. The *Frankfurter Allgemeine Zeitung* disagrees: 'The political thesis of sole responsibility of Germany for the First World War is, however, scholarly untenable: the main guilty [parties] in 1914 sat in Berlin, Vienna and St Petersburg. Schröder's grasp for Versailles was a historical mistake.'[95]

Given such continuing disagreements and differing agendas, there is no telling how the debate on the origins of the war will develop in the twenty-first century. We are almost sufficiently far removed from the event for there to be no eyewitnesses left to tell the tale. The First World War, one of the most emotive topics of modern history, will soon no longer be part of anyone's personal history. Apologists may find it easier in time to play down the importance of the question of the origins of the war, and perhaps it will indeed cease to be of particular importance, although its lessons, real or imagined, will no doubt continue to influence the way in which we react to international crises in the years following the Cold War. The controversy will no doubt remain interesting for historians, who may continue to unearth documents in their quest to understand the decisions made in July 1914 and, given that apologetic accounts continue to be published, there will remain enough contentious history for academics to debate. Potentially, revisionists can continue to revise what they consider to be the orthodox view. Ultimately, however, they will find it difficult to argue with the underlying consensus that has developed as a result of Fischer's once so controversial claims.

Notes

1 Gregor Schöllgen, *Escape into War? The Foreign Policy of Imperial Germany*, Oxford 1990, p. 4.
2 Stevenson, *The Outbreak of the First World War*, p. 12.
3 An English translation of the article, published in the *Frankfurter Allgemeine Zeitung* on 8 July 1982, and a reply by the author to a critique of his argument by Fischer can be found in Koch (ed.), *The Origins of the First World War*, pp. 371–85.
4 In April 1980, the weekly journal *Der Spiegel* devoted a cover story to the perceived parallels between the events of July and August 1914, and the conflict between China and Vietnam in 1979–80, the crisis in Iran, the Soviet invasion of Afghanistan and the naval operations of the two superpowers in the Indian Ocean, and juxtaposed images of the war of 1914 with description of current international tensions. 'Like in August 1914? Fear of the Great War', *Der Spiegel*, 21 Apr. 1980.
5 Klaus Hildebrand, 'Saturiertheit und Prestige: Das Deutsche Reich als Staat im Staatensystem 1871–1918', *Geschichte in Wissenschaft und Unterricht*, 1989/4, pp. 193–202, citations pp. 199/200. The same argument was repeated in 1994: 'Germany took on the initiating responsibility for the outbreak of the First World War, without however carrying the sole guilt.' Hildebrand, 'Reich-Großmacht-Nation: Betrachtungen zur Geschichte der deutschen Aussenpolitik 1871–1918', *Historische Zeitschrift*, 259, 1994, pp. 369–89, citation p. 379.
6 Hildebrand, 'Der deutsche Eigenweg: Über das Problem der Normalität in der modernen Geschichte Deutschlands', in M. Funke et al. (eds), *Demokratie und Diktatur: Geist und Gestalt politischer Herrschaft in Deutschland und Europa*, Festschrift für Karl Dietrich Bracher, Düsseldorf 1987, pp. 17, 21.
7 Gregor Schöllgen, '"Fischer Kontroverse" und Kontinuitätsproblem: Deutsche Kriegsziele im Zeitalter der Weltkriege', in Andreas Hillgruber and Jost Dülffer (eds), *Ploetz: Geschichte der Weltkriege*, Freiburg and Würzburg 1981, pp. 174ff.
8 Schöllgen (ed.), *Escape into War?*, p. 4; Hillgruber, 'Riezlers Theorie des kalkulierten Risikos und Bethmann Hollwegs politische Konzeption in der Julikrise 1914' in idem, *Deutsche Grossmacht- und Weltpolitik im 19. und 20. Jahrhundert*, Düsseldorf 1977, p. 92.
9 Gregor Schöllgen, 'Germany's Foreign Policy in the Age of Imperialism: A Vicious Circle?', in idem (ed.), *Escape into War?*, p. 121. Interestingly, Ludwig Dehio argued along virtually the same lines in the 1950s.

10 Schöllgen (ed.), *Escape into War?*, p. 125/p. 133, original italics.

11 Michael Stürmer, 'A Nation-State against History and Geography', in Schöllgen (ed.), *Escape into War?*, pp. 64/5. Stürmer's *Das Ruhelose Reich: Deutschland 1866–1918*, Berlin 1983, in which Stürmer refers to Germany as the 'powerful state (*Machtstaat*) in the middle', was the stimulus to wider discussions of the problem of geopolitics. See also Klaus Hildebrand, 'Staatskunst oder Systemzwang? Die "Deutsche Frage" als Problem der Weltpolitik', *Historische Zeitschrift*, 228, 1979, pp. 624ff.; idem, 'Der deutsche Eigenweg', pp. 15–34.

12 Hans-Ulrich Wehler, 'Sonderweg aus der "Sonderlage"?: Die Wiederentdeckung der "deutschen Mittellage" in Wissenschaft und Publizistik', in Landeszentrale für politische Bildung Nordrhein-Westfalen (ed.), *Streitfall Deutsche Geschichte: Geschichts- und Gegenwartsbewußtsein in den 80er Jahren*, Essen 1988, pp. 87ff.

13 Retallack, *Germany in the Age of Kaiser Wilhelm II*, p. 74. For a strong critique of the geopolitical explanation, see Helmut Böhme, '"Primat" und "Paradigmata": Zur Entwicklung einer bundesdeutschen Zeitgeschichtsschreibung am Beispiel des Ersten Weltkrieges', in Hartmut Lehman (ed.), *Historikerkontroversen*, Göttingen 2000, pp. 89–139.

14 Ibid., p. 136.

15 Ibid., p. 135.

16 Retallack, *Germany in the Age of Kaiser Wilhelm II*, p. 74. For the historical background to the shift in the debate, see particularly Böhme, '"Primat" und "Paradigmata"', pp. 135–6.

17 Mary Fulbrook, 'Dividing the Past, Defining the Present: Historians and National Identity in the Two Germanies', in Stefan Berger et al. (eds), *Writing National Histories: Western Europe since 1800*, London 1999, p. 221.

18 Although the debates were about different topics, essentially they were about the same thing – the attempt by some historians to 'rescue' German history by way of a more favourable interpretation of the country's recent past, and to draw a final line under the National Socialist history that 'would not pass'. The *Historikerstreit* began with an attack by Jürgen Habermas on the 'apologetic tendencies' in German history writing, and the debate was carried out in the national press, much like the Fischer controversy twenty years previously. Essentially, historians in the 1980s argued over the 'unique' nature of National Socialist atrocities or their alleged 'relativization' by historians who claimed that Soviet atrocities had not only preceded those of the Nazis, but that the Nazis had acted in response to them. Key texts on the *Historikerstreit* are reprinted in *Historikerstreit: Die Dokumentation der Kontroverse und die Einzigartigkeit der nationalsozialistischen Judenvernichtung*, Munich

1987, Engl. transl. by James Knowlton and Truett Cates, *Forever in the Shadow of Hitler?*, New Jersey 1993. Mary Fulbrook traces the origins and nature of the *Historikerstreit* in *German National Identity after the Holocaust*, Oxford and Cambridge 1999, pp. 118–29. See also Peter Baldwin (ed.), *Reworking the Past: Hitler, the Holocaust and the Historians' Dispute*, Boston 1990.

19 Miles Kahler, 'Rumours of War: The 1914 Analogy', *Foreign Affairs*, 2, 1979–80, pp. 374–96, p. 391.

20 Klaus Bruckmann, 'Erster Weltkrieg – Ursachen, Kriegsziele, Kriegsschuld: Fritz Fischers Thesen in deutschen Schulgeschichtsbüchern', *Geschichte in Wissenschaft und Unterricht*, 10, 1981, pp. 600–17, quote on p. 607.

21 Kahler, 'Rumors of War', p. 375.

22 See, for example, Kennedy, *The Rise of Anglo-German Antagonism*; David E. Kaiser, 'Germany and the Origins of the First World War', *Journal of Modern History*, 55/3, 1983; *Der Spiegel*, 21 Apr. 1980.

23 Williamson (ed.), *The Origins of a Tragedy*, p. v.

24 Geoffrey Barraclough, *From Agadir to Armageddon: Anatomy of a Crisis*, London 1982, pp. 180–1.

25 Stevenson, *The Outbreak of the First World War*, p. 1.

26 S.R. Williamson, Jr., 'The Origins of World War I', *Journal of Interdisciplinary History*, xviii/4, 1988, pp. 795–818, p. 796.

27 Albertini, *The Origins of the War*, vol. 2, p. 148.

28 Langdon, *The Long Debate*, p. 155.

29 Williamson, 'The Origins of World War I', pp. 795–818.

30 Williamson, *Austria-Hungary and the Origins of the First World War*, p. 215. For similar views, idem, 'Vienna and July 1914: The Origins of the Great War Once More', in S.R. Williamson, Jr. and Peter Pastor (eds), *Essays on World War I*, New York 1983.

31 R.J.W. Evans, 'The Habsburg Monarchy and the Coming of War', in Evans and Pogge von Strandmann (eds), *The Coming of the First World War*, citations on pp. 34/37.

32 Fritz Fellner, 'Die "Mission Hoyos"', in Wilhelm Alf (ed.), *Deutschlands Sonderung von Europa 1862–1945*, Frankfurt 1984, pp. 283–316; idem, 'Austria-Hungary', in Wilson (ed.), *Decisions for War*, citation p. 11.

33 John Leslie, 'The Antecedents of Austria-Hungary's War Aims', *Wiener Beiträge zur Geschichte der Neuzeit*, vol. 20, 1993, pp. 307–94, p. 309.

34 Ibid., pp. 131/318.

35 Williamson, 'The Origins of World War I', p. 815.

36 Fellner, 'Austria-Hungary', pp. 19/21/23.

37 Holger Herwig, *The First World War: Germany and Austria-Hungary, 1914–1918*, London and New York 1997, p. 18.

38 Ibid., pp. 11–12.

39 G. Kronenbitter, 'Bundesgenossen? Zur militärischen Kooperation zwischen Berlin und Wien 1912–1914', in Walther L. Bernecker and Volker Dotterweich (eds), *Deutschland in den internationalen Beziehungen des 19. und 20. Jahrhunderts: Festschrift für Josef Becker zum 65. Geburtstag*, Munich 1996, p. 165. See also Kronenbitter, 'Falsch verbunden? Die Militärallianz zwischen Österreich-Ungarn und Deutschland, 1906–1914', *Österreichische Militärische Zeitschrift*, 38, 2000, 6, pp. 743–54; idem, '"Nur los lassen": Österreich-Ungarn und der Wille zum Krieg', in Johannes Burkhardt et al. (eds), *Lange und kurze Wege in den Ersten Weltkrieg*, Munich 1996, pp. 159–87. For an interpretation of Austria-Hungary's policies before 1914, see, for example, Mark Cornwall (ed.), *The Last Years of Austria–Hungary: Essays in Political and Military History, 1908–1918*, Exeter 1990, particularly ch. 1: F.R. Bridge, 'The Foreign Policy of the Monarchy, 1908–1918', pp. 7–30; F.R. Bridge, *From Sadowa to Sarajevo: The Foreign Policy of Austria-Hungary, 1866–1914*, London 1972.

40 Bethmann Hollweg, *Betrachtungen zum Weltkriege.*

41 For a discussion of the criticism raised against Grey during and after the war see Wilson, 'Britain', in idem (ed.), *Decisions for War*, pp. 175ff.

42 Cited ibid., p. 175.

43 Cited in John Charmley, *Splendid Isolation? Britain and the Balance of Power 1874–1914*, London 1999, p. 331.

44 James Joll's introduction to Fritz Fischer, *Germany's Aims in the First World War*, pp. xv–xvi. See also Pogge von Strandmann, 'Britische Historiker und der Ausbruch des Ersten Weltkrieges', p. 941.

45 Zara Steiner, *Britain and the Origins of the First World War*, New York 1977, pp. 248/224 (a second, revised edition is forthcoming, London 2002). See also Langdon, *The Long Debate*, pp. 152–4 and S.R. Williamson, Jr., 'The Reign of Sir Edward Grey as British Foreign Secretary', *International History Review*, 1, 1979, pp. 426–38 for a summary and evaluation of Steiner's views.

46 Citations in Wilson, 'Britain', pp. 184–6.

47 Donald Kagan, *On the Origins of Wars and the Preservation of Peace*, London 1995, p. 205. See also Kahler, 'Rumours of War', pp. 374–96; Steven E. Miller, *Military Strategy and the Origins of the First World War*, Princeton 1985; Barraclough, *From Agadir to Armageddon.*

48 David Calleo, *The German Problem Reconsidered*, Cambridge, Mass. 1978, p. 6. See also Kagan, *On the Origins of Wars*, p. 206.

49 Ibid., pp. 206/209.

50 Niall Ferguson, *Pity of War*, London 1998, p. 155.

51 Calleo, *The German Problem Reconsidered*, p. 34.

52 Ferguson, *Pity of War*, p. 73.

53 See Mombauer, *Helmuth von Moltke*, e.g. pp. 109, 116, 210.

54 Ferguson, *Pity of War*, p. 67.

55 Cited in Wilson, *The Policy of the Entente*, p. 78. For a similar argument, see also Lahme, 'Das Ende der Pax Britannica', p. 190.
56 Holger H. Herwig, Review of *Pity of War, Journal of Modern History*, vol. 72, No. 3, Sept. 2000, p. 774.
57 Ferguson, *Pity of War*, pp. 64–73. For a similar argument see Wilson, *The Policy of the Entente.*
58 See e.g. Stig Förster, who argues that Ferguson underestimated the aggressive potential of German policy before 1914. 'Im Reich des Absurden: Die Ursachen des Ersten Weltkrieges', in Bernd Wegner (ed.), *Wie Kriege entstehen: Zum historischen Hintergrund von Staatenkonflikten*, Paderborn, Munich, Vienna and Zurich 2000, pp. 211–52, p. 217.
59 Charmley, *Splendid Isolation?*, pp. 1, 6.
60 Remak, '1914 – The Third Balkan War', p. 14.
61 Förster, 'Im Reich des Absurden', p. 247.
62 John Keiger, *France and the Origins of the First World War*, London 1983, pp. 1–2. For a more detailed account of the Poincaré-la-guerre myth, see Keiger's biography *Poincaré*, pp. 193ff.
63 Jules Isaac, *Un débat historique: 1914, le problème des origines de la guerre*, Paris 1933.
64 Gerd Krumeich, *Armaments and Politics in France on the Eve of the First World War: The Introduction of the Three-Year Conscription, 1913–1914*, Leamington Spa 1984 (Engl. translation of *Aufrüstung und Innenpolitik in Frankreich vor dem Ersten Weltkrieg*, Wiesbaden 1980), pp. 228–9. See also Langdon, *The Long Debate*, on Keiger and Krumeich, pp. 165–71. On the revisionist anti-Poincaré arguments of the interwar years see above, Part 2.
65 M.B. Hayne, *The French Foreign Office and the Origins of the First World War, 1898–1914*, Oxford 1993, citations on pp. 2, 269.
66 Ibid., pp. 273, 281.
67 Ibid., p. 310. For a different evaluation of Paléologue see Dominic C.B. Lieven, *Russia and the Origins of the First World War*, London 1983, p. 141: 'one can only assume that the ambassador's self-confidently vigorous line echoed the approach taken by his country's leaders in the previous week', and that it was in keeping with French policy during the previous 18 months.
68 Lieven, *Russia and the Origins*, p. 27.
69 Remak, '1914 – The Third Balkan War', p. 11.
70 Ibid., p. 12.
71 Hayne, *The French Foreign Office*, p. 294.
72 Lieven, *Russia and the Origins*, pp. 151.
73 See Mombauer, *Helmuth von Moltke*, pp. 199ff. Details of Russia's mobilization in Stephen J. Cimbala, 'Steering Through Rapids: Russian Mobilization and World War I', *Journal of Slavic Military History*, 9/2, 1996, pp. 376–98.

74 Lieven, *Russia and the Origins*, pp. 24, 26.
75 Ibid., p. 136.
76 Ibid., p. 151.
77 Keith Neilson, 'Russia', in Wilson (ed.), *Decisions for War*, p. 112.
78 Williamson, 'The Origins of World War I', p. 811. For a similar view, see Manfried Rauchensteiner, *Der Tod des Doppeladlers: Österreich-Ungarn und der Erste Weltkrieg*, Graz, Vienna and Cologne 1993, p. 85.
79 There is no doubt today that Prime Minister President Păsić and some of his colleagues, as well as the chief of the Serbian intelligence service, Colonel Dimitrijevic, and some members of the Serb military had known about the assassination plan. See Rauchensteiner, *Der Tod des Doppeladlers*, p. 77; Strachan, *The First World War*, pp. 65–8. For a detailed investigation of the events, see Friedrich Würthle, *Die Spur führt nach Belgrad: Die Hintergründe des Dramas von Sarajevo 1914*, Vienna 1974.
80 Mark Cornwall, 'Serbia', in Wilson (ed.), *Decisions for War*, pp. 83–4. In the 1960s, Vladimir Dedijer (who had been one of the editors of the Serbian documents on the war) had already investigated Serbia's role, and had found evidence of the Serbian government's complicity in the assassination of Franz Ferdinand. *The Road to Sarajevo*, London 1966.
81 Remak, '1914 – The Third Balkan War', p. 22.
82 Ibid.
83 Rauchensteiner, *Der Tod des Doppeladlers*, p. 85.
84 Williamson (ed.), *The Origins of a Tragedy*, p. xi.
85 Stevenson, *The Outbreak of the First World War*, p. 12.
86 Förster, 'Im Reich des Absurden', pp. 211–12.
87 Ibid., p. 216; Klaus Hildebrand, *Das vergangene Reich: Deutsche Aussenpolitik von Bismarck bis Hitler*, Stuttgart 1995.
88 Edward E. McCullough, *How the First World War Began: The Triple Entente and the Coming of the Great War of 1914–1918*, Montreal, New York and London 1999, citations on p. 336 and p. 329.
89 Examples include Wolfram Wette (ed.), *Der Krieg des kleinen Mannes*, Munich 1992; Jost Dülffer and Karl Holl (eds), *Bereit zum Krieg: Kriegsmentalität im wilhelminischen Deutschland, 1890–1914*, Göttingen 1986; Bernd Ulrich and Benjamin Ziemann (eds), *Frontalltag im Ersten Weltkrieg: Wahn und Wirklichkeit. Quellen und Dokumente*, Frankfurt/M. 1994; M. Stöcker, *'Augusterlebnis 1914' in Darmstadt: Legende und Wirklichkeit*, Darmstadt 1994; J.M. Winter, *Sites of Memory, Sites of Mourning: The Great War in European Cultural History*, Cambridge 1995; Roger Chickering and Stig Förster (eds), *Great War, Total War: Combat and Mobilization on the Western Front 1914–1918*, Cambridge 2000. For further references, see Strachan, *The First World War* and Stig Förster's introduction in *Great War, Total War*.

90 Hew Strachan's new authoritative study of the First World War, for example, incorporates traditional and new approaches to the history of the war. Strachan, *The First World War,* vol. I: *To Arms.*

91 Gregor Schöllgen, 'Kriegsgefahr und Krisenmanagement vor 1914: Zur Aussenpolitik des kaiserlichen Deutschland', *Neue Politische Literatur,* 267, 1998, pp. 399–413.

92 Seligmann and McLean, *Germany from Reich to Republic,* p. 140.

93 Falkenhayn quoted in Holger Afflerbach, *Falkenhayn: Politisches Denken und Handeln im Kaiserreich,* Munich 1994, p. 147; Moltke, quoted in Mombauer, *Helmuth von Moltke,* p. 182; Conrad's regret at the missed opportunity of 1908/09 in Kronenbitter, '"Nur los lassen"', p. 175.

94 Förster, 'Im Reich des Absurden', pp. 213, 243–7. On the absurd nature of Moltke's demands for war and simultaneous dread of it see also Mombauer, *Helmuth von Moltke, passim.*

95 *Frankfurter Allgemeine Zeitung,* 16 July 2001, No. 162.

Conclusion

This account has examined the evolution of the debate on the origins of the First World War from the initial, emotionally charged reactions to the carnage of the war itself, to the more measured (but still contested) academic debate at the end of the twentieth century. During and immediately after the war, national pride played an important part in the desire of all combatants to attribute the blame for the outbreak of war elsewhere, whilst exonerating their own actions. The Versailles 'war guilt' judgement, on which subsequent demands for retribution were based, was arrived at against the background of the horrors of the war, which were still fresh in the memory of the victors. Soon, however, other concerns took over from this immediate postwar desire to name and shame a guilty party. New international crises threatened the peace of Europe, and it became more pressing to try to understand why the international system had broken down in 1914, as it was now believed to have been the case. Moreover, in the light of developing East–West antagonism, it seemed politic to win over Germany, the country that had had to shoulder the blame for the outbreak of war, to the side of Britain, France and America, as an additional ally against the perceived threat emanating from the Soviet Union.

Before long, the threat and subsequent reality of the Second World War temporarily overshadowed any debate on the origins of its predecessor, and the controversy was seemingly relegated to history in the aftermath of the even greater carnage of the Second World War. However, once it was suggested that, in fact, a connection existed between the two wars, and that the unresolved issues of the First World War had contributed to the outbreak of the Second, the idea that the First World War was the seminal event of the twentieth century once again made an investigation of the war's origins imperative.

With the reassertion of German war guilt in Germany in the 1960s the topic became politically explosive again and, as in the interwar period, current political concerns influenced the nature of the historical debate. In the midst of the Cold War, the new, divided Germany had more than enough uncomfortable history to come to terms with, without the views of Fritz Fischer and his followers. The heated debate that followed finally made way to less polarized views by the 1970s, although the advancing of geopolitical arguments in the 1980s suggested a renewed willingness to downplay Germany's role in the events that had led to war in 1914. Only recently, in the reunited Germany, has the topic become less controversial. The debate over the origins of the First World War seems at last to have lost its link with many contemporary political concerns, and to reside now wholly in the realm of history. It no longer incites the same passion, but it still divides historians to some degree.

What conclusions can be drawn at the end of this investigation into the debate on the origins of the First World War, and after nearly ninety years of controversy? First, this book has demonstrated the intimate connection between the political concerns of a society and its interpretation of history. Historical controversies need to be studied against the background of contemporary political preoccupations. If we are to understand fully the motivations of the victorious Allies and defeated Germans, the revisionists and anti-revisionists, those who espoused the comfortable compromise point of view of the 1930s and those who strove to revisit the question of the origins of the First World War during the 1960s and beyond, it is vital to consider the *historical context* in which their views were formulated. Likewise, the political agendas of those who shaped the controversy need to be considered. Generally speaking, if a topic is deemed worthy of sustained debate, this is in no small measure due to the fact that it has a contemporary relevance and a popular resonance which elevate it above the status of 'mere' history. As such, the question of the origins of the First World War has been of immense importance for the history of Germany following both world wars, and for the history of Europe as a whole.

Secondly, studying and understanding historical controversies in their historical context cannot be overemphasized. This controversy proves, if proof were needed, that history is only ever the interpretation of events, formulated against the background of political agendas. History is not an objective, factual account of events as they occurred, and historical accounts have to be read with a clear understanding of their provenance. History is subject to bias, falsification and deliberate mis-interpretation on the part of individuals, even professional historians, as well as to censorship by government bodies, if the findings of history are too uncomfortable or reflect too badly on the present. For students of history, this is perhaps the most important conclusion of this book.

Is there a consensus at the end of so much debate? The Fischer controversy of the 1960s has itself become history, the outrage of those years has largely subsided, and most historians involved in the debate today carry less political baggage, but disagreements continue to this day about the origins of the First World War. Some consensus has been reached, and most historians today would no longer support Lloyd George's dictum of the European nations slithering into war accidentally. Many would agree with Fischer's once so controversial view that Germany must bear the main share of responsibility for the war that started in 1914, but there are still disagreements over the precise amount of guilt attached to Berlin, as opposed to Vienna, St Petersburg, London and Paris. Studies of individual countries show different levels of culpability – depending on the focus of the historian, different countries appear more or less prominently responsible for a policy that led directly or indirectly to the outbreak of war. The Balkan tensions that 'plagued' Europe in the prewar years clearly are of crucial importance in this context, as are the decisions taken by the individual European governments in July 1914. In the main, however, Fischer's theses have been accepted by historians, with the notable exception of his views on German war aims. Equally, most historians have found it difficult to accept Fischer's interpretation of the importance of the December 1912 war council.

While today no one would seriously maintain any more that Germany had been an innocent party, surprised by events and attacked by Russia and France (and be able to back up such a claim with evidence), equally no one would say that Germany had acted in complete isolation, a belligerent power that was to blame to the exclusion of everyone else. The current consensus is thus that Germany bore the main share, or at least a very large share of the blame, but that the policies of other European governments also need to be considered for a fair judgement. Such a measured conclusion seems substantiated by the available evidence. And yet, in the course of this study we have encountered many such confident statements. During the 1950s it was felt that historians moved 'on safe ground' regarding the First World War, as Walther Hubatsch asserted, just as in the 1930s George P. Gooch had been similarly confident that the riddle of the origins of the war had been solved. As long as the origins, nature and conduct of the First World War continue to occupy historians, and while the flood of books on the war continues unabated, it is still possible that today's consensus will be tomorrow's contested ground.

Bibliography

Adler, Selig, 'The War-Guilt Question and American Disillusionment, 1918-1928', *Journal of Modern History*, xxiii, No. 1, March 1951, pp. 1–28

Afflerbach, Holger, *Falkenhayn: Politisches Denken und Handeln im Kaiserreich*, Munich 1994

Afflerbach, Holger, '"... nearly a case of Italy contra mundum?" Italien als Siegermacht in Versailles 1919', in Gerd Krumeich (ed.), *Versailles 1919: Ziele – Wirkung – Wahrnehmung*, Essen 2001, pp. 159–73

Albertini, Luigi, *Le origini della guerra del 1914*, 3 vols, Milan 1942–43 (English translation: *The Origins of the War of 1914*, 3 vols, Oxford 1952–57)

Auswärtiges Amt (ed.), *Deutschland Schuldig? Deutsches Weissbuch über die Verantwortlichkeit der Urheber des Krieges*, Berlin 1919; *The German White Book Concerning the Responsibility of the Authors of the War*, New York 1924

Baldwin, Peter (ed.), *Reworking the Past: Hitler, the Holocaust and the Historians' Dispute*, Boston 1990

Barker, E., *Britain's Reasons for Going to War*, London 1915

Barker, E., Davis, H.W.C., Fletcher, C.R.L., Hassal, A., Wickham Legg, L.G. and Morgan, F., *Why We Are at War: Great Britain's Case*, Oxford 1914

Barnes, H.E., *The Genesis of the War: An Introduction to the Problem of War-Guilt*, New York 1926

Barraclough, Geoffrey, *From Agadir to Armageddon: Anatomy of a Crisis*, London 1982

Baumgart, Winfried (ed.), *Die Julikrise 1914 und der Ausbruch des Ersten Weltkriegs 1914*, Darmstadt 1983

Bell, Philip, 'Origins of the War of 1914', in Paul Hayes (ed.), *Themes in Modern European History 1890–1945*, London and New York 1992

Berber, Fritz, *Das Diktat von Versailles. Enstehung – Inhalt – Zerfall. Eine Darstellung in Dokumenten,* 2 vols, Essen 1939

Berger, Stefan, *The Search for Normality: National Identity and Historical Consciousness in Germany since 1800*, Providence and Oxford 1997

Berger, Stefan, 'The German Tradition of Historiography, 1800–1995', in Mary Fulbrook (ed.), *German History since 1800*, London 1997, pp. 477-92

Berger, Stefan et al. (eds), *Writing National Histories: Western Europe since 1800*, London 1999

Berghahn, Volker R., *Der Tirpitz-Plan: Genesis und Verfall einer innenpolitischen Krisenstrategie unter Wilhelm II*, Düsseldorf 1971

Berghahn, Volker R., *Germany and the Approach of War in 1914*, London 1973, 2nd edn London 1993

Berghahn, Volker R., *Imperial Germany 1871–1914: Economy, Society, Culture and Politics*, Oxford 1994

Bethmann Hollweg, Theobald von, *Betrachtungen zum Weltkrieg*, 2 vols, Berlin 1919

Bittner, L. and Übersberger, H. (eds), *Österreich-Ungarns Aussenpolitik von der Bosnischen Krise bis zum Kriegsausbruch 1914*, 9 vols, Vienna 1930

Blänsdorf, Agnes, 'Der Weg der Riezler-Tagebücher: Zur Kontroverse über die Echtheit der Tagebücher Kurt Riezlers', *Geschichte in Wissenschaft und Unterricht*, 35, 1984, pp. 651–84

Boemke, M.F., Feldmann, G.D. and Glaser, E. (eds), *The Treaty of Versailles: A Reassessment after 75 Years*, Cambridge 1998

Böhme, Helmut, '"Primat" und "Paradigmata": Zur Entwicklung einer bundesdeutschen Zeitgeschichtsschreibung am Beispiel des Ersten Weltkrieges', in Hartmut

Lehman (ed.), *Historikerkontroversen*, Göttingen 2000, pp. 87–139

Bourne, John, Liddle, Peter and Whitehead, Ian (eds), *The Great World War, 1914-1945*, vol. I: *Lightning Strikes Twice*, London 2000

Boyce, Robert (ed.), *French Foreign and Defence Policy, 1918–1940: The Decline and Fall of a Great Power*, London and New York 1998

Bridge, Francis R., *From Sadowa to Sarajevo: The Foreign Policy of Austria-Hungary, 1866–1914*, London 1972

Bruckmann, Klaus, 'Erster Weltkrieg – Ursachen, Kriegsziele, Kriegsschuld: Fritz Fischers Thesen in deutschen Schulgeschichtsbüchern, *Geschichte in Wissenschaft und Unterricht*, 10, 1981, pp. 600–17

Burz, Ulfried, 'Austria and the Great War: Official Publications in the 1920s and 1930s', in Keith M. Wilson (ed.), *Forging the Collective Memory: Government and International Historians through Two World Wars*, Providence and Oxford 1996

Calleo, David, *The German Problem Reconsidered*, Cambridge, Mass. 1978

Canis, Conrad, *Von Bismarck zur Weltpolitik: Deutsche Aussenpolitik 1890–1902*, Berlin 1997

Carsten, Francis L., Review of *Griff nach der Weltmacht*, in *English Historical Review*, 78, 1963, pp. 751–3

Charmley, John, *Splendid Isolation? Britain and the Balance of Power 1874–1914*, London 1999

Chickering, Roger, *Imperial Germany and the Great War, 1914–1918*, Cambridge 1998

Chickering, Roger and Förster, Stig (eds), *Great War, Total War: Combat and Mobilization on the Western Front, 1914–1918*, Cambridge 2000

Cimbala, Stephen J., 'Steering Through Rapids: Russian Mobilization and World War I', *Journal of Slavic Military History*, 9/2, 1996, pp. 376–98

Clark, Christopher, *Kaiser Wilhelm II*, London 2000

Clark, M., *Modern Italy 1971–1995*, 2nd edn, London and New York 1996

Cline, Catherine A., *E.D. Morel, 1873–1924: The Strategies of Protest*, Belfast 1980

Cohen, Warren I., *The American Revisionists: The Lessons of Intervention in World War I*, Chicago and London 1967

Conrad von Hötzendorf, Franz, *Aus meiner Dienstzeit 1906–1918*, 5 vols, Vienna, Leipzig and Munich 1921–25

Cornwall, Mark (ed.), *The Last Years of Austria-Hungary: Essays in Political and Military History, 1908–1918*, Exeter 1990

Cornwall, Mark, 'Serbia', in Keith M. Wilson (ed.), *Decisions for War, 1914*, London 1995, pp. 83–4

Crampton, R.J., *The Hollow Detente: Anglo-German Relations in the Balkans, 1911–1914*, London 1980

Dedijer, Vladimir, *The Road to Sarajevo*, London 1967

Dehio, Ludwig, *Gleichgewicht oder Hegemonie?*, Krefeld 1948

Dehio, Ludwig, *Deutschland und die Weltpolitik im 20. Jahrhundert*, Munich 1955

Demartial, Georges, 'La Guerre de 1914: Comment on mobilisa les consciences', *Current History*, 1922

Die Denkschrift des Fürsten Lichnowsky, edited by 'a group of peace lovers', Bern 1918

Derez, Mark, 'The Experience of Occupation: Belgium', in John Bourne, Peter Liddle and Ian Whitehead (eds), *The Great World War, 1914–1945*, vol. I: *Lightning Strikes Twice*, London 2000, pp. 511–32

'Deutsch-französische Vereinbarung über strittige Fragen europäischer Geschichte' (May and October 1951), *Geschichte in Wissenschaft und Unterricht*, 3, 1952, pp. 288–99

Dickmann, Fritz, 'Die Kriegsschuldfrage auf der Friedenskonferenz von Paris 1919', *Historische Zeitschrift*, 197, 1963, pp. 1–100

Dorpalen, Andreas, 'Gerhard Ritter', in H.-U. Wehler (ed.), *Deutsche Historiker*, Göttingen 1973, pp. 86–99

Dorpalen, Andreas, *German History in Marxist Perspective: The East German Approach*, London 1985

Droz, Jaques, *Les Causes de la Première Guerre mondiale: Essai d'historiographie*, Paris 1973

Dülffer, Jost and Holl, Karl (eds), *Bereit zum Krieg: Kriegsmentalität im wilhelminischen Deutschland, 1890–1914*, Göttingen 1986

Duroselle, Jean-Baptiste, *La Grande Guerre des Français, 1914–1918: L'incompréhensible*, Paris 1994

Eckardstein, Hermann von, *Lebenserinnerungen und politische Denkwürdigkeiten*, 3 vols, Leipzig 1919

Epkenhans, Michael, *Die wilhelminische Flottenrüstung 1908–1914: Weltmachtstreben, industrieller Fortschritt, soziale Integration*, Munich 1991

Epstein, Klaus, 'Die deutsche Ostpolitik im Ersten Weltkrieg', *Jahrbücher für die Geschichte Osteuropas*, 10, 1962, pp. 381ff.; reprinted in Ernst W. Lynar (ed.), *Deutsche Kriegsziele 1914–1918*, Frankfurt/M. 1964, pp. 158–74

Erdmann, Karl Dietrich, 'Zur Beurteilung Bethmann Hollwegs', *Geschichte in Wissenschaft und Unterricht*, 15, 1964, pp. 525–40

Erdmann, Karl Dietrich (ed.), *Kurt Riezler: Tagebücher, Aufsätze, Dokumente*, Göttingen 1972

Erdmann, Karl Dietrich, 'Die Tagebücher sind echt. Streit um ein historisches Dokument, das ins Zwielicht geraten ist. Eine Antwort', *Die Zeit*, No. 28, 8 July 1983

Erdmann, Karl Dietrich, 'War Guilt 1914 Reconsidered: A Balance of New Research', in H.W. Koch (ed.), *The Origins of the First World War: Great Power Rivalry and German War Aims*, 2nd edn, London 1984, pp. 342–70

Evans, R.J.W., 'The Habsburg Monarchy and the Coming of War', in R.J.W. Evans and Hartmut Pogge von Strandmann (eds), *The Coming of the First World War*, Oxford 1988, pp. 33–55

Evans, R.J.W. and Pogge von Strandmann, Hartmut (eds), *The Coming of the First World War*, Oxford 1988

Evans, Richard J., *In Hitler's Shadow: West German Historians and the Attempt to Escape from the Nazi Past*, London 1989

Fabre-Luce, Alfred, *La Victoire*, Paris 1924

Fay, S.B., *The Origins of the World War*, 2 vols, New York 1929, 2nd revised edn, New York 1930

Fellner, Fritz, Review of *Kurt Riezler: Tagebücher, Aufsätze, Dokumente*, in *Mitteilungen des Österreichischen Instituts für Geschichte*, 1973, pp. 490–5

Fellner, Fritz, 'Die "Mission Hoyos"', in Wilhelm Alf (ed.), *Deutschlands Sonderung von Europa 1862–1945*, Frankfurt 1984, pp. 283–316

Fellner, Fritz, 'Austria-Hungary', in Keith M. Wilson (ed.), *Decisions for War, 1914*, London 1995, pp. 9–25

Ferguson, Niall, *Pity of War*, London 1998

Fischer, Fritz, 'Deutsche Kriegsziele, Revolutionierung und Separatfrieden im Osten 1914–1918, *Historische Zeitschrift*, 188, 1959

Fischer, Fritz, *Griff nach der Weltmacht: Die Kriegszielpolitik des kaiserlichen Deutschland 1914/18*, 1st edn Düsseldorf 1961 (English translation: *Germany's Aims in the First World War*, London 1967)

Fischer, Fritz, 'Weltpolitik, Weltmachtstreben und deutsche Kriegsziele', *Historische Zeitschrift* 199, 1964, pp. 265–346

Fischer, Fritz, *World Power or Decline: The Controversy over Germany's Aims in the First World War*, New York 1974 (translation of *Weltmacht oder Niedergang? Deutschland im Ersten Weltkrieg*, Frankfurt 1965)

Fischer, Fritz, *Krieg der Illusionen: Die deutsche Politik von 1911–1914*, 1st edn, Düsseldorf 1969 (English translation: *War of Illusions: German Policies from 1911–1914*, London 1975)

Fischer, Fritz, *Juli 1914: Wir sind nicht hineingeschlittert. Das Staatsgeheimnis um die Riezler-Tagebücher. Eine Streitschrift*, Reinbek 1983

Förster, Stig, 'Der deutsche Generalstab und die Illusion des kurzen Krieges, 1871–1914. Metakritik eines Mythos', *Militärgeschichtliche Mitteilungen*, 54, 1/1995, pp. 61–98

Förster, Stig, 'Im Reich des Absurden: Die Ursachen des Ersten Weltkrieges', in Bernd Wegner (ed.), *Wie Kriege entstehen: Zum historischen Hintergrund von Staatenkonflikten*, Paderborn, Munich, Vienna and Zurich 2000, pp. 211–52

Freund, Michael, 'Bethmann-Hollweg: Der Hitler des Jahres

1914? Zu einer Spätfrucht des Jahres 1914 in der Geschichtsschreibung', in Ernst W. Lynar (ed.), *Deutsche Kriegsziele 1914–1918*, Frankfurt/M. 1964, pp. 175–82

Fry, Michael Graham, 'British Revisionism', in M.F. Boemke, G.D. Feldmann and E. Glaser (eds), *The Treaty of Versailles: A Reassessment after 75 Years*, Cambridge 1998, pp. 565–601

Fulbrook, Mary (ed.), *German History since 1800*, London 1997

Fulbrook, Mary, 'Dividing the Past, Defining the Present: Historians and National Identity in the Two Germanies', in Stefan Berger et al. (eds), *Writing National Histories: Western Europe since 1800*, London 1999, pp. 217–29

Fulbrook, Mary, *German National Identity after the Holocaust*, Oxford and Cambridge 1999

Gasser, Adolf, *Preußischer Militärgeist und Kriegsentfesselung 1914: Drei Studien zum Ausbruch des Ersten Weltkrieges*, Basel and Frankfurt/M. 1985

Gatzke, H.W., Review of *Griff nach der Weltmacht*, in *American Historical Review*, 68, 1962, pp. 443–5

Geiss, Imanuel, *Der Polnische Grenzstreifen 1914–1918: Ein Beitrag zur deutschen Kriegszielpolitik im Ersten Weltkrieg*, Lübeck and Hamburg 1960

Geiss, Imanuel (ed.), *Julikrise und Kriegsausbruch: Eine Dokumentensammlung*, 2 vols, Hanover 1963/64

Geiss, Imanuel (ed.), *Juli 1914: Die europäische Krise und der Ausbruch des Ersten Weltkrieges*, 3rd edn 1986 (1st edn 1965) (English translation: *July 1914: The Outbreak of the First World War. Selected Documents*, London and New York 1967)

Geiss, Imanuel, *Studien über Geschichte und Geschichtswissenschaft*, Frankfurt/M. 1972

Geiss, Imanuel, 'Die manipulierte Kriegsschuldfrage. Deutsche Reichspolitik in der Julikrise 1914 und Deutsche Kriegsziele im Spiegel des Schuldreferats des Auswärtigen Amtes, 1919–1939', *Militärgeschichtliche Mitteilungen*, 34, 2/1983

Goldstein, Erik, 'Great Britain: The Home Front', in M.F. Boemke, G. D. Feldmann and E. Glaser (eds), *The Treaty of Versailles: A Reassessment after 75 Years*, Cambridge 1998, pp. 147–66

Gooch, George P., *Before the War: Studies in Diplomacy*, vol. 2: *The Coming of the Storm*, London 1938

Görlitz, Walther (ed.), *Der Kaiser ... Aufzeichnungen des Chefs des Marinekabinetts Admiral Georg Alexander von Müller über die Ära Wilhelm II.*, Göttingen 1965

Grelling, Richard, *J'accuse ...*, Lausanne 1915

Grelling, Richard, *Le Campagne 'innocentiste' en Allemagne et le traité de Versailles*, Paris 1925

Grey of Fallodon, Viscount, *Twenty-Five Years*, 2 vols, New York 1925

Gutsche, Willibald, *Sarajevo 1914: Vom Attentat zum Weltkrieg*, Berlin 1984

Gutsche, Willibald, *Der gewollte Krieg: Der deutsche Imperialismus und der Erste Weltkrieg*, Berlin 1984

Gutsche, Willibald, 'The Foreign Policy of Imperial Germany and the Outbreak of the War in the Historiography of the GDR', in Gregor Schöllgen (ed.), *Escape into War? The Foreign Policy of Imperial Germany*, Oxford 1990

Hamilton, Keith, 'The Historical Diplomacy of the Third Republic', in Keith M. Wilson (ed.), *Forging the Collective Memory: Government and International Historians through Two World Wars*, Providence and Oxford 1996

Hamilton, Keith, 'The Pursuit of Enlightened Patriotism: The British Foreign Office and Historical Researchers During the Great War and its Aftermath', in Keith M. Wilson (ed.), *Forging the Collective Memory: Government and International Historians through Two World Wars*, Providence and Oxford 1996

Hayne, M.B., *The French Foreign Office and the Origins of the First World War, 1898–1914*, Oxford 1993

Headlam-Morley, J.W., *The History of Twelve Days*, London 1915

Headlam-Morley, J.W., *The German Chancellor and the Outbreak of War*, London 1917

Heinemann, Ulrich, *Die Verdrängte Niederlage: Politische Öffentlichkeit und Kriegsschuldfrage in der Weimarer Republik*, Göttingen 1983

Helfferich, Karl, *Die Vorgeschichte des Weltkrieges*, Berlin 1919

Henig, Ruth, *Versailles and After 1919–1933*, London 1984, 2nd edn 1995

Herrmann, David G., *The Arming of Europe and the Making of the First World War*, Princeton, 1997

Herwig, Holger (ed.), *The Outbreak of World War I: Causes and Responsibilities*, 5th revised edn, Lexington and Toronto 1991

Herwig, Holger, 'Clio Deceived: Patriotic Self-Censorship in Germany after the War', first published in *International Security*, 12, 1987, reprinted in Keith M. Wilson (ed.), *Forging the Collective Memory: Government and International Historians through Two World Wars*, Providence and Oxford 1996, pp. 87–127

Herwig, Holger H., *The First World War: Germany and Austria-Hungary 1914–1918*, London 1997

Herwig, Holger H., Review of *Pity of War*, *Journal of Modern History*, vol. 72, No. 3, September 2000

Hildebrand, Klaus, 'Staatskunst oder Systemzwang? Die "Deutsche Frage" als Problem der Weltpolitik', *Historische Zeitschrift*, 228, 1979

Hildebrand, Klaus, 'Der deutsche Eigenweg: Über das Problem der Normalität in der modernen Geschichte Deutschlands', in M. Funke et al. (eds), *Demokratie und Diktatur: Geist und Gestalt politischer Herrschaft in Deutschland und Europa*, Festschrift für Karl Dietrich Bracher, Düsseldorf 1987

Hildebrand, Klaus, 'Saturiertheit und Prestige: Das Deutsche Reich als Staat im Staatensystem 1871–1918', *Geschichte in Wissenschaft und Unterricht*, 1989/4, pp. 193–202

Hildebrand, Klaus, 'Reich-Großmacht-Nation. Betrachtungen zur Geschichte der deutschen Aussenpolitik 1871-1918', *Historische Zeitschrift*, 259, 1994, pp. 369–89

Hildebrand, Klaus, *Das Vergangene Reich: Deutsche Aussenpolitik von Bismarck bis Hitler*, Stuttgart 1995

Hillgruber, Andreas, 'Riezlers Theorie des kalkulierten Risikos und Bethmann Hollwegs politische Konzeption in der

Julikrise 1914', in idem, *Deutsche Grossmacht- und Weltpolitik im 19. und 20. Jahrhundert*, Düsseldorf 1977

Hinsley, F.H. (ed.), *British Foreign Policy under Sir Edward Grey*, London 1997

Historikerstreit. Die Dokumentation der Kontroverse um die Einzigartigkeit der nationalsozialistischen Judenvernichtung, Munich 1987 (English translation by James Knowlton and Truett Cates, *Forever in the Shadow of Hitler?*, New Jersey 1993)

Hofer, Walter, *Die Entfesselung des Zweiten Weltkrieges*, 2nd edn, Stuttgart 1955

Hubatsch, Walther, *Der Weltkrieg 1914/1918*, in Leo Just (ed.), *Handbuch der deutschen Geschichte*, vol. IV, 2nd Section, Konstanz 1955, 2nd revised edn, *Der Erste Weltkrieg*, Bundesministerium der Verteidigung (ed.), Bonn 1966

Iggers, Georg (ed.), *The Social History of Politics: Critical Perspectives in West German Historical Writing Since 1945*, Leamington Spa 1985

Isaac, Jules, *Un débat historique: 1914, le problème des origines de la guerre*, Paris 1933

Jäger, Wolfgang, *Historische Forschung und politische Kultur in Deutschland*, Göttingen 1984

Jagow, Gottlieb von, *Ursachen und Ausbruch des Weltkrieges*, Berlin 1919

Janssen, Karl-Heinz, 'Aus Furcht und Verzweiflung: Das deutsche Angriffsmotiv im August 1914', *Die Zeit*, No. 12, 21 March 1969

Janssen, Karl-Heinz, 'August '14: Wahrheit auf Raten. Zwei Historiker streiten um Tagebücher: Wurde die deutsche Kriegsschuld am Ersten Weltkrieg im nationalen Interesse verschleiert?', *Die Zeit*, No. 24, 10 June 1983

Jarausch, Konrad H., 'The Illusion of Limited War: Chancellor Bethmann Hollweg's Calculated Risk, July 1914', *Central European History*, vol. II, 1969, pp. 48–76

Jarausch, Konrad H., 'World Power of Tragic Fate? The Kriegsschuldfrage as Historical Neurosis', *Central European History*, 5, 1972, pp. 72–92

Jarausch, Konrad H., *The Enigmatic Chancellor: Bethmann Hollweg and the Hubris of Imperial Germany*, New Haven, 1973

Jerábek, Rudolf, 'Die österreichische Weltkriegsforschung', in Wolfgang Michalka (ed.), *Der Erste Weltkrieg: Wirkung, Wahrnehmung, Analyse,* Munich and Zurich 1994, pp. 953–71

Joll, James, '1914: The Unspoken Assumptions', in H.J. Koch (ed.), *The Origins of the First World War: Great Power Rivalry and German War Aims*, New York, 1st edn 1972

Joll, James, 'The 1914 Debate Continues: Fritz Fischer and his Critics', in H.W. Koch (ed.), *The Origins of the First World War: Great Power Rivalry and German War Aims*, 2nd edn, London 1984, pp. 30–45

Joll, James, *The Origins of the First World War*, 2nd edn, London and New York 1992

Kaes, Anton, Jay, Martin and Dimenberg, Edward (eds), *The Weimar Republic Sourcebook*, Berkeley and London 1994

Kagan, Donald, *On the Origins of Wars and the Preservation of Peace*, London 1995

Kahler, Miles, 'Rumours of War: The 1914 Analogy', *Foreign Affairs*, 2, 1979–80, pp. 374–96

Kaiser, David E., 'Germany and the Origins of the First World War', *Journal of Modern History*, 55/3, 1983

Kann, Robert A., Review of *Gutachten zur Kriegsschuldfrage,* in *Central European History*, 1, 1968

Kanner, Heinrich, *Kaiserliche Katastrophenpolitik*, Vienna 1922

Kanner, Heinrich, *Der Schlüssel zur Kriegsschuldfrage,* Munich 1926

Kantorowicz, Hermann, *Der Geist der englischen Politik und das Gespenst der Einkreisung Deutschlands*, Berlin 1929

Kantorowicz, Hermann, *Gutachten zur Kriegsschuldfrage,* ed. I. Geiss, Frankfurt 1967

Kautsky, Karl, Montgelas, Max and Schücking, Walter (eds), *Die deutschen Dokumente zum Kriegsausbruch*, 4 vols, Berlin 1919 (English translation: *The Outbreak of the World War,* London 1924)

Keiger, John F.V., *France and the Origins of the First World War*, London 1983

Keiger, John F.V., 'France', in Keith M. Wilson (ed.), *Decisions for War, 1914*, London 1995, pp. 121–49

Keiger, John F.V., *Raymond Poincaré*, Cambridge 1997

Keiger, John F.V., 'Raymond Poincaré and the Ruhr Crisis', in Robert Boyce (ed.), *French Foreign and Defence Policy, 1918–1940: The Decline and Fall of a Great Power*, London and New York 1998, pp. 49–70

Kennan, George F., *The Decline of Bismarck's European Order: Franco-Russian Relations, 1875–1890*, Princeton 1979

Kennedy, Paul M., 'The Development of German Naval Operations Plans against England, 1896–1914', in idem (ed.), *The War Plans of the Great Powers, 1880–1914*, London 1979

Kennedy, Paul M., *The Rise of the Anglo-German Antagonism*, London 1980

Kent, Bruce, *The Spoils of War: The Politics, Economics, and Diplomacy of Reparations 1918–1932*, Oxford 1989

Kettenacker, Lothar, *Germany since 1945*, Oxford 1997

Klein, Fritz, 'Über die Verfälschung der historischen Wahrheit in der Aktenpublikation "Die Grosse Politik der Europäischen Kabinette 1871–1914"', *Zeitschrift für Geschichtswissenschaft*, 7, 1950, pp. 318–30

Klein, Fritz, 'Die westdeutsche Geschichtsschreibung über die Ziele des deutschen Imperialismus im ersten Weltkrieg', *Zeitschrift für Geschichtswissenschaft*, 10/8, 1962, pp. 1808–36

Klein, Fritz, 'Der Erste Weltkrieg in der Geschichtswissenschaft der DDR', *Zeitschrift für Geschichtswissenschaft*, 42, 1994, pp. 293–301.

Klein, Fritz, 'Between Compiègne and Versailles: The Germans on the Way from a Misunderstood Defeat to an Unwanted Peace', in M.F. Boemke, G.D. Feldmann and E. Glaser (eds), *The Treaty of Versailles: A Reassessment after 75 Years*, Cambridge 1998, pp. 203–20

Klein, Fritz, *Drinnen und Draussen. Ein Historiker in der DDR. Erinnerungen*, Frankfurt/M. 2000

Klein, Fritz et al. (eds), *Deutschland im Ersten Weltkrieg*, 3 vols, Berlin 1968–69

Koch, H.W. (ed.), *The Origins of the First World War: Great Power Rivalry and German War Aims*, 1st edn London 1972, 2nd edn London 1984

Kohut, Thomas A., *Wilhelm II and the Germans: A Study in Leadership*, New York and Oxford 1991

Kramer, Alan, 'Der Umgang mit der Schuld: Die "Schuld im Kriege" und die Republik von Weimar', in Dietrich Papenfuss and Wolfgang Schieder (eds), *Deutsche Umbrüche im 20. Jahrhundert*, Cologne 2000

Kronenbitter, Günther, 'Bundesgenossen? Zur militärischen Kooperation zwischen Berlin und Wien 1912–1914', in Walther L. Bernecker and Volker Dotterweich (eds), *Deutschland in den internationalen Beziehungen des 19. und 20. Jahrhunderts. Festschrift für Josef Becker zum 65. Geburtstag*, Munich 1996

Kronenbitter, Günther, '"Nur los lassen." Österreich-Ungarn und der Wille zum Krieg', in Johannes Burkhardt et al. (eds), *Lange und kurze Wege in den Ersten Weltkrieg*, Munich 1996, pp. 159–87

Kronenbitter, Günther, 'Falsch verbunden? Die Militärallianz zwischen Österreich-Ungarn und Deutschland, 1906–1914', *Österreichische Militärische Zeitschrift*, 38, 2000, 6, pp. 743–54

Krumeich, Gerd, *Armaments and Politics in France on the Eve of the First World War: The Introduction of the Three-Year Conscription, 1913–1914*, Leamington Spa 1984 (English translation of *Aufrüstung und Innenpolitik in Frankreich vor dem Ersten Weltkrieg*, Wiesbaden 1980)

Krumeich, Gerd, 'Vergleichende Aspekte der "Kriegsschulddebatte" nach dem Ersten Weltkrieg' in Wolfgang Michalka (ed.), *Der Erste Weltkrieg: Wirkung, Wahrnehmung, Analyse*, Munich and Zurich 1994, pp. 915–28

Krumeich, Gerd, 'Das Erbe der Wilhelminer', *Frankfurter Allgemeine Zeitung*, 4 Nov. 1999, p. 56

Lahme, Rainer, 'Das Ende der Pax Britannica: England und die europäischen Mächte 1890–1914', *Archiv für Kulturgeschichte*, vol. 73, No. 1, 1991, pp. 169–92

Lambert, Peter, 'Friedrich Thimme, G.P. Gooch and the Publication of Documents on the Origins of the First World War: Patriotism, Academic Liberty and a Search for Anglo-German Understanding, 1920-1938', in Stefan Berger, Peter Lambert and Peter Schumann (eds), *A Dialogue of the Deaf? Historiographical Connections between Britain and Germany, c. 1750–2000*, forthcoming, Göttingen 2002

Langdon, John W., *July 1914: The Long Debate 1918–1990*, New York and Oxford 1991

Langhorne, R.T.B., 'Great Britain and Germany, 1911–1914', in F.H. Hinsley (ed.), *British Foreign Policy under Sir Edward Grey*, London 1997, pp. 288–311

Lee, Marshall and Michalka, Wolfgang, *German Foreign Policy 1917–1933: Continuity or Break?*, Leamington Spa 1987

Lehmann, Hartmut (ed.), *Historikerkontroversen*, Göttingen 2000

Lenin, V.I., *Imperialism – The Last State of Capitalism*, in *Selected Works*, English translation, Moscow 1968, pp. 169–257

Lentin, Antony, *Lloyd George, Woodrow Wilson and the Guilt of Germany*, Leicester, 1984

Lepsius, J., Mendelssohn Bartholdy, A. and Thimme, F. (eds), *Die Grosse Politik der Europäischen Kabinette, 1871–1914: Sammlung der Diplomatischen Akten des Auswärtigen Amtes*, 40 vols, Berlin 1922–27

Leslie, John, 'The Antecedents of Austria-Hungary's War Aims', *Wiener Beiträge zur Geschichte der Neuzeit*, vol. 20, 1993, pp. 307–94

Lichnowsky, Karl Max von, *Heading for the Abyss*, English translation, London 1928

Lieven, Dominic, *Russia and the Origins of the First World War*, London 1983

Lloyd George, David, *War Memoirs*, vol. I, London 1924

Longerich, Peter (ed.), *Die Erste Republik: Dokumente zur Geschichte des Weimarer Staates*, Munich and Zurich 1992

Lorenz, Chris, 'Beyond Good and Evil? The German Empire of 1871 and Modern German Historiography', *Journal of Contemporary History*, 30, 1995, pp. 729–65

Luckau, Alma, *The German Delegation at the Paris Peace Conference*, New York 1941

Lynar, Ernst W. (ed.), *Deutsche Kriegsziele 1914–1918*, Frankfurt/M. 1964

Mack Smith, Denis, *Modern Italy: A Political History*, New Haven and London 1997

Mann, Golo, 'Der Griff nach der Weltmacht', in Ernst W. Lynar, (ed.), *Deutsche Kriegsziele 1914–1918*, Frankfurt/M. 1964, pp. 189–90

Marchand, René, *Un livre noir*, 3 vols, Paris 1921–22

Marks, Sally, 'Smoke and Mirrors: In Smoke-Filled Rooms and the Galerie des Glaces', in M.F. Boemke, G.D. Feldmann and E. Glaser (eds), *The Treaty of Versailles: A Reassessment after 75 Years*, Cambridge 1998, pp. 337–70

Martel, Gordon, *The Origins of the First World War*, 2nd edn, London 1996

Marx, Wilhelm, 'The Responsibility for the War', *Foreign Affairs*, 4, 1926

McCullough, Edward, *How the First World War Began: The Triple Entente and the Coming of the Great War of 1914–1918*, Montreal, New York and London 1999

McCurdy, C.A. *Guilty! Prince Lichnowsky's Disclosures*, National War Aims Committee, London, no date [1918]

McDonough, Frank, *The Origins of the First and Second World Wars*, Cambridge 1997

Michalka, Wolfgang (ed.), *Der Erste Weltkrieg: Wirkung, Wahrnehmung, Analyse*, Munich and Zurich 1994

Miller, Steven E., *Military Strategy and the Origins of the First World War*, Princeton 1985

Mombauer, Annika, *Helmuth von Moltke and the Origins of the First World War*, Cambridge 2001

Mommsen, Wolfgang J., 'Domestic Factors in German Foreign Policy before 1914', *Central European History*, vol. 6, No. 1, 1973

Mommsen, Wolfgang J., 'Der Topos vom unvermeidlichen Krieg: Außenpolitik und öffentliche Meinung im Deutschen Reich im letzten Jahrzehnt vor 1914', in idem, *Der autoritäre Nationalstaat*, Frankfurt/M. 1990, pp. 380ff.

Mommsen, Wolfgang J., 'Max Weber and the Peace Treaty of Versailles', in M.F. Boemke, G.D. Feldmann and E. Glaser (eds), *The Treaty of Versailles: A Reassessment after 75 Years*, Cambridge 1998, pp. 535–46

Morel, Edmund D., *Morocco in Diplomacy*, London 1912, republished during the war as *Ten Years of Secret Diplomacy: An Unheeded Warning*, London 1915

Morel, Edmund D., *Truth and the War*, London 1916

Morhardt, Mathias, *Les Vrais Coupables*, German translation *Die wahren Schuldigen*, Leipzig 1925

Moser, John E., *Twisting the Lion's Tail: Anglophobia in the United States, 1921–1948*, London 1999

Moses, John A., *The War Aims of Imperial Germany: Professor Fritz Fischer and his Critics*, University of Queensland Papers, vol. I, No. 4, St Lucia 1968

Moses, John A., *Politics of Illusion: The Fischer Controversy in German Historiography*, London 1975

Neck, R., 'Kriegszielpolitik im Ersten Weltkrieg', in Ernst W. Lynar (ed.), *Deutsche Kriegsziele 1914–1918*, Frankfurt/M. 1964, pp. 145–57

Neilson, Keith, 'Russia', in Keith M. Wilson (ed.), *Decisions for War, 1914*, London 1995, pp. 175–208

Niedhart, Gottfried (ed.), *Kriegsbeginn 1939: Entfesselung oder Ausbruch des Zweiten Weltkrieges*, Darmstadt 1976

Peukert, Detlef, *The Weimar Republic: The Crisis of Classical Modernity*, New York 1992

Pogge von Strandmann, Hartmut, 'Britische Historiker und der Ausbruch des Ersten Weltkrieges', in Wolfgang Michalka (ed.), *Der Erste Weltkrieg. Wirkung: Wahrnehmung, Analyse*, Munich and Zurich 1994, pp. 929–52

Pogge von Strandmann, Hartmut, 'Germany and the Coming of War', in R.J.W. Evans and Hartmut Pogge von

Strandmann (eds), *The Coming of the First World War*, Oxford 1988, pp. 87–123

Poincaré, R., *Au Service de la France*, Paris 1926

Rauchensteiner, Manfried, *Der Tod des Doppeladlers: Österreich-Ungarn und der Erste Weltkrieg*, Graz, Vienna and Cologne 1993

Remak, Joachim, '1914 – The Third Balkan War: Origins Reconsidered', *Journal of Modern History*, 43, 1971, reprinted in H.W. Koch (ed.), *The Origins of the First World War: Great Power Rivalry and German War Aims*, 2nd edn London 1984, pp. 101–27

Renouvin, Pierre, *Les Origines immédiates de la guerre*, Paris 1925 (English translation: *The Immediate Origins of the War*, New York 1927)

Renouvin, Pierre, 'How the War Came', *Foreign Affairs*, April 1929

Renouvin, Pierre, 'Les Buts de guerre de l'Allemagne (1914–1918) d'après les travaux de Fritz Fischer', *Revue Historique*, 80, 1962, pp. 381–90

Retallack, James, *Germany in the Age of Kaiser Wilhelm II*, Basingstoke and London 1996

Ritter, Gerhard, 'Eine neue Kriegsschuldthese? Zu Fritz Fischers Buch "Griff nach der Weltmacht"', *Historische Zeitschrift*, 194, 1962, pp. 667–8, reprinted in Ernst W. Lynar (ed.), *Deutsche Kriegsziele 1914–1918*, Frankfurt/M. 1964, pp. 121–44

Ritter, Gerhard, *Der Erste Weltkrieg: Studien zum deutschen Geschichtsbild*, Bundeszentrale für politische Bildung, Heft 64, Bonn 1964

Ritter, Gerhard, *Staatskunst und Kriegshandwerk: Das Problem des Militarismus in Deutschland*, 4 vols, Munich 1959–68, vol. 3 *Die Tragödie der Staatskunst*, 1964. English translation: *The Sword and the Scepter: The Problem of Militarism in Germany*, translated by Heinz Norden; vol. 3, *The Tragedy of Statesmanship – Bethmann Hollweg as War Chancellor 1914–1917*, 3rd edn Miami 1972

Robbins, Keith, *The Abolition of War: The 'Peace Movement' in Britain, 1914–1919*, Cardiff 1976

Rochat, Giorgio, 'Die italienische Historiographie zum Ersten Weltkrieg', in Wolfgang Michalka (ed.), *Der Erste Weltkrieg: Wirkung, Wahrnehmung, Analyse,* Munich and Zurich 1994, pp. 972–90

Röhl, John C.G., 'Admiral von Müller and the Approach of War, 1911–1914', *Historical Journal,* XII 4, 1969

Röhl, John C.G. (ed.), *1914: Delusion or Design? The Testimony of Two German Diplomats,* London 1973, translation of *Zwei deutsche Fürsten zur Kriegsschuldfrage. Lichnowsky und Eulenburg und der Ausbruch des Ersten Weltkrieges. Eine Dokumentation,* Düsseldorf 1971

Röhl, John C.G., 'An der Schwelle zum Weltkrieg: Eine Dokumentation über den "Kriegsrat" vom 8. Dezember 1912', *Militärgeschichtliche Mitteilungen,* 21, 1/1977

Röhl, John C.G., 'Germany', in Keith M. Wilson (ed.), *Decisions for War, 1914,* London 1995, pp. 27–54

Röhl, John C.G., *The Kaiser and his Court,* London 1995

Russell, Bertrand, 'Experiences of a Pacifist in the First World War', in *Portraits from Memory and other Essays,* London 1956

Schivelbusch, Wolfgang, *Eine Ruine im Krieg der Geister: Die Bibliothek von Löwen, August 1914 bis Mai 1940,* Frankfurt/M. 1993

Schmitt, B.E., 'July 1914', *Foreign Affairs,* No. 1, Oct. 1926

Schmitt, B.E., *The Coming of the War, 1914,* 2 vols, New York, 1930

Schmitt, B.E., *The Origins of the First World War,* London 1958

Schöllgen, Gregor, '"Fischer Kontroverse" und Kontinuitätsproblem: Deutsche Kriegsziele im Zeitalter der Weltkriege', in Andreas Hillgruber and Jost Dülffer (eds), *Ploetz: Geschichte der Weltkriege,* Freiburg and Würzburg 1981

Schöllgen, Gregor, 'Griff nach der Weltmacht? 25 Jahre Fischer-Kontroverse', *Historisches Jahrbuch,* 106, 1986, pp. 386–406

Schöllgen, Gregor, 'Germany's Foreign Policy in the Age of Imperialism: A Vicious Circle?', in idem (ed.), *Escape into War? The Foreign Policy of Imperial Germany,* Oxford 1990

Schöllgen, Gregor, 'Kriegsgefahr und Krisenmanagement vor 1914: Zur Aussenpolitik des kaiserlichen Deutschland', *Neue Politische Literatur*, 267, 1998, pp. 399–413

Schulte, Bernd Felix, *Die Verfälschung der Riezler Tagebücher: Ein Beitrag zur Wissenschaftsgeschichte der 50er und 60er Jahre*, Frankfurt/M., Bern and New York 1985

Schumann, Wolfgang and Nestler, Ludwig (eds), *Weltherrschaft im Visier*, Berlin 1975

Schwabe, Klaus, *Woodrow Wilson, Revolutionary Germany and Peacemaking, 1918–1919: Missionary Diplomacy and the Realities of Power*, Chapel Hill and London 1985

Schwertfeger, Bernhard (ed.), *Dokumentarium zur Vorgeschichte des Weltkrieges, 1871–1914*, Berlin 1928

Seligmann, Matthew S. and McLean, Roderick R., *Germany from Reich to Republic 1871–1918*, London 2000

Sharp, Alan, 'Lloyd George and Foreign Policy, 1918–1922', in Judith Loades (ed.), *The Life and Times of David Lloyd George*, Bangor 1991

Sladen, Douglas, *Germany's Great Lie: The Official German Justification of the War*, London 1914

Smith, Munroe (ed.), *The Disclosures from Germany*, New York 1918

Sösemann, Bernd (ed.), *Theodor Wolff. Tagebücher 1914–1918. Der Erste Weltkrieg und die Entstehung der Weimarer Republik in Tagebüchern, Leitartikeln und Briefen des Chefredakteurs am 'Berliner Tageblatt' und Mitbegründer der 'Deutschen Demokratischen Partei'*, 2 vols, Boppard-am-Rhein 1984

Spring, Derek, 'The Unfinished Collection: Russian Documents on the Origins of the First World War', in Keith Wilson (ed.), *Forging the Collective Memory: Government and International Historians through Two World Wars*, Providence and Oxford 1996

Steiner, Zara, *Britain and the Origins of the First World War*, New York 1977, 2nd edn London 2001

Stevenson, David, *Armaments and the Coming of War: Europe 1904–1914*, Oxford 1996

Stevenson, David, *The Outbreak of the First World War: 1914 in Perspective*, London 1997

Stieve, Friedrich, *Der diplomatische Schriftwechsel Iswolskis 1911–1914*, 4 vols, Berlin 1925

Stöcker, M. *'Augusterlebnis 1914' in Darmstadt: Legende und Wirklichkeit*, Darmstadt 1994

Strachan, Hew, *The First World War*, vol. I: *To Arms*, Oxford 2001

Stürmer, Michael, *Das Ruhelose Reich: Deutschland 1866–1918*, Berlin 1983

Stürmer, Michael, 'A Nation-State against History and Geography', in Gregor Schöllgen (ed.), *Escape into War? The Foreign Policy of Imperial Germany*, Oxford 1990

Swartz, Marvin, *The Union of Democratic Control in British Politics During the First World War*, Oxford 1971

Sywotteck, Arnold, 'Die Fischer-Kontroverse: Ein Beitrag zur Entwicklung des politisch-historischen Bewußtseins in der Bundesrepublik', in Imanuel Geiss and Bernd Jürgen Wendt (eds), *Deutschland in der Weltpolitik des 19. und 20. Jahrhunderts*, Düsseldorf 1973

Taylor, A.J.P., *The Course of German History*, London 1945

Taylor, A.J.P., *The Struggle for Mastery in Europe, 1848–1918*, New York and Oxford 1954, reprint 1988

Taylor, A.J.P., *War by Time-Table: How the First World War Began*, London and New York 1969

Temperley, H.W.V., *A History of the Peace Conference of Paris*, 5 vols, London 1920

Thoss, Bruno, 'Der Erste Weltkrieg als Ereignis und Erlebnis: Paradigmenwechsel in der westdeutschen Weltkriegsforschung seit der Fischer-Kontroverse', in Wolfgang Michalka (ed.), *Der Erste Weltkrieg: Wirkung, Wahrnehmung, Analyse*, Munich and Zurich 1994, pp. 1012–43

Turner, L.C.F., *The Origins of the First World War*, London 1970

Ullrich, Volker, *Die nervöse Grossmacht: Aufstieg und Untergang des deutschen Kaiserreichs 1871–1918*, Frankfurt/M. 1997

Ulrich, Bernd and Ziemann, Benjamin (eds), *Frontalltag im*

Ersten Weltkrieg: Wahn und Wirklichkeit. Quellen und Dokumente, Frankfurt/M. 1994

Versammlung deutscher Historiker in Berlin, 7.–11. Oktober 1964. Beiheft zur Zeitschrift Geschichte in Wissenschaft und Unterricht, Stuttgart 1965

Wegerer, Alfred von, *Die Widerlegung der Versailler Kriegsschuldthese*, Berlin 1928 (English translation: *A Refutation of the Versailles War-Guilt Thesis*, New York 1930), 2nd edn Berlin 1936

Wegerer, Alfred von, *Wie es zum Grossen Krieg kam: Vorgeschichte des Weltkrieges*, Leipzig 1930

Wegerer, Alfred von, *Im Kampf gegen die Kriegsschuldlüge: Ausgewählte Aufsätze*, Berlin 1936

Wegerer, Alfred von, *Der Ausbruch des Weltkrieges*, 2 vols, Berlin 1939

Wehler, Hans-Ulrich, *Das deutsche Kaiserreich, 1871–1918*, Göttingen, 1973 (English translation: *The German Empire, 1871–1918*, Leamington Spa 1985)

Wehler, Hans-Ulrich, 'Sonderweg aus der "Sonderlage"?: Die Wiederentdeckung der "deutschen Mittellage" in Wissenschaft und Publizistik', in Landeszentrale für politische Bildung Nordrhein-Westfalen (ed.), *Streitfall Deutsche Geschichte. Geschichts- und Gegenwartsbewußtsein in den 80er Jahren*, Essen 1988

Wehler, Hans-Ulrich, *Deutsche Gesellschaftsgeschichte*, vol. 3: *Von der 'Deutschen Doppelrevolution' bis zum Beginn des Ersten Weltkrieges*, 1849–1914, Munich 1995

Wendt, Bernd Jürgen, 'Fritz Fischer: Leben, Werk und Wirkung', in Kersten Krüger (ed.), *Fritz Fischer (1908–1999): Schenkung der Gelehrtenbibliothek Fritz Fischer an die Fachbibliothek Geschichte*, Veröffentlichungen der Universitätsbibliothek Rostock 2000, pp. 13–29

Wette, Wolfram (ed.), *Der Krieg des kleinen Mannes*, Munich 1992

Williamson, Samuel R., Jr., 'The Reign of Sir Edward Grey as British Foreign Secretary', *International History Review*, 1, 1979, pp. 426–38

Williamson, Samuel R., Jr. (ed.), *The Origins of a Tragedy: July 1914*, Chapel Hill 1981

Williamson, Samuel R., Jr., 'Vienna and July 1914: The Origins of the Great War Once More', in S.R. Williamson and Peter Pastor (eds), *Essays on World War I*, New York 1983

Williamson, Samuel R., Jr., 'The Origins of World War I', *Journal of Interdisciplinary History*, xviii/4, 1988, pp. 795–818

Williamson, Samuel R., Jr., *Austria-Hungary and the Origins of the First World War*, London 1991

Wilson, Keith M., *The Policy of the Entente: Essays on the Determinants of British Foreign Policy 1904–1914*, Cambridge 1985

Wilson, Keith M. (ed.), *Decisions for War, 1914*, London 1995

Wilson, Keith M. (ed.), *Forging the Collective Memory: Government and International Historians through Two World Wars*, Providence and Oxford 1996

Winter, Jay M., *Sites of Memory, Sites of Mourning: The Great War in European Cultural History*, Cambridge 1995

Wittgens, Hermann, 'Senator Owen, the Schuldreferat and the Debate over War Guilt in the 1920s', in Keith M. Wilson (ed.), *Forging the Collective Memory: Government and International Historians through Two World Wars*, Providence and Oxford 1996

Wolfrum, Edgar, *Geschichtspolitik in der Bundesrepublik Deutschland: Der Weg zur bundesrepublikanischen Erinnerung, 1948–1990*, Darmstadt 1999

Würthle, Friedrich, *Die Spur führt nach Belgrad: Die Hintergründe des Dramas von Sarajevo 1914*, Vienna 1974

Zechlin, E., 'Die Adriakrise und der "Kriegsrat" vom 8. Dezember 1912', in idem, *Krieg und Kriegsrisiko: Zur Deutschen Politik im Ersten Weltkrieg*, Düsseldorf 1979

Zechlin, Egmont, 'Probleme des Kriegskalküls und der Kriegsbeendigung', in idem, *Krieg und Kriegsrisiko: Zur deutschen Politik im Ersten Weltkrieg*, Düsseldorf 1979

Ziemann, Benjamin, *Front und Heimat: Ländliche Kriegserfahrungen im südlichen Bayern*, Essen 1997

Zilliacus, Konne, *The Mirror of the Past: Lest it Reflect the Future*, London 1944

Index